IN DEFENSE OF

Thomas Jefferson

THE SALLY HEMINGS SEX SCANDAL

WILLIAM G. HYLAND JR.

THOMAS DUNNE BOOKS
St. Martin's Press ✖ New York

THOMAS DUNNE BOOKS.
An imprint of St. Martin's Press.

IN DEFENSE OF THOMAS JEFFERSON. Copyright © 2009 by William G. Hyland Jr. All rights reserved. Printed in the United States of America. For information, address St. Martin's Press, 175 Fifth Avenue, New York, N.Y. 10010.

www.thomasdunnebooks.com
www.stmartins.com

Frontispiece: *Jefferson, 1975*, mixed media on board, collection of Mrs. Jane Wyeth, courtesy of artist Jamie Wyeth

Library of Congress Cataloging-in-Publication Data

Hyland, William G.
   In defense of Thomas Jefferson : the Sally Hemings sex scandal / by William G. Hyland Jr.—1st ed.
            p. cm.
   Includes bibliographical references and index.
   ISBN-13: 978-0-312-56100-0 (alk. paper)
   ISBN-10: 0-312-56100-8 (alk. paper)
   1. Hemings, Sally.   2. Jefferson, Thomas, 1743–1826—Relations with women.
3. Jefferson, Thomas, 1743–1826—Relations with slaves.   4. Hemings family.
5. Jefferson family.   I. Title.
   E332.2.H95   2009
   973.4'6092—dc22

                                                                    2009007588

First Edition: June 2009

10   9   8   7   6   5   4   3   2   1

To the memory of my father,

diplomat, scholar, author, loving husband,

father, and grandfather.

Mr. Jefferson would have been proud of the life you led.

CONTENTS

LIST OF WITNESSES

Key Witnesses

EDMUND BACON—Jefferson's overseer at Monticello from 1806 to 1823; testified that Jefferson was not the father of Sally Hemings's children, because he saw another man coming out of her room "many a morning."

JAMES THOMSON CALLENDER—alcoholic, muckraking journalist who first published the allegation that Jefferson had fathered the children of Sally in 1802.

PETER CARR—favorite nephew of Thomas Jefferson. Alleged lover of Sally and father of her children.

SAMUEL CARR—nephew of Thomas Jefferson. Brother of Peter. Alleged lover of Sally and father of her children. Born in 1771, died in 1855. Jefferson acted as devoted mentor to both boys.

ELLEN WAYLES RANDOLPH COOLIDGE—granddaughter of Thomas Jefferson. Wrote letter to her husband, Joseph Coolidge, implying that Samuel Carr was the father of Sally's children.

MARIA COSWAY—recipient of Jefferson's love letter in Paris, "A Dialogue Between My Head and My Heart." It was thought the relationship was romantic, but platonic, after the death of Jefferson's wife.

DR. ROBLEY DUNGLISON—Jefferson's twenty-seven-year-old English physician who treated Jefferson for migraine headaches, rheumatoid arthritis, intestinal and urinary infections, and was present at his deathbed.

MARY JEFFERSON EPPES—youngest surviving daughter of Jefferson and Martha Wayles Jefferson. Also called Maria or Polly. Born in 1778, died in 1804. Unbeknownst to Jefferson, Sally was sent with Mary on the voyage to France in 1787.

BEVERLY HEMINGS—full name William Beverly Hemings. Born in 1798. Son of Sally Hemings. Ran away from Monticello in 1822.

CRITTA HEMINGS—sister of Sally Hemings. Daughter of Elizabeth Hemings ("Betty") and allegedly John Wayles, Jefferson's father-in law, yet she was not listed as a "mulatto" in the 1833 census.

ELIZABETH HEMINGS—mother of Sally Hemings. Had twelve children by three different men.

ESTON HEMINGS—born in 1808. Son of Sally Hemings. Alleged son of Thomas Jefferson based on DNA match, which also matched the DNA of Jefferson's younger brother, Randolph and eight other Jefferson males.

MADISON HEMINGS—born in 1805, died in 1877. Son of Sally Hemings. Gave an "interview" to a partisan editor in 1873 alleging that Jefferson was his father.

SALLY HEMINGS—alleged mistress of Jefferson. Born in 1773, died in 1835. Daughter of Elizabeth Hemings and, allegedly, John Wayles. Never commented publicly or privately on the father of her children.

MARTHA WAYLES SKELTON JEFFERSON—beloved wife of Jefferson. Born in 1748, died at age thirty-three in 1782. Daughter of John Wayles. Mother of six children, two who survived to adulthood, Martha ("Patsy") and Mary ("Maria/Polly").

ISAAC JEFFERSON—former slave. He worked as a tinsmith and blacksmith at Monticello until seven years before Jefferson's death and dictated his recollections. Isaac never alluded or even hinted at Sally's relationship to Jefferson. His memoirs were not rediscovered until 1951, and published in modernized editions.

ISRAEL JEFFERSON—gave a statement to the *Pike County* (Ohio) *Republican* affirming Madison Hemings's hearsay assertion that Jefferson had a sexual relationship with Sally Hemings, "but do not positively know."

RANDOLPH JEFFERSON—Thomas Jefferson's younger brother, and most likely the father of one or more of Sally's children. He shared the same DNA match with Jefferson and was at Monticello nine months before Sally gave birth to Eston, the DNA matched son.

GEORGE WYTHE RANDOLPH—youngest grandson of Thomas Jefferson. Son of Martha Jefferson Randolph and Thomas Mann Randolph, Jr. His mother attempted to prove to him that Jefferson could not have been the father of Sally's children.

MARTHA JEFFERSON RANDOLPH—oldest daughter of Thomas Jefferson. Also called "Patsy." Married to Thomas Mann Randolph, Jr. Mother of twelve children, including Thomas Jefferson Randolph, Ellen Randolph Coolidge, and George Wythe Randolph. Vehemently denied that Jefferson had any relationship with Sally.

THOMAS JEFFERSON RANDOLPH—oldest grandson of Thomas Jefferson. Son of Martha Jefferson Randolph. Told his grandfather's biographer that Peter Carr, Jefferson's nephew, had admitted to being the father of Sally's children. Told his sister, Ellen Randolph Coolidge, that he overheard Peter Carr say that "the old gentleman had to bear the blame of his and Sam's (Colonel Carr) misdeeds."

JOHN WAYLES—father-in-law to Thomas Jefferson, and alleged father of Sally Hemings.

S. F. WETMORE—Political editor of the *Pike County* (Ohio) *Republican*. He was an abolitionist census taker for Pike County. Wrote down, published, and unduly influenced Madison Hemings's memoirs in 1873.

EXPERT WITNESSES (HISTORIANS)— FOR JEFFERSON'S DEFENSE

DOUGLASS ADAIR—author of "The Jefferson Scandals," an essay published in a collection of his works entitled *Fame and the Founding Fathers*. The piece, exonerating Jefferson, was written in the early 1960s but was not published until 1974, after Adair's death.

CYNTHIA BURTON—historian, researcher, genealogist, and author of the book, *Jefferson Vindicated*.

VIRGINIUS DABNEY—historian, author, journalist, and a winner of the Pulitzer Prize for editorial writing. He authored the 1981 book, *The Jefferson Scandals: A Rebuttal*, a defense to Fawn Brodie's biography of Thomas Jefferson and Barbara Chase-Riboud's novel *Sally Hemings*.

FORREST MCDONALD—Distinguished Research Professor of History (Emeritus), University of Alabama. Professor McDonald has also taught at Brown and was the James Pinckney Harrison Professor of History at the College of William & Mary. His many awards and prizes include Thomas Jefferson Lecturer with the National Endowment for the Humanities. Author of *The Presidency of Thomas Jefferson*, considered one of the leading historians on the old South.

DUMAS MALONE—Malone was a former professor of history at the University of Virginia, who spent thirty-five years writing a six-volume, Pulitzer Prize–winning biography of Jefferson, published between 1948 and 1981. Considered the foremost authority on Thomas Jefferson.

JAMES PARTON—early biographer of Jefferson. Published *The Life of Thomas Jefferson* in 1874. Recipient of a letter from Henry Stephens Randall alleging that one of Jefferson's nephews fathered Sally Hemings's children.

MERRILL PETERSON—Professor Emeritus, University of Virginia, the greatest living Jefferson expert, author of the Pulitzer Prize–winning book, *The Jefferson Image in the American Mind,* published in 1960, in which he dealt explicitly and extensively with Madison Hemings's statement to the *Pike County* (Ohio) *Republican.*

HENRY STEPHENS RANDALL—nineteenth-century biographer of Jefferson; published a three-volume biography of Jefferson in 1858. Wrote a letter to James Parton stating that Jefferson's grandson T. J. Randolph said that one of the Carr brothers, not Jefferson, was the father of Sally Hemings's children.

WILLARD STERNE RANDALL—Visiting Professor of History, Champlain College.

ROBERT TURNER—University of Virginia professor. Turner holds both professional and academic doctorates from the University of Virginia School of Law, and is a former Charles H. Stockton Professor of International Law at the U.S. Naval War College and a Distinguished Lecturer at West Point. A former president of the congressionally established U.S. Institute of Peace, he has had a strong professional interest in Jefferson for three decades.

Expert Witnesses for the Plaintiff—Hemings

FAWN BRODIE—professor of history, UCLA. Wrote controversial biography on Jefferson entitled *Thomas Jefferson: An Intimate History* published in 1974.

ANDREW BURSTEIN—professor of history, University of Tulsa.

BARBARA CHASE-RIBOUD—author of *Sally Hemings*, a historical novel based upon the Thomas Jefferson–Sally Hemings story, published 1979.

ALAN PELL CRAWFORD—writer, author.

JOSEPH ELLIS—professor of history, Mount Holyoke College.

ANNETTE GORDON-REED—professor of law, New York Law School.

JON KUKLA—historian, writer.

PETER ONUF—professor of history, University of Virginia.

LUCIA CINDER STANTON—senior researcher, Monticello.

DIANNE SWANN-WRIGHT—former Monticello researcher and Director of "Getting Word" Oral History Project at Monticello.

PREFACE

*The moment a person forms a theory, his imagination sees, in every object,
only the traits which favor that theory.*
                    —Thomas Jefferson to Charles Thompson, 1787[1]

I was encouraged to write this book by my late father. He felt Jefferson's
reputation had been unfairly eviscerated by a misrepresentation of the
DNA results in the Hemings controversy. The exhumation of discredited, prurient embellishments has not only deluded readers, but impov-
erished a fair debate. In fact, with the possible exception of the Kennedy
assassination, I am unaware of any major historical controversy riddled
with so much misinformation and outright inaccuracies as the sex-
oriented Sally Hemings libel. When the public is forced to accept an "official story" by means of a process more political than scientific, driven
by a desire to follow hearsay, gossip, and innuendo, we do so at the expense of truth.

The "Sally" story is pure fiction, possibly politics, but certainly not
historical fact or science. It reflects a recycled inaccuracy that has metas-
tasized from book to book, over two hundred years. I insist on stabiliz-
ing the record, separating revisionist ideology from accuracy. Let me state
clearly that I am neither a professional historian, nor a preeminent Jefferson scholar as was Dumas Malone, who spent thirty-five years writing a
Pulitzer Prize–winning six-volume biography of Jefferson. Having been

born and raised in Virginia, I have a personal affinity for Jefferson and have been fascinated with his life. The man who led the footsteps of an infant Republic into the path of civilization is one of the few historical figures whose absence can not be fathomed. As my father and I sifted through the research and interviews, we realized that books alone could not give the full measure of Jefferson. For that you need to visit Monticello, (old Italian for "little mountain") the visible projection of its resident. Jefferson spent most of his life building (and rebuilding) his five thousand-acre Palladian estate nestled in the rolling Blue Ridge Mountains. One can visualize an absorbed Jefferson, tall and slender in a blue frock coat, standing at the east entrance, supervising his busy carpenters, the aroma of rich maple wood pressed against his skin. He would register the spring frost blanketing the peach orchard, his grapes inclining toward purple, pale rows of peas bursting upon Monticello's garden.

For the past twenty-six years the modicum of my expertise has been yoked to the courtroom, presenting the most persuasive evidence to a jury. As a civil litigator and former prosecutor, I do not claim mastery of all the facts of Jefferson's celebrated life and career. However, I have attempted to research and evaluate every scholarly book, article, Committee report, eighteenth-century letters, and ancillary material relevant to the singular, inflammatory subject of whether Thomas Jefferson had an exotic, sexual liaison with his "servant" Sally Hemings.[2] For the first time, the public will gain access to personal interviews and correspondence with two Jeffersonian experts: Dr. White McKenzie (Ken) Wallenborn, a former professor at the University of Virginia medical school and tour guide at Monticello,[3] and genealogist Herbert Barger.[4] Both gentlemen are Jefferson "insiders" intimately involved in the distorted DNA study and the subsequent misleading report, fueled by the energies of cosseted slave historians at official Monticello and the University of Virginia. They reveal how evidence was manipulated into a censored, predetermined "official" conclusion, giving a false stigma of Jefferson's guilt to the American public.

The fevered debate about Sally and Jefferson changed radically in 1998. Science exploded a historical bombshell, confirming that a male carrying Jefferson DNA had fathered Sally Hemings's last child, Eston. The British science journal *Nature*'s distortion of that news led to a worldwide misrepresentation that DNA had specifically proven Thomas Jefferson was the father. In fact, at least two dozen male Jeffersons could have fathered Eston. Historians understood this, but certain scholars marginalized evidence pointing toward any paternity candidate but Jefferson. At a vitriolic college forum on DNA, one professor insisted, with withering scorn, that denial of Jefferson's guilt is either "an act of religious faith or belief in superstition."[5]

This book is neither patriotic haze, nor a free fall into Jeffersonian idolatry. It is historical hygiene by print, an attempt to marshal facts, rationally dissect the evidence, and prove beyond reasonable doubt that Jefferson is completely *innocent* of this sordid charge.[6] In contrast to the blizzard of recent books spinning the controversy as a miniseries version of history, I found that layer upon layer of direct and circumstantial evidence points to a mosaic distinctly away from Jefferson. My research, evaluation, and personal interviews led me to one inevitable conclusion: the revisionist grip of historians have the wrong Jefferson—the DNA, as well as other historical evidence, matches perfectly to his younger brother, Randolph and his teenage sons, as the true candidates for a sexual relationship with Sally. A monopoly of books (all paternity believers) written since the DNA results have gone far beyond the evidence and transmuted conjecture into apparent fact, and in most instances, engaged in a careless misreading of the record. They have raised speculative "possibilities," not concrete facts "within a reasonable degree of historical certainty." This is the standard for expert opinion in a court of law, and should be the standard for the court of public opinion as well.

In short, upon close scrutiny the various sexual/romantic theories against Jefferson turn out to be weightless and devoid of substance. I have found logical, plausible, sensible explanations for the paternity of Sally's children that do not inculpate Jefferson. In my view, belief in the paternity allegation is literally a concocted myth, a symptom of a disconcerting trend injected not only into the Jefferson-Hemings controversy, but academia as well. I was particularly troubled in my research by the fact that some biographers have mangled professional standards in seizing upon the emotionally charged DNA results. Any knowledgeable Jefferson historian knows full well that he was accused of the "crime against nature" that he *most abhorred*—miscegenation (race mixing).[7] In fact, only six months before he died in 1826, Jefferson wrote of his "aversion" to "the mixture of colour."[8]

Some partisan historians have accepted unreliable hearsay as the connective tissue to establish fact. Along the way, they have split hairs, drawn far-fetched inferences, and literally invented other facts from the grist of rumor, casting the relationship in a romantic glow. Some slavery historians have abjured the potent testimony of Jefferson's grandchildren, his own private denials of the charge, the fact that this behavior would be in fundamental contradiction to his towering character and tight rein over his emotions. In the process, a few scholars negligently presumed, ignored, omitted, or misrepresented the findings that exonerate Jefferson, to mine their own simmering dyspepsia about slavery. Perhaps, this whole unsettling controversy is another reminder that history is a tragedy, not a morality tale.

The foremost living Jefferson scholar, Professor Merrill Peterson, grasped the nettle: "American history has sometimes seemed a protracted litigation—hearings, negotiations, trials, and appeal in endless number—on Thomas Jefferson." Unfortunately, they have all presumed "Mr. Jefferson" guilty of the paternity charge. Yet, what troubles me most about the remnants of this "revisionist Sally" mood, is that some of Jefferson's more interesting accomplishments have been overlooked:

- Jefferson was the president who abolished the slave trade with Africa.
- The indefatigable Virginian taught himself to read and write Spanish, while on his nineteen-day voyage across the ocean to France.
- Though born a wealthy man, he died a debtor, having spent the majority of his fortune on launching our nation, a stark contrast to today's politicians.
- In 1814, after British warships burned the White House and the Library of Congress, Jefferson sold the majority of his personal books to the Library to jump-start its recovery.
- Gore Vidal wrote that "Thomas Jefferson was the most intricate character—and in a corrupt moment, he allowed his cook to give birth to that unique dessert later known as Baked Alaska."[9]

Quite obviously, the debate over Jefferson-Hemings, as well as the moral abomination of slavery, will continue. Yet the truth about Jefferson must be gleaned in the life he led, not what his political enemies poured into his life as a tonic for their own purposes. Let a sensible, fair-minded public decide where the truth lies, mindful of Jefferson's own words:

> When tempted to do anything in secret, ask yourself if you would do it in public; if you would not, be sure it is wrong.[10]

—WILLIAM G. HYLAND JR.
Tampa, Florida
November 2008

For at least 25 years, we've been raising young Americans who are by and large, historically illiterate ... history has not just been pushed to the back burner, it's been pushed off the stove.

—David McCullough[11]

[A] myth's power does not depend on its plausibility.

—George Will[12]

IN DEFENSE OF
THOMAS JEFFERSON

INTRODUCTION

All should be laid open to you without reserve, for there is not a truth existing which I fear, or would wish unknown to the whole world.
> —Thomas Jefferson to Henry Lee, May 15, 1826
> (fifty days prior to Jefferson's death)[1]

Thomas Jefferson is either the most prolific, hypocritical liar in American history or the victim of the most profane, two-hundred-year-old defamation of character allegation in legal annals.

There is no gauzy middle ground in this historical tableau.

A small universe of historians contend that whether the consanguinitory allegations are true is a peripheral issue, since the renown of Jefferson as a votary of liberty is so monumental that nothing can affect it. Perhaps. Yet the "Sally" charges have permeated the national consciousness, and remain a demonizing blot on Jefferson's character. In the interest of justice and historical accuracy, the charges need to be appraised in a "mock" legal context/trial and, if proven false, vigorously refuted.

No other person in the public domain has been studied, debated, and written about more than the man who penned the charter of American independence. Of all the Founding Fathers, Jefferson, statesman, diplomat, naturalist, apostle of freedom, has fared the worst at the hands of barbed revisionists.[2] In fact, Jefferson's personal reputation has been all but assassinated for the last ten years, since the 1998 DNA. The face on Mount Rushmore has been vilified as a slave-owning hypocrite, misogynist, and racist.

The DNA findings darkened the portrait of "Jefferson, the man" that has been incubating ever since. Writer Dinesh D'Souza describes a conversation he had with several college students: "On Jefferson, the three were agreed: he was, in various descriptions, a 'hypocrite,' a 'rapist' . . . , and a 'total racist.' Jeffersonian principles of individualism, reason, science, and private property, all become tainted."[3]

For over two hundred years, Jefferson has been accused of a sexual relationship with one of his servants, Sally Hemings. According to DNA interpretive results, it is now widely accepted that Jefferson fathered one or more of Sally's children. Are the accusations true? And if so, could they be proven in a court of law or, more importantly, in the panoramic court of public opinion?

The Sally story can be made authentic only by an incredible suspension of disbelief. I have found that the threadbare arguments against Jefferson are a proverbial throw at the dartboard of history. The foggy allegation consists of a mixture of gossip, hearsay, and speculation, bordering on willful opacity. One would have to assume Jefferson transformed himself into a schizophrenic Jekyll and Hyde to maintain two different families, and lead an emotionally repressed double life.

The following chapters reveal a whirlpool of salient facts, separating the proverbial wheat from the chaff, and prove Jefferson's innocence:

- the virulent rumor was first started by the unscrupulous, scandal-mongering journalist James Callender, who burned for political revenge against Jefferson. Callender was described as "an alcoholic thug with a foul mind, obsessed with race and sex," who intended to defame the public career of Jefferson. Historian James Truslow Adams wrote: "[A]lmost every scandalous story about Jefferson which is still whispered or believed may be traced to the scurrilous writings of Callender."[4]
- the one, credible eyewitness to this sexual allegation was Edmund Bacon, Jefferson's overseer at Monticello, who saw another man (not Jefferson) leaving Sally's room "many a morning." Bacon wrote: "I have seen him come out of her mother's room [Sally's] many a morning when I went up to Monticello very early."[5]
- Jefferson's deteriorating health would have prevented any such sexual relationship. He was sixty-four at the time of the alleged

affair and suffered debilitating migraine headaches that incapacitated him for weeks, as well as severe intestinal infections and
rheumatoid arthritis. He complained to John Adams: "My health
is entirely broken down within the last eight months."

- Jefferson owned three different slaves named Sally, adding to the
historical confusion. Yet, he never freed his supposed lover and
companion of thirty-seven years, "Sally Hemings" from her enslavement, or mentioned her in his will.

- Randolph Jefferson, his younger brother, would have the identical Jefferson Y chromosome as his older brother, Thomas, that
matched the DNA. Randolph had a reputation for socializing
with Jefferson's slaves and was expected at Monticello *approximately nine months* before the birth of Eston Hemings, Sally's
son who was the DNA match for a "male Jefferson."

- The DNA match was to a male son of Sally's. Randolph had *six*
male sons. Thomas Jefferson had all *female* children—except for
a nonviable male infant—with his beloved wife, Martha.[6]

- Until 1976, the oral history of Eston's family held that they descended from a Jefferson "uncle." Randolph was known at Monticello as "Uncle Randolph."

- Unlike his brother, by taste and training Thomas Jefferson was
raised as the perfect Virginia gentleman, a man of refinement
and intellect. The personality of the man who figures in the
Hemings soap opera cannot be attributed to the known nature
of Jefferson. Having an affair with a house servant would be preposterously out of character for him.

The alleged affair between Jefferson and Hemings began as a vindic-
tive political attack during Jefferson's first term as president. It first swirled
into publication in 1802 by an alcoholic, bellicose journalist by the name
of James Callender. He was a disappointed office seeker, the "most deadly
of all political animals."[7] In common with the licentious practice of those
times, the allegations were spread for political purposes, even though the
accusations had no foundation in fact. The pestering rumors were pro-
moted by Jefferson's Federalist enemies. They have been accepted
through handed-down gossip, distorted scientific results, and offered to
the public as "fact." But what is presented as historical fact is based on a

singular misleading headline in the 1998 science journal *Nature*: "Jefferson Fathered Slave's Last Child."[8]

Rumored for centuries, the affair was allegedly "confirmed" when a retired pathologist named Eugene Foster collected DNA samples from descendants of Jeffersons (his uncle, Field Jefferson) and the Hemings's families.[9] The condemnation of Jefferson's guilt was a huge story, prompting tabloid headlines. Media accounts contained strong language such as "proves conclusively," "demonstrated," or "resolved," and included the following incredible headline: "Adulterer on Mt. Rushmore" claimed the *Des Moines Register*, which included a charge of "statutory rape." Two authors wrote churlish books calling for the dismantling of the Jefferson Memorial and the removal of his face from Mount Rushmore.[10]

Unfortunately, this is one fraying legend that truth will never catch up to. When facts contradict a salacious story, it is the story that survives. Betsy Ross may have her American flag, so we can let Sally have Thomas Jefferson's love child.

Joseph Ellis, an award-winning historian, proclaimed in 1996 (pre-DNA) that: "[T]he likelihood of a liaison with Sally Hemings is remote," and the story is "a tin can tied to Jefferson's reputation . . . that has rattled through the ages and pages of history books ever since."[11] After the DNA study, however, Ellis veered and enthused to *Newsweek*: "For all intents and purposes, this ends the debate." Ellis also referred to Jefferson as a "white supremacist" in the *New Republic* and *William and Mary Quarterly*.[12]

All too often, the news stories, commentary, and analysis transformed an intriguing, but indeterminate scientific finding, into dead certainty. Some historians turned these abridged results into a referendum on slavery and race relations, as well as presidential politics at the time. (Impeachment of President Clinton was at the height of its frenzy, and the DNA story broke the weekend before Election Day.) Yet, there was little notice of a subsequent thirteen-member, blue-ribbon panel of prominent historians and scientists (white, black, male, and female) named to reconfirm the DNA conclusions (the "Scholars Commission"). After a year of investigating history's most famous paternity case, the independent historians tamped down the simmering allegation: *"our conclusions range from serious skepticism about the charge to a conviction that it is almost certainly false."*[13]

"Thomas Jefferson was simply not guilty of the charge," said the preeminent historian Professor Forrest McDonald, who served on the panel. McDonald and other panel members pointed to the real suspect—Jefferson's brother, Randolph. In fact, the most logical and credible evidence points to Randolph, unmarried in his early fifties and known for socializing with the Monticello slaves. Randolph, unlike his accomplished brother, was easily influenced by others. An old militia list reveals connections between Randolph and white men with black mistresses—in two cases, Hemingses.[14] And what about Randolph's sons? These unmarried eighteen- to twenty-six-year-olds also were near Monticello at the right conception times. In fact, two letters found by Charlottesville genealogist Cynthia Burton suggest Jefferson's unmarried cousin, George Jefferson, also made periodic visits to Monticello.[15]

In writing this book, my greatest concern is that those who wish to villainize Jefferson think they have a license to do so with the deceptive DNA results. After examining all the credible, documented, and corroborated evidence, it is hard to escape the singular conclusion that Jefferson has been enlisted on the losing side in a battle where racial creeds have been allowed to predominate, turning a quest for evidence into a paroxysm of rage on slavery. No doubt, historians are not bound by the legal rules of evidence. Yet the divisive character of the historical debate has curdled the facts into a predetermined mantra: Jefferson's guilt.

What I have found in my research was a type of shape-shifting, investigative scholarship. The most dominant, compelling evidence proving Jefferson's innocence was misinterpreted, masqueraded, or manipulated to fit a predetermined blueprint. This two-hundred-year-old, cascading fabrication embodies a not so subtle shift away from Jefferson and on to his racial views. Some scholars are exclusively imbued with the subject of slavery, and the Hemings family in general. Like many critical studies of historical figures, the Jefferson-Hemings debate is fundamentally flawed due to "presentism." By taking Jefferson's statements out of context and judging him by present-day standards, several historians have misinterpreted evidence to indict Jefferson. "Presentism" has plagued this controversy by its inability to make allowances for prevailing historical conditions.[16]

It has been said that journalism "is the first rough draft of history."[17] Some truth lies in this statement. Unfortunately, this standard has been misapplied to the Jefferson-Hemings debate, which has dissolved into a second and third draft of a politicized novel. Jefferson is, as Pulitzer Prize–winning historian Virginius Dabney wrote: "[O]ne of the principle historical victims of the current orgy of debunking" our heroes.[18]

Thus, I offer this book as "Jefferson's lawyer," attempting to relegate this legend to the dustbin of history. I will advance his vigorous, full-throated defense against a fabricated allegation, illuminating the most rational, credible evidence and omissions in this disconnected controversy. Jefferson's health, his activities, his younger brother, the misleading forensic DNA are all carefully cross-examined and dissected to set the "record" straight in the Jeffersonian tradition.

Former Monticello President Daniel Jordan believes "honorable people can disagree" in the Hemings paternity debate. He believes new evidence might be discovered to fill the ruptured lacunae in the historical record. Acting on those beliefs, however, can earn authors a label of "Jefferson canonizer" or worse, a racist. I am neither. I have spent over three years conducting research, sifting my way through a thicket of social fictions and historical gossip, motivated by a fundamental sense of fair play to Jefferson. To paraphrase one scholar, it is frequently so tempting to read the past backward—and very dangerous. Historians cannot rob Jefferson of his laurels, but they can scribble graffiti on his statute. It is unfortunate that sexual innuendo is so hard to erase.[19]

Jefferson died on the Fourth of July, 1826, the fiftieth anniversary of the Declaration of Independence, killed by a wasting, internal infection. His final words were, "Is it the Fourth?" On the same day, John Adams died hours earlier and uttered, "Jefferson still lives." Whether these words were literal or apocryphal, it reminded me of a story I share with my juries in closing argument ("borrowed" from the finest trial lawyer in the country, Gerry Spence):

> Once, there was a wise old man who lived in a small fishing village. The villagers would seek him out for sage advice. One day some young boys visited him, trying a ruse. One of the boys concealed a baby bird in his hands, and called to the wrinkled gentleman: "Hey old man! If you're so smart, tell me if the bird in my hand is alive or dead." The man glinted at the boy, for he knew the bird was alive. The old man also knew that if he declared the bird was alive, the boy would crush his hands together,

killing the tiny creature. Yet, if he said the bird was dead, the boy would release his hands and let the bird fly away, mocking him for being wrong. The sage drew closer to the boy, hooked eyes with him and whispered: *"The fate of the bird, my son, is in your hands."*

Just as the fate of Thomas Jefferson is now in your hands.

I

James Callender:
"Human Nature in a Hideous Form"

Refutation can never be made.
—James Callender, 1802[1]

The rotting corpse bobbed up and down in a muddy, shallow stretch of the James River. Through peeling flesh and hair matted like seaweed, the man's gray face was still recognizable. He was the eighteenth-century version of a tabloid reporter, devoid of honor or decency. Hours earlier, the combustible personality of this man staggered in and out of Richmond's finest taverns, slurring words of rage against President Thomas Jefferson. The next day a coroner heaved the alcohol injected body onto the autopsy table. The cause of death was registered: drowning. Amid rumors of foul play, the formal inquest noted that the deceased had been drunk, his waterlogged body recorded as drowned in three feet of water on a Sunday in July 1803. The coroner then scrawled a name on the death certificate: *James Thomson Callender.*

Ten days later, the *Richmond Examiner* newspaper regarded Callender's death as a drunken suicide, and wrote that "this unfortunate man had descended to the lowest depths of misery after having been fleeced by his partner."[2] His onetime collaborator recalled years later that Callender had resorted to "unwarrantable indiscretions" begun amid "paroxysms of inebriety."[3] And so the foul life of the most ignoble James Callender came to an end, self-destructing like an overloaded circuit without a breaker.

But this is where the embryo of the "Sally" story begins.

The most direct statement that can be made about the alleged sexual relationship between Jefferson and Hemings is this: It was invented by the fractured psyche of an alcoholic, hack journalist, James Callender.

In 1804, Jefferson's fierce political enemies lacked a substantial issue to use against him as he sought reelection as America's third president. The country was prosperous, peaceful, and the historic Louisiana Purchase had been finalized. So his opponents turned personal. The previous election between incumbent John Adams and Jefferson had also descended into a vicious affair in which Federalists attacked Jefferson's character in a fevered pitch. Jefferson cheated British creditors, they charged, obtained property by fraud, and robbed a widow of £10,000, and if elected: "Murder, robbery, rape, adultery, and incest will openly be taught and practiced," according to the federalist *Connecticut Courant.*[4]

James Callender surged onto the scene and represented, as one historian put it, a "darker and more personal kind of trouble for the president."[5] He distinguished himself by the fierceness and scurrility of his attacks on Jefferson, as well as on John Adams and Alexander Hamilton. In 1802, the sexual accusation against Jefferson first appeared in a slashing, vituperative article written by Callender, an initial supporter of the president who later became a bitter political enemy. Published in the *Richmond Recorder* on September 1, 1802:

> [I]t is, well known that the man, whom it delighteth the people to honor, keeps and for many years past has kept, as his concubine, one of his own slaves. Her name is SALLY. The name of her eldest son is TOM. His features are said to bear a striking although sable resemblance to those of the president himself. The boy is ten or twelve years of age. His mother went to France in the same vessel with Mr. Jefferson and his two daughters. . . . By this wench Sally, our president has had several children.[6]

Among other things, the scandalmonger referred to Sally as an "African Venus," a "black Venus," "Dusky Sally," "wooly-headed concubine," a member of Jefferson's "Congo harem," and having a "complection between mahogany and dirty greasy yellow."[7] The vile accusation released into a receptive political world of Jefferson enemies, who said the president's involvement with "Black Sal" made him unfit for the nation's highest office.

Ultimately, Jefferson won the 1804 election in a landslide, capturing all but two of the then seventeen states and 92 percent of the electoral vote.

As for Callender, his origins and early life remain a "mystery." A political refugee from Scotland, he began his career as a blistering writer in the 1780s. He was one of those men "who never in his life beheld with equanimity a greater than himself."[8] Full of pride and jealousy, Callender embarked on writing political pamphlets, leading to *The Political Progress of Britain,* which criticized powerful British politicians. He libeled Lord Gardenstone, his mentor, Dr. Samuel Johnson, and the crown itself. Callender, hearing rumors of his imminent arrest for his seditious writings, fled Britain in 1793. He escaped to the New World, leaving his wife and child behind.

On May 27, 1800, Callender was arrested under the Sedition Act, for attacking President John Adams as a "hoary headed incendiary and a man who had deserted and reversed all principles."[9] He was put on trial in Richmond. Having learned of the indictment, and framed by his vehement opposition to the Federalist Sedition laws, Jefferson wrote to future President James Monroe: "I think it essentially just and necessary that Callendar [*sic*] should be substantially defended."[10] Jefferson associated with Callender against his own better judgment, not because he approved of Callender but because he needed Callender to rebut newspaper attacks on his policies. In June 1800, Judge Samuel Chase fined Callender two hundred dollars and sentenced him to nine months in jail.

When Jefferson became president, he pardoned Callender, allowing him to claim compensation for his fine. The muckraker began a campaign for money and a presidential appointment to postmaster of Richmond. He complained to James Madison that "Jefferson has not returned one shilling of my fine. I now begin to know what Ingratitude is."[11]

Jefferson denied Callender his appointment to postmaster concluding that he was "unworthy."[12] Callender turned to Monroe, who tried to "tranquilize his mind" but began to suspect that Callender would attack the "Executive." Monroe had a sharper eye to Callender's potential threats than did Jefferson. He expressed concern that Jefferson had given Callender money, and advised the president to "get all the letters however unimportant from him . . . Your resolution to terminate all communication with him is wise, yet it will be well to prevent even a serpent doing one an injury."[13]

Madison also became suspicious of Callender's motives, observing: "It had been my lot to bear the burden of receiving and repelling [Callender's] claims. . . . [I]t is impossible to reason concerning a man, whose imagination and passions have been so fermented."[14]

As Jefferson moved to the political center, Callender remained on the infested, radical fringe. Jefferson refused to become any closer to a man most readers would soon recognize as a "bitter, ranting mercenary."[15] He sent the journalist fifty dollars, a paltry sum that incensed Callender as "hush money." Jefferson, in turn, became insulted by Callender's "base ingratitude" and denied any close relationship with him:

> I am really mortified at the base ingratitude of Callender. It presents human nature in a hideous form. It gives me concern because I perceive that relief which was afforded him on mere motives of charity, may be viewed under the aspect of employing him as a writer.[16]

Furious at Jefferson's parsimony, Callender trembled with rage. His political idol, Jefferson, had spurned his efforts to cultivate their friendship. The perceived slight stimulated Callender's imagination for revenge, and it was in this state of mind that Callender retaliated by publishing Jefferson's friendly letters and payments to him. In fact, Jefferson had not only paid for copies of Callender's pamphlets, but had given him money to sustain him—"mere motives of charity" Jefferson had claimed to Monroe.

In August 1802, one of Jefferson's partisans accused Callender of causing his wife's death from a venereal disease. Callender counterattacked with character assassination, and accused Jefferson of keeping a slave "concubine." He denigrated Sally as a "[s]lut common as the pavement," who was "romping with half a dozen black fellows," and having "fifteen, or thirty gallants of all colours."[17] He referred to Jefferson as a man who would lecherously summon Sally from "the kitchen or perhaps the pigsty," using animal comparisons of bestiality for Jefferson's mixing of the races.[18]

Callender excoriated Jefferson in the journal the *Richmond Recorder*. The tawdry revelations spread rapidly, appearing in the cheering Federalist press—the *New York Evening Post*, the *Washington Federalist*, and the *Gazette of the United States*. Although sexual abuses by masters inflicted on female slaves were common in the old South, the widower Jefferson had never before been suspected or accused of such improper behavior. Callender's scandalous revelation dramatically changed that.

Callender himself was not only a "drunken ruffian," but a racist.[19] He always referred to Sally by her race ("Dusky Sally," "Black Sal," "mahogany colored charmer") and wrote "if eight thousand white men in Virginia followed Jefferson's example you would have FOUR HUNDRED THOUSAND MULATTOES in addition to the present swarm. The country would no longer be habitable."[20] Callender also believed that accusing Jefferson of miscegenation would fatally ruin his career. As one authority commented: "Jefferson's offense was held to be mixture of the races, and Callender and his fellow scandalmongers strummed the theme until it was dead tired."[21] At one point, Callender boasted that he had done more harm to Jefferson's reputation in five months than all of Jefferson's critics in ten years.

A prophetic statement.

Callender's libel was not limited to Jefferson. He called John Adams a "repulsive pedant," a "gross hypocrite," and in his "private life, one of the most egregious fools upon the continents." Adams was a "hideous hermaphroditical character who has neither the force and firmness of a man, nor the gentleness and sensibility of a woman." John Adams had no use for Callender. "I believe nothing that Callender said any more than if it had been said by an infernal spirit. I would not convict a dog of killing sheep upon the testimony of two such witnesses," Adams wrote with characteristic candor. He concluded that Callender's charges against Jefferson were "mere clouds of unsubstantiated vapour."[22]

Abigail Adams also described Callender as "a libeler whom you could not but detest and despise."[23] Abigail took personally Callender's characterizations of her husband—"the basest Libel, the lowest and vilest slander which malice could invent," she called it. Abigail, after learning Jefferson had initially supported Callender, would later write that it was as though the serpent Jefferson had "cherished and warmed" had turned and "bit the hand that nourishes him."[24]

The obscenity and vulgarity of these extracts from Callender and others, serve to illustrate the low taste of the journalism of the era. Factual accuracy was of no concern to him. He had a caustic pen that rankled those he pilloried. The menacing Callender had already besmirched the reputations of Alexander Hamilton when he publicized Hamilton's affair with Maria Reynolds to her blackmailing husband.

Two potential sources for Callender's vulgarity also had a clear motive against Jefferson: David Meade Randolph and his wife Mary (Molly), disaffected, distant cousins who were Callender's informants. Before the appearance of Callender's articles, Randolph had been fired by Jefferson as federal marshal in Richmond, allegedly for rigging the Callender jury. Randolph's dismissal outraged him, and the couple's grandiose lifestyle disintegrated. They became outspoken enemies of Jefferson and fed hearsay and gossip to Callender, as well as others.

Jefferson's friends vehemently denied the disparagement in print, but the president bore this vilification without public comment. Privately, he wrote that a formal refutation was beneath him. "I have determined to contradict none," he wrote to Monroe.[25] A statement made to Dr. George Logan indicates Jefferson's mature judgment with regard to such extreme slanders: "As to Federal slanders, I never wished them to be answered, but by the tenor of my life. . . . [T]he man who fears no truths has nothing to fear from lies."[26] Jefferson explained his position to William A. Burwell:

> Many of the [federal] lies would have required only a simple denial, but I saw that even that would have led to the infalliable inference, that whatever I had not denied was to be presumed true. I have, therefore, never done even this, but to such of my friends as happen to converse on these subjects, and I have never believed that my character could hang upon every two-penny lie of our common enemies.[27]

Jefferson's silence on the subject was in accord with his "rule of life" not to respond to newspaper attacks: "Their approbation has taught a lesson, useful to the world. . . . I should have fancied myself guilty had I condescended to put pen to paper in refutation of their falsehoods, or drawn to them respect by a notice from myself."[28] In a letter to Samuel Smith of Maryland, Jefferson said: "At a very early period of my life, I determined never to put a single sentence into any newspaper. I have religiously adhered to the resolution through my life . . . were I to undertake to answer the calumnies of the newspapers, it would be more than all my own time and that of twenty aids could affect. For while I should be answering one, twenty new ones would be invented."[29]

Privately, however, Jefferson alluded to and, in fact, denied the charges. For example, he wrote to Dr. Benjamin Rush: "The Morals of Jesus," with a Syllabus, Washington, April 21, 1803: "And in confiding it to you, I know it will not be exposed to the malignant perversions of those who make every word from me a text for new misrepresentations & calumnies."[30]

"I know," he explained to a friend in Connecticut, "that I might have filled the courts of the Untied States with actions for these slanders, and have ruined, perhaps, many persons who are not innocent. But this would be no equivalent for the loss of character. I leave them, therefore, to the reproof of their own consciences. If these do not condemn them, there will come a day when the false witness will meet a judge who has not slept over his slanders."[31] Edward Coles, a friend and neighbor of Jefferson's, confirmed to a friend that Jefferson denied the "Black Sal" charges to him and to a Kentuckian stranger. Coles referred to the charges as "vacuous."[32]

"With the aid of a lying renegade from Republicanism, the Federalists have opened all their sluices of calumny," Jefferson complained.[33] Perhaps Jefferson offered the best refutation of this tale of seduction when he said that if a biographer dealing with a person whose character was "well known and established on satisfactory testimony, imputes to it things incompatible with that character, we reject without hesitation, and assent to that only of what we have better evidence."[34] More importantly, it simply defies common sense that Jefferson would have been so reckless as to impregnate Sally *after* the charges surfaced, while he remained president.

"James Callender dreamt up the myth of Sally Hemings," according to historian Willard Sterne Randall. "The only thing that he got right out of that one paragraph . . . was Sally Hemings' name."[35] Jefferson, two years before his own death, reflected on Callender's bespatterment and seemed to pity him: "He was a poor creature, sensible [oversensitive], hypochondriac, drunken, penniless & unprincipled."[36] Dumas Malone, the most respected Jeffersonian scholar, was less forgiving of the malignment: "The evil that he did was not buried with him: some of it has lasted through the generations."[37]

2

Misleading DNA

[T]his whole affair's been conducted by amateurs. I include myself.
—Dr. Eugene Foster, who performed the Jefferson DNA test[1]

[B]ecause the story of Sally Hemings and Thomas Jefferson has always been about blood and race and land.
—Lucian Truscott IV[2]

Two hundred years later, James Callender's historical libel intersected with Winifred Joyce Bennett. Mrs. Bennett's name should be registered in every history book. Who was she and what did she have to do with Thomas Jefferson and Sally Hemings?

Winifred was born on July 12, 1935, in Columbus, Ohio, earned a bachelor's degree in philosophy from Cornell in 1957, then moved to New York City. While studying philosophy and art history at New York University, she modeled for the Ford agency, framed by honey blonde hair and stunning good looks. In 1993, divorced after thirty years, the refined socialite moved to Charlottesville and, as an amateur historian, had an inquisitive mind. One evening in 1996, over a casual dinner at the home of Dr. Eugene Foster, the conversation turned to DNA. For years, a Charlottesville woman had claimed to be Anastasia, the long-lost daughter of Czar Nicholas II. Years later, DNA testing had debunked her claim. Mrs. Bennett wondered whether DNA might resolve the Jefferson-Sally controversy. And the rest of the story is, literally, history.[3]

The tumultuous DNA Project was conducted by Dr. Eugene Foster, a retired pathologist working at the University of Virginia Hospital. Foster was urged to undertake the 1998 DNA investigation by a "friend," later revealed to be Winifred Bennett, who was planning a book about the controversy. After some study, Foster embarked on a search for male candidates for testing.

One of the biggest misconceptions is that the DNA was drawn from Jefferson himself, or his heirs. This is false. Jefferson had no male, surviving children, so Foster turned to five male-line descendants of Jefferson's uncle, Field Jefferson. With the assistance of a Jefferson historian and genealogist Herbert Barger, a wizened former Air Force and Pentagon official, they located the individuals to be tested and included the descendants of the Carr family (Jefferson's nephews, both of whom were alleged to be Sally's lovers), and the Woodson family (the baby supposedly fathered by Jefferson in Paris).

When contacted about the DNA tests, the Woodson family was wary. They later wrote that they found Dr. Foster "befuddled."[4] The Woodsons also wanted access to half of the DNA samples involved in the study, so that their own geneticist could conduct independent tests. Dr. Foster refused. Byron Woodson, a Woodson descendant, states that his family "still puzzles over the inconclusive results."[5]

Finally, one male-line descendant of Eston Hemings, Sally's youngest child, was located and agreed to be tested. Blood samples were also obtained from several white descendants of Jefferson's neighbors, raising the possibility that they might have been Sally's partner.

At the University of Virginia, DNA was extracted from the blood samples. After Foster tried to negotiate a publication deal with the U.S. journal *Science* magazine (which refused to publish his article), the extracts were then flown to England (creating a legal issue, termed "chain of custody"[6]) by Dr. Foster in December 1997. Foster said that he rode a bus from Heathrow Airport to Oxford and handed over his samples to a researcher, who stored them in a refrigerator, after which the two "toddled" off to a pub.[7] Three laboratories at Oxford (University of Leicester) performed the analysis, and some tests were performed as far away as the Netherlands (Leiden University). The results were completed in June 1998 and published in *Nature* magazine on November 5, 1998.

Not *one* historian reviewed the findings, or the article, on behalf of *Nature* before it was published.

According to Dr. Foster, the results were threefold: (1) the analysis found *no match* between the DNA of Jefferson and Woodson descendants—thus, Woodson was not fathered by *any* Jefferson, debunking any gossip that Jefferson and Sally had a sexual relationship in Paris; (2) no match was found between the DNA of the Carrs (Jefferson's nephews) and Hemings descendants—thus, exonerating the Carr brothers, Peter and Samuel, as the father of Eston Hemings *only*; and (3) most controversial, the Y chromosome "haplotypes" of the descendants of Field Jefferson (Jefferson's uncle) and Eston Hemings did match, implicating *a male* Jefferson (not Thomas Jefferson, as the public was led to believe) as the father of Eston.[8]

Yet, the misleading and sensationalized headline in *Nature* pronounced Jefferson guilty: "Jefferson Fathered Slave's Last Child." The *Nature* article was signed by Dr. Foster and six other European biologists, none of them U.S. board-certified doctors, molecular scientists, or historians. Foster later wrote that he was embarrassed by the blatant spin of the *Nature* article, but had to admit that he had negotiated the text with the magazine, including the lead—"Jefferson Fathered Slave's Last Child."

Had the headline stated, "A Male Jefferson Fathered Slave's Last Child" it would have been accurate, but as Foster was quick to point out the published version was misleading. Nevertheless, the damage had been done. Although in some early reports the press conveyed the speculative and limited nature of the DNA study, the subtleties were gradually lost. Matters were complicated by solipsistic revisionists spreading the word that Jefferson's paternity was now scientific fact.

After the study was completed, Mrs. Bennett, the friend of Dr. Foster's who had prompted him to undertake the DNA tests, read in the newspaper that Foster had published the results in *Nature*. Much to her surprise, Foster did not give her any credit for her contribution, which she had planned to take to the official Jefferson Memorial Foundation (legal owners of Monticello) for financial support, research, and a possible book. Mrs. Bennett, in a conversation with Foster, questioned why Foster would do such a thing. *"Gene, what is it that you want? Do you want money?"* Foster replied, *"No, I want fame."* Mrs. Bennett related these statements to Jefferson historian Herbert Barger, adding: "Well, he was just willing to sacrifice me for his fame."[9]

Barger also related an interesting side note to the controversy:

After several months of research I was able to locate and identify a second Hemings DNA source, William Hemings, a son of Madison Hemings [Sally's eldest son], in a Veteran's Cemetery in Leavenworth, Kansas. I notified the Hemings family, gave them forms and urged them to permit a gathering of that valuable DNA. At the same time I advised Monticello President Dan Jordan, and suggested he urge the Hemings to permit the gathering of a second Hemings DNA. He [Jordan] refused to contact them, suggested that I contact them, but cautioned me against undue pressure. All eight Hemings family members refused to permit the test and their spokesperson, Shay Banks-Young, informed me that they are happy with their oral family history and will never give permission.[10]

"My family doesn't need to prove themselves," said Shay Banks-Young, fifty-five, a great-great-great-granddaughter of Madison Hemings, who lives in Columbus, Ohio. "If they dig up Thomas Jefferson at the same time, maybe I'll reconsider."[11] The Woodson family, if called to testify, would be particularly critical of Dr. Foster. They would allege that he rejected their requests for certain assurances. They wanted the blood samples to be independently tested for accuracy. Apparently, Dr. Foster circumvented their requests and found people who claimed they were male-line descendants of Thomas Jefferson through Thomas Woodson.

The Woodson DNA result is of extreme historical significance, and often overlooked: If Tom Woodson was Sally's Paris-conceived son, and shown to have the Jefferson Y chromosome, it would be a *certainty* that Jefferson was his father, since he was the only Jefferson in Paris. But there was no match. In fact, the one thing the DNA proves beyond all doubt is that whoever was Woodson's father, his Y chromosome was one common among white Europeans, not sub-Saharan blacks. Thus, Tom's father was surely someone Sally had met in France—but not Jefferson.[12]

Dr. Foster felt compelled to disavow his advocacy of the deceptive headline, but stood by his DNA analysis:[13]

[T]he genetic findings my collaborators and I reported in NATURE, Nov. 5, 1998 do not prove that Thomas Jefferson was the father of one of Sally Hemings' children. We have never made that claim. Furthermore, we do not believe that the Y-chromosome type we found in one of Sally

Hemings descendants occurs only in members of the Jefferson family. . . . There are many possible explanations for our findings and it may turn out that some highly complicated and improbable theories are true. . . .

Foster was obviously conflicted by his role in the subsequent rush to judgment maelstrom, as indicated in the following correspondence to Barger in 1998:

Dear Mr. Barger:
. . . I continue to understand your distress at what has happened with the media, but I would like you to understand my role more fully. First of all, you must understand that I had no control over the headline in Nature and had no knowledge whatever of the content of Ellis and Lander's companion piece. The title of our piece submitted to NATURE was "Genetic Evidence That Thomas Jefferson Fathered a Slave Child" . . . When NATURE accepted the article they told me that the format of the Scientific Correspondence articles required a very short title. The galley proof they sent me was titled, "Jefferson fathered his slave's child". . . . I regret that they chose the title they did, but I did my best to have a title that more accurately reflected the content of the article. Furthermore, we stated that we understood that there were other possible explanations. The discussion of the other possible explanations has to be left to historians . . . As you know, I have said publicly, both before and after publication of our article, that our results could not be conclusive. I have already sent you a copy of my letter to the New York Times in which I repeat that message . . . My experience with this matter so far tells me that no matter how strongly I say that the study is not conclusive and no matter how often I repeat it, it will not stop the media from saying what they want to in order to try to increase their circulation. And I truly regret that. In fact, I am angered by it . . . Your evidence on Randolph Jefferson and his sons, now that it has been made public, will be evaluated by other historians and will eventually be accepted if it is found to be valid. Eventually, and I don't think it will be soon, there will be enough solid scientific and historical evidence for people to be able to make an informed judgment . . . It has been painful to me to see my work over interpreted

and sensationalized by the media. *But I know that this will all die down* [emphasis added], that sober reconsideration of the issues will take place over the years, and that new scientific and historical knowledge will be accepted . . .

Sincerely,

Gene Foster[14]

After the DNA results were published, historian Willard Sterne Randall called the FBI DNA lab to question the inferences of Foster's conclusion, since no DNA was used from Jefferson himself:

> I don't deal in inferences. As a former journalist, I got on the phone and called the head of the DNA lab at the FBI, Jennifer Smith, who told me this case wouldn't hold up in court because the DNA has to be direct from the father. That is an impossibility because his [Jefferson's] only son died, and as long as there are other possibilities of people who had access to Sally Hemings the case would be thrown out of court on those grounds.[15]

Science writer Steven Corneliussen also disputes Foster's scientific methodology in an article written for the *Richmond Times-Dispatch*. He called the DNA results "science abuse." According to Corneliussen, scientific participants in the controversy, who were not scholars to put the results into historical perspective, abused science's special authority. Corneliussen criticized misreporting of the DNA evidence—misreporting that hobbled public understanding. According to Corneliussen, the statistical (Monte Carlo) study contributed nothing, not even evidence and it has no merit whatsoever. In fact, "it constitutes an abuse of the special authority of science."[16]

Dr. Edwin M. Knights, Jr., a doctor and genealogist, describes the problems of the DNA study:

> The worst case scenario is that in which DNA testing is properly performed on the appropriate individuals and then individuals who profess to be authorities in genealogy, choose their personal bias and ignore the scientific results. Unfortunately, this is what happened in the highly publicized DNA studies done to explore a possible relationship between Thomas Jefferson and one of his slaves, Sally Hemings.[17]

From a legal standpoint, Dr. Foster would be subjected to a scathing cross-examination. Important legal questions would have to be answered. For example, what was the "chain of custody" (reliably packaged and preserved) of the blood samples from Charlottesville, Virginia, while traveling through international airports to Oxford, England? Where and how were the samples stored? At what temperature were they stored? Would the method of storage maintain the integrity of the sample? Was there any security to prevent tampering? On a transatlantic trip, how would atmospheric radiation degrade the samples? Why was a laboratory in England and not the United States selected? How were the DNA extracts transported there? Were they examined and passed through customs? What was the chain of custody at the laboratories? Were the samples X-rayed at the airport and, if so, what effect did that have on the integrity of the samples? Where are the samples now? What independent controls were used to conduct the tests? Were the results "peer"-reviewed by U.S. scientists and if not, why not? And finally, how was the entire project financed and by whom? What was their bias or motivation?

Foster's own admission impeaches the entire DNA result:

> They were hurried into print. All of [the confusion over headlines] probably would have gotten straightened out if there had not been this frantic rush to beat the leaks. . . . [18]

In court, the Jefferson DNA analysis would be subject to a legal challenge under the case of *Daubert v. Merrell Dow Pharmaceuticals, Inc.*,[19] which holds that scientific evidence must be reliable (in form and substance), and not "junk science," but that is beyond the scope of this book. For example, a scientist from MIT, Dr. David Page, opined there was a problem of accurate bookkeeping, including the danger of mixing samples. Dr. Page suggested drawing more blood from the Eston Hemings's descendant and retyping it (which was never done).[20]

In the final analysis, the entire DNA test would be excluded from a real trial. More importantly, the DNA interpretations were completely misleading to the public as to Jefferson's paternity.

3

SALLY HEMINGS AND RANDOLPH JEFFERSON: "THE UNKNOWN BROTHER"

As to Randolph, I think it would not be improbable . . . he was clearly an earth bound farmer of no intellectual interest whatsoever. He liked hunting and fishing and that was about the size of it . . . I could imagine such a man doing this, but Jefferson was exactly the contrary.

—Historian Frank Berkeley[1]

The historians have the wrong Jefferson. Randolph Jefferson, Thomas's unaccomplished younger brother by twelve years, was the father of Eston Hemings, within a reasonable degree of certainty. All of the overwhelming, credible, corroborative evidence leads to Randolph as Sally's sexual partner, including the most important fact: Randolph was at Monticello exactly nine months before Eston's birth.

How, and what, did Randolph know of Sally? In fact, who was Sally Hemings?

SALLY HEMINGS

Sally is a constricted, historical enigma. As biographer John C. Miller commented: "[W]e know virtually nothing of Sally Hemings, or her motives [and] she is hardly more than a name."[2]

Born in 1773 at a Charles City plantation, Sally was the alleged illegitimate daughter of John Wayles, Jefferson's father-in-law. Her mother was Elizabeth (Betty) Hemings, a "chattel" of Wayles's, who was a well-known businessman, lawyer, and occasional slave trader for a British supplier. It was rumored that Wayles took his slave, Betty, (Sally's mother) as his "concubine," linking Jefferson's wife, Martha, as Sally's half sister.[3]

And here is where the debate begins. Those who believe that Wayles was Sally's father accelerate the argument that Jefferson had a personal affinity for Sally due to this fact, and that Sally may have "looked" like Jefferson's deceased wife, Martha, her potential "half sister." Once again, this is facile hearsay that is not only unproven, but directly refuted in the book *Anatomy of a Scandal* by Rebecca and Dr. James McMurry. The McMurry's spent over two years analyzing every record, newspaper, and family letter, finding no reference to Wayles having "mulatto" children or a "concubine." In fact, John Wayles was sick the last two years of his life and did not travel far, if at all. Sally was born several months after Wayles died, and was born at Guinea Plantation, about three days of hard travel from Wayles's home near Williamsburg.

Jefferson's slave, Isaac Jefferson, said, "Folks said that these Hemingses was old Mr. Wayles children."[4] Isaac is quoted in clear terms describing many people at Monticello where he lived as a boy and young man. However, he made an exception to his usual direct statements, qualifying his words by saying "Folks said" when he spoke of "old Mr. Wayles." Isaac had not been a Wayles family slave, and he was born about the same time John Wayles died.

Some scholars refer to an 1805 publication of a letter written by "Thomas Turner" (apparently a pseudonym), which claimed that Wayles was Sally's father. This October 1805 letter was signed as *T. Turner, Wheatland., Jefferson County*, yet expresses no personal knowledge of the charges, *saying they occurred before his birth*. In fact, young Thomas Turner of Wheatland, Jefferson County, was about twelve at the time.

Quite simply, the most credible evidence concludes that Wayles was not Sally's father. Thus, Sally and Martha were not half sisters, and did not "look or act like each other." Even official Monticello concludes that "there are no documentary records relating to Wayles's possible paternity of any Hemings children."[5] Yet this false rumor directly affected Jefferson and the way he treated the Hemings family. Jefferson, completely innocent of Callender's allegations in the newspaper, could only have defended himself publicly by revealing who the Hemings were and how they came to Monticello. His own father-in law, John Wayles, had been alleged to be Sally's father, making his wife (Martha), Sally's half sister.[6] Although the allegation was untrue, as an honorable man, Jefferson was prepared to absorb the venomous charge and kept his silence rather than embarrass his late father-in-law, and dishonor his beloved wife's memory.[7]

As to Sally's mother, Betty, a Monticello slave described her as a "bright mulatto woman."[8] The list of her children, as recorded later by Jefferson, included several children, some fathered by someone other than Wayles. The oldest child was Mary, born in 1753, Nance born in 1761, and the youngest of this group, Bob, born in 1762. Betty's other children were born in the year John Wayles died, including Sally Hemings, born in 1773 (month unknown).

In that same year Jefferson inherited, on his wife's behalf, all of Betty Hemings's family (including Sally as an infant) as well as several large parcels of land and 135 slaves from Wayles. Most of the Hemings, including Betty, became house servants at Monticello, which seemed to confirm their special status. It seems clear that the Hemingses were trusted and indispensable servants to Jefferson's family as nannies, cooks, carpenters, dress makers, seamstresses, and almost everything else that could be physically made to self-support Monticello.[9] Historian Donald Jackson explains this special relationship:

> That the Hemings matriarchy was well thought of by the Jefferson family made the children and grandchildren more conspicuous than the other slaves in the Monticello neighborhood. Add the facts that miscegenation [race mixing] did exist in the South; that men of such probity as George Washington were falsely but commonly believed to engage in it; and that Sally and her children were all but white in appearance, and it is little wonder that Jefferson's opponent would eventually produce a story conferring on him the paternity for those children.[10]

It appears that Sally was illiterate, and one can only speculate as to the relationship she had with the Jefferson family. No recorded evidence suggests that it was hostile. A reasonable inference would be that Sally must have left Monticello after it was sold. By 1830, she was living with her sons, Madison and Eston, in or around Charlottesville. It is interesting to note that in one census, Sally was listed as free and in another she was designated "white."[11]

Some slave historians have speculated that Sally lived inside the house at Monticello, or had a secret "room" at the main house (discussed subsequently). This is false. After her return from Paris as maid to Jefferson's daughter, Sally lived with her older sister, Critta, on Mulberry Row, the slave quarters closest to the big house. Four years later, they moved, in all probability, into one of the three new log cabins built in 1793. Finally between 1803 and 1807 Sally moved into a masonry room near the "south dependency," then the kitchens and stables. There is not a shred of credible evidence that Sally lived inside Monticello, or occupied some secret rendezvous room there.[12]

Sally died in 1835 at age sixty-two. She had no burial marker or obituary in the newspaper. There is no recorded evidence or letters suggesting that she ever addressed her relationship, if any, with Jefferson. Nor is there any evidence about her activities in the post-Monticello period. If Sally was Jefferson's sexual partner, there is no indication that she was approached by anyone on this subject.[13]

Jefferson once called the letters of a person "the only full and genuine journal of his life." In an ocean of words, he wrote and received nearly fifty thousand letters to family, friends, experts on varied subjects, and to many people he did not even know. He also kept fastidious records, an epistolary record, in his own hand, which runs 656 pages. He listed chronologically every letter written and received from November 1783 until his death on July 4, 1826.[14]

Some of the voluminous letters are chronicled by Princeton University Press's exhaustive Papers of Thomas Jefferson, one colossal diary. Yet, there are only a few *passing mentions* of Sally in these thousands of Jefferson letters, chronicled at Princeton, Yale, the Library of Congress, and the University of Virginia libraries. And in fact one casual reference of Sally was not even by her specific name. She was referred to as "Maria's maid"—Maria being Jefferson's young daughter.[15]

There is evidence that other slaves were jealous of the Hemingses' special treatment. Jefferson's grandson, Jeff Randolph, said the Hemings family was "a source of bitter jealousy to the other slaves who liked to account for it with other reasons than the true one viz. superior intelligence capacity and fidelity to trusts."[16] Their special treatment caused rivalry with the other servants, and probably was a catalyst for the "Sally" rumor.

Sally herself was described by her son, Madison, as a chambermaid and seamstress. Thus, she and her family would have been Jefferson's natural choice to take charge inside Monticello.[17] It was also Jefferson's practice to keep family units together, so as the other Hemingses matured they were given house assignments also. But there is a more important reason for the Hemingses' particular treatment: Jefferson's knowledge of Betty Hemings, Sally's mother. Betty was a house servant for Wayles and she had been part of Martha Jefferson's life since birth. Since Martha's own mother died young, Betty may have acted as a surrogate mother to her. Naturally, Thomas Jefferson's guiding principle in his relationship with the Hemingses, revealed by his actions and thereafter in every decision he made, was to accept responsibility for their welfare. He wished to give them his fullest protection, and place them in a safe environment, Monticello.[18]

Jefferson's policy of freeing the Hemings men on his death, who were able, mature carpenters practicing a trade with their uncle, did not apply to the Hemings girls, especially not to Sally. Historian Douglass Adair argues in his famous essay that if Jefferson had freed Sally at his death, there was no place for her to go. She would have been displaced in eighteenth-century America, as she was described as nearly white. In such southern cities as New Orleans young women like Sally would have two choices— to work in a brothel or to become a mistress of a young, wealthy Creole. Both choices would have been abhorrent to Jefferson. Adair suggests that since there was no venue for Sally to travel if she was freed, Jefferson kept her where he thought he could keep her safe—with his own family at Monticello.[19]

Jefferson died on the Fourth of July, 1826, killed by a wasting diarrhea and an infection of the urinary tract.[20] It has been alleged that Sally was present at Jefferson's deathbed. In the recent HBO production of *John Adams* (based on historian David McCullough's seminal biography), a light-skinned black female servant weeps, while seated at Jefferson's bedside. Standing on the other side of the bed is a young black male, assumed to be one of Sally's sons.

Simply put, this is Hollywood's bleached version of the historical record.

At seven o'clock on the night of July 3, 1826, Jefferson awakened and uttered a declaration, "This is the Fourth," or "This is the fourth of July." Told that it would be soon, he slept again. Two hours later, at about nine,

Jefferson was roused to be given a dose of laudanum, which he refused saying, "No doctor, nothing more." According to a throng of authoritative Jefferson scholars, including Dumas Malone and Henry Randall, the only people present at Jefferson's deathbed were: 1) his beloved and loyal daughter Martha, 2) his grandson Jeff Randolph, 3) Dr. Robley Dunglison, Jefferson's twenty-seven-year-old personal physician, 4) Nicholas Trist, his grandson-in-law, and 5) Jefferson's long serving adult butler, Burwell Colbert.

Historian Henry S. Randall writing in *The Life of Thomas Jefferson— Volume III* (1858), confirms this in a narrative written by Colonel Thomas Jefferson Randolph (Jefferson's grandson) to Randall regarding the death of Jefferson. The narrative records that Colonel Randolph, Nicholas Trist, and Dr. Robley Dunglison were at Jefferson's bedside on July 3 and July 4, 1826. Burwell Colbert was the only black servant at Jefferson's bedside that Colonel Randolph mentioned by name. Randolph states that as Jefferson neared death, Martha Randolph (Jefferson's daughter), Mr. Trist, and Dr. Dunglison spent much of their time with Jefferson. Randall adds: "Mr. Trist's written recollection of the closing death scene coincides too closely with Colonel Randolph's in all material particulars, to require their transcription."[21]

The historical record is clear: No Sally at Jefferson's deathbed. Even if we assume, *arguendo,* that she was present, this was not uncommon in the old South. Favorite house servants huddling around the deathbed of their owner was the custom in the South. When Martha Jefferson died, several servants also surrounded her deathbed, including Betty Hemings and four of her children. Thus, even if Sally was present, which no evidence establishes, this was common practice in the South, not evidence of a sequestered lover.

Jefferson had his wish and he survived until Tuesday, July 4, 1826, the fiftieth anniversary of the Declaration of Independence. Before his death he had directed his daughter, Martha, to a drawer in which he had placed a final poem entitled "A Death-bed Adieu from Th. J. to M. R.":

> *Life's visions are vanished, its dreams are no more;*
> *Dear friends of my bosom, why bathed in tears?*
> *I go to my fathers; I welcome the shore,*
> *Which crowns all my hopes or which buries my cares.*

Then farewell, my dear, my lov'd daughter, adieu!
The last pang of life is in parting from you!
Two seraphs await me long shrouded in death;
I will bear them your love on my last parting breath.[22]

The "two seraphs await me" is a clear reference to his dear wife "Patty" and his deceased daughter, Maria.[23] At the end of his life, Jefferson allowed himself to acknowledge one woman and one woman only: his most faithful and loyal daughter Martha, the "nurse of my age."[24]

RANDOLPH JEFFERSON: THE UNKNOWN BROTHER

It is against this historical backdrop that Randolph Jefferson enters the controversy. Unfortunately, neither a portrait nor physical description of Randolph exists. But Jefferson described Randolph after his death in an 1815 deposition:

[T]hat he considered his said brother as not possessing skill for the judicious management of his affairs, and that in all occasions of life a diffidence in his own opinions. . . . and an easy pliancy to the wishes and urgency of others made him very susceptible of influence from those who had any views upon him. . . . [25]

Randolph was born on October 1, 1755, about thirteen years after his famous brother. Dumas Malone described Randolph as a "very amiable man" that "never amounted to anything much" even though the brothers were similarly educated and reared. They even took violin lessons from the same tutor.[26]

Randolph served in the Revolutionary War and was commissioned a captain in the Buckingham Militia in 1794. It was in this militia that he served with a number of white men who were involved in interracial relationships—two of whom worked at Monticello. In fact, Randolph served with Captain Wingfield's Company in the Albemarle Militia in 1776 along with white men like William Fossett, Stephen Hughes, Joseph Nielson, and Thomas West, all of whom were involved in sexual, interracial relationships. Fossett and Nielson were hired workers at Monticello and specifically cohabitated with members of the Hemings family. Mary

Hemings (Sally's sister) was Fossett's mistress, and Nielson fathered a child with Betty Hemings, Sally's mother.[27]

The DNA study of the Y chromosome found that there was a link between Eston and some male Jefferson. In fact, the DNA tests indicated that any one of seven Jeffersons could have been the father of Eston. The seven possibilities identified are: Thomas [Jefferson], Randolph (Jefferson's brother), Randolph's four sons, and a cousin George.

Cynthia Burton, a slight, soft-spoken Charlottesville genealogist and meticulous researcher, notes in her book, *Jefferson Vindicated*, the probability that Hemings's children were fathered by Randolph. "Other analyses that I had read, they kind of overlooked Randolph Jefferson," she declared in an interview. "That was kind of shocking to me." According to Professor Robert Turner, law professor and Jefferson scholar at the University of Virginia, Randolph fathered children by his own slaves, and reportedly spent time with slaves at Monticello.[28] Randolph, according to Turner and a blue-ribbon panel of independent scholars that he chaired, is a far more likely suspect. Randolph visited Monticello often, and his years as a widower corresponded with the years in which Hemings had children. "We know that Randolph had a habit of socializing at night with the slaves," Turner added and he "would fiddle and dance in slave quarters." According to the former Monticello slave, Isaac Jefferson: "Old Master's brother, Mass Randall, was a mighty simple man: used to come out among black people, play the fiddle and dance half the night; hadn't much more sense than Isaac."[29] Historian Forrest McDonald describes Randolph more bluntly: a "half wit."[30]

Thomas Jefferson, on the other hand, seemed amiable and pleasant, but was nonetheless "a man of almost impenetrable emotional reserve."[31] He separated himself from his slaves, and by some historical accounts considered them inferior in the exercise of reason and intellect. As author Andrew Burstein comments: "He was a fair master, but not uncomfortable in the role of master."[32]

Additional research by Burton provides a number of compelling reasons why Randolph is considered the father of Eston:[33]

- Randolph was expected at Monticello to visit his family *during Eston's exact conception period*; his twin sister, Lucy, and her family, who lived near Monticello, were preparing to move west that fall, so Randolph would have visited before they left.

- Randolph had the same Jefferson Y chromosome as his older brother Thomas Jefferson and other Jefferson males. Randolph had the same parents as Thomas, and carried the same genes that determine appearance.
- Randolph had a reputation for socializing with Jefferson's slaves and was counseled about his use of alcohol.
- Randolph lived less than twenty miles from Monticello and had a pattern of visiting his brother in the spring and late summer. Randolph and his sons owned more than enough horses for them to visit Monticello.
- Randolph was a widower in 1807, only fifty-one years old in contrast to the frail and in declining health, sixty-four-year-old Thomas Jefferson. All of Sally's children were born between 1795 and 1808, when Randolph was single.
- Randolph made his will at Monticello six days *following* the birth of Eston, leaving his estate to his five *legitimate* sons, apparently severing any future paternity claims.
- Randolph was rumored among descendants of former slaves connected to Monticello to have fathered "colored children." Until 1976, the oral history of Eston's heirs maintained that they descended from a Jefferson "uncle." Randolph was known at Monticello as "Uncle Randolph."[34]
- Most importantly, Randolph produced six "male" children; Jefferson, on the other hand, produced all girls—except for a nonviable male infant—making it much more likely from a genetic standpoint that Randolph was the father of Eston Hemings.

The evidence is clear that Randolph was present at Monticello at the time of Eston's conception (the DNA match). In fact, Jefferson wrote an invitation to his brother dated August 12, 1807, approximately nine months before Sally's pregnancy:

Dear brother
I did not recieve your letter of July 9 till the 8th. inst. and now, by the first post inclose you 20.D. to pay for the clover and greenswerd seed; which goes by post to Warren. The greenswerd seed I wish to have

here; but the white clover seed is to go to Bedford. I must thereefore get you to make interest with Mr. Crouch to have it conveyed to the care of Mr. Brown mercht. of Lynchburg for Burgess Griffin at Poplar Forest. This he can do I expect by his batteaux which go to Lynchburg.

Our sister Marks arrived here last night and we shall be happy to see you also. I salute you affectionately.

Th:Jefferson[35]

The letter references Burgess Griffin, who was an overseer at Poplar Forest, Jefferson's farm in Bedford County. Anna Scott (Mrs. Hastings) Marks was Randolph's twin sister. The Markses lived in Louisa County, adjacent to Albemarle County on the east.[36]

Thus, documentary evidence places Randolph, *with his sons most probably*, at Monticello to see his sister before she departed. Since the trip to Monticello was less than a day's ride, this was an easy journey in good weather. And since Randolph and Thomas Jefferson had the same Y chromosome, he would also match the DNA in the 1998 study.

Yet, the official Monticello Foundation report (discussed and dissected subsequently) rejected this possibility. Why? Because the committee concluded that "Randolph Jefferson and his sons are not *known* [emphasis added] to have been at Monticello at the time of Eston Hemings' conception."[37] The Foundation's report concludes, in essence, that there is no written evidence that Randolph actually visited Jefferson.

There is also no evidence he did not go.

According to Jefferson researcher and scholar Eyler Coates, a former assistant Librarian of Congress:[38] "An invitation should be enough evidence, because there just weren't those kinds of records kept on family visits. Only when something special happened, like when Thomas Jefferson made out Randolph's last will and testament, do we have actual documented evidence that Randolph was present. Ordinary visits would be noted only incidentally."[39]

Other evidence suggests that Randolph was also present at Monticello when Harriet I was conceived by Sally in January 1795. Both Jefferson and his young daughter Mary were at Monticello with Martha's two eldest children during this period. Specifically, on January 22, 1795, Jefferson wrote a letter to his daughter Martha that referred to his "sister" Anne, a clear reference to Randolph's wife. This means that Randolph's wife was in the neighborhood visiting her family, and most probably Randolph traveled with her since their oldest child was only fourteen at the time.[40]

Other than Randolph Jefferson, twenty-five other adult male descendants of his father Peter (1707–1757) and his uncle Field (1702–1765) lived in Virginia during the 1794–1807 period of Sally Hemings's pregnancies:

- His brother Randolph Jefferson (1755–1815) and five of his sons.
- His first cousin John Robertson Jefferson (1743–1809) and six of his sons.
- Seven sons of Peter Field Jefferson (1735–1794), his first cousin.
- Five sons of George Jefferson (1739–1780), his first cousin.[41]

Historian Cynthia Burton's methodical research indicates that all of Randolph's sons had been at or near Monticello during the various times of Sally's conceptions.[42] In fact, an 1884 book in Todd County, Kentucky, records that Isham Randolph Jefferson (1781–1852) was "reared" at Monticello. Barger's research corroborated Burton. He found an important historical statement in J. H Battle's *The History of Todd Co., Ky.*[43] According to the entry, Isham lived at Monticello and was "reared" and under the supervision of his famous uncle, Thomas Jefferson. Isham would have been about fifteen when Sally's first child was born and approximately twenty-seven when Eston was born in 1808. In fact, his age would make him eligible for the paternity of all Sally's children.[44] Jefferson himself stated in his 1815 deposition that Isham came to see him about financial problems related to his father, and his father's second wife. Needless to say, this visit was not recorded in any formal registry, but Jefferson's deposition confirmed Isham's visit.[45]

As to Randolph's other sons, it is known that Thomas Jefferson, Jr. (1783–1876) resided at Monticello for extended periods of schooling in 1799, 1800, and possibly 1801. Robert Lewis Jefferson (1787–1808) carried a letter to Monticello in July or August 1807; dated July 9, it was not received by Jefferson until August 8.[46]

Most importantly, Randolph was a widower at the time of Sally's pregnancies, and between wives when shortly after his own wife's death, Sally became pregnant with her first child, Harriet I. It had been more than five years since Sally had arrived at Monticello from Paris with Jefferson. *No pregnancies resulted in those years.* She continued having children until 1808 when Eston was born. Randolph married his second wife the very next year, 1809, and had a child, John, born about 1810, proving beyond all doubt that he was sexually active and capable. Most telling, however, is the fact that three of Sally's children, Harriet, Beverly, and Eston had uncommon names, and were the given family names of Randolph Jefferson's mother, after whom Randolph was named.[47] In fact, David Mead Randolph, Jefferson's cousin who fed malicious gossip to the journalist James Callender, had three children by these same names.

Other evidence concretely connects Randolph as Sally's sexual partner. For example, when Jefferson finally came home to Monticello after his second term as president (1809), Sally *stopped* having children. Randolph was widowed at the time, probably as early as 1795, but as soon as he remarried in late 1808 or early 1809, Sally *had no more children.* Thomas Jefferson, Jr., Randolph's son, married on October 3, 1808, and after this date, Sally did not produce any more children as well.

Author Rebecca L. McMurry, whose family resided in Charlottesville during Jefferson's time, wrote in the preface of her book *Jefferson, Callender and the Sally Story,* that her family affirmed that Randolph Jefferson was the father of Sally's "yellow" children:

> In late 1974, Aunt Rose spoke excitedly of reading a new book about Thomas Jefferson [Fawn Brodie's]. My mother listened for a few minutes and then said, "That's trash!" She went on to explain how her grandmother had told of the "Sally story." Her grandmother lived for the first several years of her married life about 15 miles north of Monticello. Though these events had taken place decades earlier, her "in-laws" had purchased items at the great sales at Monticello and Montpelier . . . My mother continued, saying the rumors concerning the father of Sally Hemings' children had placed the blame on Jefferson's "half-wit brother," though commenting that the "Carr boys" were "too familiar" with her as well.[48]

Some scholars have concluded that Sally's children had more than one father. A similar argument was advanced by Dr. James McMurry and Mrs. McMurry in their book, *Anatomy of a Scandal.* "It is quite possible that she (Sally Hemings) has carried on an affair with one or more of the Carr nephews, but met with Randolph, the much younger Jefferson brother at the time of Eston's conception."[49] In fact, Sally's mother, her role model, had at *least two and possibly three lovers*, at least one white: Englishman Joseph Nelson (or Neilson, a white carpenter at Monticello), who fathered most of her twelve children. Betty produced two more children (John or "Johnny" and Lucy) *after* her arrival at Monticello by Nelson. Thus, it is highly probable that Sally took her queue from her mother, and had more than one father for her children.[50]

As the DNA revelations unfolded, Herbert Barger, the noted researcher and Jefferson historian, urged Dr. Foster to examine the descendants of Randolph Jefferson and his sons as DNA candidates. Foster thanked Barger for the information and did nothing. Barger also located the burial site of Madison Hemings's son in Kansas, but the family refused to permit an exhumation.[51]

After seven years of Jefferson research, Karyn Traut, a playwright and adjunct professor in the Department of Social Medicine at the University of North Carolina, also reached the conclusion that Randolph was the prime suspect. She spent two years writing a play based on this research, called *Saturday's Children*. For her, the DNA study indicated that her research had been correct. A "Jefferson" did father at least one of Sally's children. Randolph Jefferson, not Thomas.

"One day I asked myself: 'What if everyone were telling the truth?'" Traut said in an interview. "What if Sally Hemings had told her sons that Jefferson was their father? No one called him 'Thomas Jefferson.' Everyone called him 'Mr. Jefferson.' Suddenly everything fit because there were two Mr. Jeffersons."[52] Traut learned of Randolph while reading a book titled *Thomas Jefferson and Music*, in which a reference is made to Randolph. Apparently Jefferson paid for Randolph's violin lessons, but Randolph used his skill for "country fiddling" with the servants. Traut also learned that Randolph had been married twice, unlike his older brother who promised Martha on her deathbed never to remarry. "Hmmmm," Traut wondered, "I'm starting to see Randolph as possibly a rebel to his older more famous and authoritative brother. By 'dancing with the servants,' Randolph seemed to be living with the times rather than trying to change them as was Thomas Jefferson." Digging further, she revealed more facts in favor of Randolph as father of Sally's children, including that Randolph lived a mere twenty miles from Monticello, within easy visiting distance.

"Ah ha," Karyn recalled thinking. "I have an original answer to an historical question. There were two Mr. Jeffersons."[53]

In short, within a reasonable degree of historical certainty, the most credible, direct, and circumstantial evidence proves Randolph Jefferson fathered Eston Hemings: Randolph had the identical Jefferson Y chromosome as his older brother, Thomas, that matched the DNA; Randolph had a reputation for socializing with Jefferson's slaves and was expected at Monticello approximately nine months before the birth of Eston Hemings; the DNA match was to a male son of Sally's. Randolph had six male sons. Thomas Jefferson had all female children—except for a nonviable male infant—with his beloved wife, Martha; and finally, until 1976, the oral history of Eston's family held that they descended from a Jefferson "uncle." Randolph was known at Monticello as "Uncle Randolph."

4

"An American in Paris"

In every scheme of happiness, she is placed in the foreground of the picture, as the principal figure. Take that away, and it is no picture for me.
—Jefferson to Robert Skipwith, August 3, 1771[1]

September 6, 1782, was the worst day of Thomas Jefferson's life. His beloved wife, Martha Wayles Skelton Jefferson, died at age thirty-three, from complications following child birth in the previous spring. As she lay dying, Jefferson promised her he would never marry again, a remarkable pledge of love, since most eighteenth-century widowers quickly remarried. Shortly before her death, Martha copied some poignant lines from one of Jefferson's favorite books, Laurence Sterne's *Tristram Shandy*:

> . . . the days and hours of it are flying over our heads like clouds of a windy day never to return . . .

Martha was too weak to complete the lines, so Jefferson completed it for her in his own hand:

> —and every time I kiss thy hand to bid adieu, every absence which follows it, are preludes to the eternal separation which we are shortly to make.[2]

Jefferson lovingly wrapped a lock of Martha's hair with a scrap of paper containing the poem, and stored the token in his desk. It remained there for the rest of his life, only discovered by his daughter upon his death.[3] He also took some of Martha's hair and sealed it in a locket. Jefferson wore it around his neck, and into his grave.[4]

As the story was related to John and Abigail Adams, Jefferson was led from his wife's deathbed incoherent with grief. For weeks, he "confined himself from the world," pacing back and forth, seeing no one but his daughter Patsy. Nabby Adams, John's daughter, wrote in her journal what Patsy described: Jefferson "rode out . . . incessantly on horseback, rambling about the mountains." Patsy was his "solitary witness to many a violent burst of grief."[5]

After ten short years of "unchequered happiness,"[6] the death of Martha was the most devastating chapter in Jefferson's life. She had given him his emotional identity with love, affection, and children. Psychologically, he never fully recovered from this tragedy. The shock of Martha's death was so grave that he found it almost unbearable to speak her name, and he burned every letter that had passed between them.[7] As one historian noted, Jefferson's grieving had the feeling of "injustice inflicted on the living survivor."[8]

The tall, soft-spoken Virginian was a deeply feeling man when it came to his adored Martha, described as quite "beautiful, a little above medium height and with a lithe and exquisitely formed figure, with a graceful and queenlike carriage."[9] Jefferson, who regarded conjugal love, like religion, as a private matter, hid the emotional bonds of his life with Martha from the world. As one historian, concluded, "it was clearly a happy marriage even with its sorrows."[10]

Jefferson did not sit for a canvassed portrait until after his wife's death, and he never permitted Martha's portrait to be painted.[11] In a letter expressed to his friend, Major General Marquis de Chastellux, Jefferson wrote: "A single event wiped away all of my plans and left me a blank which I had not the spirits to fill up."[12] He described himself emerging from a "stupor of mind which had rendered me as dead to the world as she." At thirty-nine, he had been widowed with three young children, his political career seemingly dissolved. He lost all interest in Monticello and believed he could never be happy there again. When Congress nominated him as minister to France, he immediately accepted, although his appointment was ultimately postponed.

It is against this emotional backdrop that one must analyze the accusation that Jefferson began an affair with a fourteen-year-old Sally in Paris, less than two years after Martha's death. That Sally became Jefferson's "concubine" while he was minister to France is not corroborated by any other evidence or witness. Indeed, all the reasonable evidence contradicts this allegation.

In fact, Jefferson was completely unaware that Sally was accompanying his young daughter, Polly, on the voyage to France. He only learned this later when they arrived in London, at the Adams's residence. Jefferson had asked his sister-in-law, Elizabeth Eppes, to send an escort that was "some good lady passing from America to France, or even England, would be most eligible . . . [or] a careful Negro woman, as Isabel for instance if she has had the small pox, would suffice under the patronage of a gentleman."[13]

"Isabel" referred to Isabel Hern, thirty, an experienced caregiver with several children of her own. Her husband was David Hern, one of the skilled artisans at Monticello. Both were familiar to Jefferson, however Isabel was not available due to physical complications from childbirth. Thus, Jefferson's sister-in-law chose Sally to accompany Polly, not Jefferson. She did so most probably because she knew Sally's brother (James) was already in Paris, and Polly seemed fond of Sally.

An apprehensive Polly, described as "timid and clinging . . . a querulous beauty," was taken on board the ship, with Sally, on the Appomattox River. Polly was distracted by her cousins until she fell asleep and awoke to find the *Robert* under sail. The only familiar face with her was her nurse, Sally Hemings.[14] Abigail Adams, already in London, received Polly and Sally on their way to Paris. Abigail was in a unique position to observe Sally. In fact, she would record in a letter to Jefferson:

[T]he Girl who is with her is quite a child, and [the ship's] Captain Ramsey is of the opinion will be of so little Service that he had better carry her back with him. But of this you will be a judge. She [Sally] seems fond of the child and appears good natured [*sic*].[15]

In her next letter, Abigail wrote: "The Girl [Polly] has with her, wants more care than the child, and is wholly incapable of looking properly after her, without some superiour [*sic*] to direct her."[16]

This is a unique, firsthand observation of young Sally, in stark contrast to the alluring seductress she has been portrayed in movies and novels.

Once Sally arrived in Paris, given the size and layout of Jefferson's residence, the Hotel de Langeac, scant opportunity existed for a sexual liaison. The house functioned as the "equivalent of an embassy, flowing over with visitors, guests, tutors, and servants" none of whom left a single piece of recorded evidence of an affair.[17]

Moreover, the Paris residence was relatively small with only two bedrooms and a larger oval office, plus a bedroom that Jefferson occupied on the second floor. William Short, his secretary, lived in one bedroom, leaving only one room for guests. After April 1789, Polly and Patsy (Jefferson's daughters) returned from their convent school and lived at home with no spare bedroom. James Hemings, Sally's brother, lived in a servant's quarter. And the record is vague where Sally actually resided.

While in Paris, Jefferson placed both his daughters in the most fashionable and expensive convent school, the Abbaye Royale de Panthemont, on the left bank. The girls wore crimson uniforms and were soon speaking French better than their father, who visited them frequently enjoying the walk over the Seine by the Pont Neuf. "She [Patsy] is a sweet girl, delicacy and sensibility are read in every feature," Nabby Adams wrote of Patsy, "and her manners are in unison with all that is amiable and lovely; she is very young."[18] In a letter written shortly after Polly's arrival in Paris, Jefferson recorded that she was "now in the same convent with her sister and will come and see me once or twice a week." The two daughters remained in the convent school until shortly before the Jefferson family returned to Virginia. It is reasonable to believe that Sally was not with Jefferson at this time, but rather went with his daughters.[19]

In contrast, there exists almost no record of Sally's activities in Paris. The more reasonable view is that she did not even live in the same building with James Hemings or Thomas Jefferson during most of her stay. She was, after all, their servant to Jefferson's daughters. Thus, it would be natural for her to live near them at Abbaye Royale de Panthemont convent. Monticello researcher Lucia Cinder Stanton concludes that: "It was not uncommon for the servants of boarding students to continue to attend their mistresses in the Abbaye and some of the Jefferson sisters' schoolmates knew Sally well enough to send her greetings in their correspondence."[20]

Not a shred of evidence exists that any of Jefferson's friends in Paris, or anyone on his staff, ever mentioned a relationship with Sally. One might expect such gossip to be found in the diary of either the Parisians or expatriate Americans who knew Jefferson. Nor did two men in a position to observe Jefferson in close quarters, William Short, or his majordomo Adrien Petit, ever advance such testimony.

Jefferson's business records are helpful. The president kept meticulous records of his plantation, but there is *no record* of any child born to Sally in 1790, if she became pregnant in Paris and returned to America.[21] One further mystery surrounds Sally's alleged Paris pregnancy. Callender charged that Jefferson fathered a son with Sally that resembled Jefferson. The muckraking journalist referred to the boy as "President Tom"; he later wrote that the boy circulated and put on "airs" in Charlottesville. Callender admitted that he never saw or met "Tom," and never visited Monticello.

A slave named Thomas Woodson might have been the young boy Callender referred to as "President Tom."[22] A host of paternity historians contend that Woodson was in fact the child of Sally and Jefferson conceived in Paris. The evidence that destroys this contention is overwhelming: (1) The 1998 DNA completely *eliminated* Thomas Jefferson, or any Jefferson, as Woodson's father; (2) Woodson is not attributed to Sally in any of Jefferson records; (3) nor is "Tom's" existence even recorded in the 1790s; (4) his Woodson name was adopted later, so if he was a slave at Monticello born in 1790–1792, under what name was he listed?; (5) there is no "Tom" in any list of slaves; and (6) no child, other than those well known, were associated with Sally in such lists.

Nevertheless, the Woodson family has adamantly claimed Jefferson as "Tom's" father. According to their hearsay, Thomas Woodson was the son Sally conceived in Paris (contrary to Madison's account [Sally's son] that the infant died soon after she returned to Virginia).[23] A reasonable argument could be made that both the Woodson oral history, as well as the DNA are correct. Taken together, this evidence strongly suggests that a man other than Jefferson impregnated Sally in Paris. This could explain why Sally, or Madison, may have invented her story, although she remained silent her entire life. It seems probable that the fabrication, given the available evidence, was Madison's alone. Moreover, she had a certain freedom in Paris. Sally lived in proximity to Adrien Petit, as well as

William Short, Jefferson's secretary, and several other male servants, when not boarding with Jefferson's daughters at the fashionable convent school, the Abbaye Royale de Panthemont.

What of Madison's accusation that Sally refused to return to Virginia with Jefferson? Common sense dictates this is simply not plausible. Is it likely that a young girl of sixteen, living in a foreign country for only two years would rebel and insist on staying there? Where would she live? How would she survive? Sally did not possess any special trade or skills to support herself. She may have learned elementary French, but was scarcely fluent. Madison recalled that after two full years in Paris Sally "was just beginning to understand the French language well."[24] Some would argue, unsoundly in my view, that Sally, a sixteen-year-old slave, in a foreign land with no family support, no special friends or protectors in Paris, and no visible means of support, would choose to stay and live out her years in Paris.

In fact, there is little evidence of Sally's life in Paris. According to Jefferson's records, Sally was inoculated against smallpox. Afterward, she spent several weeks away from the Jefferson home in isolation, somewhere outside the city during her convalescence.[25] Again, this was no special favor, but a prudent precaution. In fact, Jefferson had a history with vaccines. He used a vaccine for smallpox on his Monticello slaves almost as early as did the medical profession in England.[26] In his first presidential year he had his family and "people" (slaves) in Virginia inoculated with a virus he obtained from Dr. Benjamin Waterhouse, and his sons-in-law followed his example. Jefferson exchanged letters frequently with doctors on this medical subject. In his third year as president, he had brought a vaccine from Washington to personally inoculate an entire neighborhood for smallpox, thirty miles from Monticello.[27]

A cryptic reference in Jefferson's account books recorded a payment on April 22, 1789, to "Dupre 5 weeks board of Sally washing &c" for Sally's board and washing.[28] Nothing substantive is known of this note. Did Sally board away from the Jefferson home after Martha and Polly were withdrawn from school and lived at the Hotel de Langeac, or was this for Sally's services at their school? Some historians have argued that Jefferson bought Sally an elaborate wardrobe as proof of their relationship. This is a gross misinterpretation and takes the evidence out of context. When Patsy Jefferson began to participate in French society, Sally's role naturally increased. Jefferson spent money on clothing and accessories for both his daughters and their servant, Sally, who would have needed a better wardrobe for her new social milieu.[29]

Sally's refusal to return to the United States, if true, was probably instigated by her brother, James. His history may have been the backdrop for Sally's rebellion and Jefferson's alleged inducements. James trained as a chef, studied French with a tutor, and desired to remain in Paris. However, some years later, he was given his freedom as a result of a written agreement signed by Jefferson. It is probable that James negotiated his freedom before returning to Virginia. This could have led Sally to request concessions from Jefferson—that her children would be freed at age twenty-one.

Some historians have tried to make a persuasive case for Sally's "treaty" with Jefferson. He "induced" her to come back to Virginia with him and promised her "extraordinary privileges" according to her son, Madison. These "extraordinary privileges" are not visible in the lists of Jefferson's *Farm Book*, the only source of Sally's subsequent life at Monticello. In it, Jefferson recorded, just as he did for the other slaves, the births of Sally's children, the clothing she and other "house-maids" received, as well as her meat and cornmeal rations—the usual allotment.[30] No special privileges.

Some also argue that the freeing of Sally's children by Jefferson, though not exactly at age twenty-one, was a promise he made to Sally in Paris. In fact, both Beverly and Harriet (Sally's children) actually "ran away," an eighteenth-century term suggesting they left with Jefferson's acquiescence.[31] Edmund Bacon, Jefferson's overseer, wrote that he gave Harriet a ticket to Philadelphia and some money when she departed. The law in Virginia, at the time, required a freed slave to move out of the state. According to Madison Hemings, Harriet and Beverly disappeared into the white community. Madison and Eston obtained their freedom at age twenty-one, as provided by Jefferson's will.[32]

Although the freeing of the Hemings children provides substance to Madison's version of a "treaty," no other source, including Jefferson's daughters, alludes to this bargain between Jefferson and Sally. In fact, they suggested other reasons for freeing the Hemingses: loyalty to the Jefferson family and for their excellent work and service over forty years.[33] Yet Sally, Jefferson's alleged lover and paramour, was *never* freed by Jefferson during his lifetime, or by his will.

While in Paris, Jefferson also met a beautiful and talented twenty-six-year-old: Maria Louisa Caterina Cecilia Hadfield Cosway. Maria was artistic, musical, and intelligent, a woman much like his late wife, Martha. The lovely wife of a British portrait painter, Maria was introduced to Jefferson through the artist John Trumbull. Jefferson became infatuated with Maria, spending time with her exploring the environs of Paris. He eventually wrote her a 4,600-word essay, a sensitive and revealing "love" letter.

Yet, the Hemings proponents would have you believe that the author of "A Dialogue Between My Head and My Heart" would decline the delectable Maria Cosway, to seduce a semi-educated, teenage virgin. Sally stood in a dependant relation to Jefferson both as a servant and maid to his young daughters. The Hemings advocates argue that having seduced Sally—a mere child—after she conceived a daughter, Jefferson was so callous that when Sally pleaded to remain in France cloaked in freedom, he beguiled her into returning to Virginia and slavery.[34] This is beyond common sense.

If one wanted to engage in dime store psychology, as Douglass Adair construes in his famous essay: "A recurring pattern in Jefferson's behavior is his taste for *married women*: his wife was a widow. Cosway was married, and the only known instance of a youthful gallantry before his marriage was the unsuccessful attempt to make love to a married woman, Mrs. John Walker."[35] Sally, in short, did not fit his penchants, or Jefferson's apparent physical type: Rebecca Burwell (his first love), his wife Martha, and Maria Cosway were all petite, blonde, blue eyed, charming, artistic, educated, and with a proper social background.[36]

When Jefferson sailed from Paris back to Virginia, some have speculated that he had Sally sleep with him in his cabin. This is patently false. "I shall have occasion for three master b[e]rths for [my]self and two daughters of 17 and 11 years of age, and b[e]rths for a man and woman servant, the latter convenient to that of my daughters," Jefferson specified. For almost eight years after they returned to Monticello, Jefferson still referred to Sally simply as "Maria's maid."[37]

Thus, no credible or substantial evidence exists that Jefferson had any relationship with Sally in Paris, let alone a sexual affair with a fourteen-year-old child, amid his two young, impressionable daughters. More importantly, what deterred Jefferson and limited any romantic foray was the shadow of his beloved wife, Martha, who had died two years earlier. Maria Cosway sensed this limit to their relationship. As to Jefferson's alleged vulnerability to Sally, the opposite was closer to the truth. The restraints on his relationships with Maria and Angelica Church would apply more strictly to any temptation for Sally.

In Paris, Jefferson kept his deathbed promise of fidelity to Martha.

5

TIMING AND CONCEPTION

This rings absolutely true, proving that sloth often alters truth more than mendacity.

—Gore Vidal, *Inventing a Nation*[1]

According to Jefferson's own business records, Sally gave birth to five children in Virginia, only four of whom survived: Harriet, Beverly, Madison, and Eston. The other child died in infancy.[2] The paternity adherents rely heavily on the sketchy, circumstantial evidence of the birth records of Sally's children to prove that Jefferson was present at Monticello during *all* of Sally's conceived pregnancies. They *assume* that Sally was also present at *all the times* that Jefferson was at Monticello.

Sally's simultaneous physical presence at Monticello with Jefferson is completely unknown by any recorded evidence. This false and misleading assumption skews the entire "timing" debate. Tangentially, Patsy, Jefferson's daughter, lived at Monticello during this period, which certainly would have dissuaded any intimacy between Jefferson and Sally.

A more important point, perhaps, has been overlooked by some historians: They have not considered the probability that the excited joy of Jefferson's presence at Monticello would have changed family sleeping or scheduling arrangements in such a way as to leave Sally more available, and vulnerable, for sexual intimacy with others.[3] As historian Winthrop Jordan concluded:

His presence at Monticello might well have resulted in rearrangements concerning who occupied what room and most certainly would have altered the pattern of visits to the plantation not only from distant admirers and acquaintances but also from relatives and friends from the neighborhood.[4]

All of the birth dates of Sally's children are taken from Jefferson's *Farm Book*, yet precisely when he entered each date is completely unknown, since he was not present for all the births. This is a critical fact because the birth dates are the controlling factor in estimating the dates of Sally's conception.[5]

Leaving aside the possible birth of a child conceived in France, Sally's first birth, (probably at Monticello), was a girl named Harriet, born October 5, 1795.[6] She died within two years. The date of her conception is calculated on or about January 11, 1795. Jefferson resided at Monticello from January 1794, after he resigned as secretary of state, through early March 1797 when he was sworn in as vice president in Philadelphia. However, this period—from the time he left to become secretary of state in 1790 to Harriet's conception—consumed over five years. Jefferson visited Monticello during this period, but if there were sexual liaisons with Sally, they did not bear fruit. Indeed, Jefferson was in residence at Monticello for almost a year before Sally is believed to have conceived Harriet.

These long intervals cast severe doubt on claims of a sexual affair. Moreover, an interesting chronological pattern can easily be seen. Jefferson had access to Sally at two different times in the year in which she conceived her son, Eston, in 1807. He was at Monticello between April 10 and May 16, and between August 4 and October 3. But Sally did not conceive Eston during this time period, where there is no evidence of anyone except Thomas Jefferson as being in residence. Rather, Sally conceived in August 1807, when there is solid, credible evidence that his brother Randolph *was* present.

Sally's next child, Beverly (a boy), offers a more complicated case. He was born in April 1798, probably on April 1. Beverly's conception is dated to July 8, 1797. Jefferson had been in Philadelphia since May of that year. The record shows that he left Philadelphia the morning of July 6 and arrived at Monticello on the morning of July 11. It is improbable that Jefferson was present when Sally conceived Beverly.

For many years it was assumed that Sally's next birth was the second Harriet (II).[7] It was discovered from a letter written by Jefferson on December 21, 1799, to his son-in-law, John Wayles Eppes, that "Maria's maid produced a daughter about a fortnight ago [and] is doing well."[8] This child, possibly named Thena or Thenia, lived only a few years. Her birth was on or about December 7, 1799, and her conception period was mid-March 1799. There is a window of sexual opportunity here, but a very narrow one. Jefferson arrived at Monticello on March 8, 1799, barely within the conception period, more likely too late. In fact, the existence of this child was not discovered for years. A few scholars attribute this child to Sally, on the assumption that she was "Maria's maid."[9] Yet Thena's name is listed with Sally's, but then crossed out. But this reference raises the interesting question of where Sally was living at this time. With Polly at Eppington (Jefferson's sister-in-law's home), and not at Monticello?[10]

The paternity scholars *assume* Sally was at Monticello, because there is no written evidence that she was elsewhere. Again, this is a gross and unsubstantiated assumption to sustain their conclusion: Jefferson's paternity. In fact, there is a specific letter in 1802 that reasonably implies that Sally, as well as her sister Critta, may have been elsewhere besides Monticello. Jefferson wrote to his daughter, Maria, at Eppington, on July 2, 1802:

> P.S. I have always forgotten to answer your apologies about Critta, which were very unnecessary. I am happy she has been with you and useful to you. At Monticello there could be nothing for her to do; so that her being with you is exactly as desirable to me as she can be useful to you.[11]

Moreover, another historian, based on Mary Randolph's letter, finds that Sally's absences from Monticello lasted as long as a year, and "certainly for some months before Jefferson's death."[12] Apparently Sally was hired out to a family called the Keys in 1825 or 1826, as evidence by the following letter to Ellen Coolidge: "Your maid Sally was here lately with Mrs. Key, begged me also to deliver a message of love to her mistress and to say how much she wanted to see you and the baby both. She thinks of you with much affection and I always have a long chat with her on your account as often as she comes here. She makes a very good nurse, and Mrs. Key seems to have perfect confidence in her ability and fidelity."[13]

Corroborating this leave of absence, in January 1802, one of the hired workers wrote that some housekeeping was needed at Monticello, but "Critty" (Critta, Sally's sister) was absent, and no one else was there to finish the task. Where were the other house servants, including Sally?[14]

Two years later, in May 1801, shortly after Jefferson became president, Sally gave birth to her next child, Harriet (II). Jefferson's *Farm Book*, recorded later, lists her birth as May, but the day is indistinct.[15] Her probable conception period was August 1800. Jefferson was at Monticello from May 29 through November 1800. Yet, his exact whereabouts in August through early September cannot be confirmed. This was a crucial election period for Jefferson. When he was at Monticello, he often traveled to his other plantations or to nearby neighbors. His records suggest that he was in Charlottesville, Albemarle Old Courthouse (now Scottsville), Lynchburg, and probably his second home at Poplar Forest.

Once again, the records prove that Jefferson was not present for the actual birth of Harriet, who was later described as "very handsome" by the slave Isaac Jefferson.[16] Harriet eventually "ran away" (freed with acquiescence) to Philadelphia in 1822 and apparently lived there as "white."[17] Following Harriet's birth, a *three-year* interval ensued with no known births by Sally. So where is the ongoing sexual affair between Jefferson and Sally? The paternity believers cannot explain these long intervals between pregnancies.

In January 1805, Sally gave birth to Madison Hemings (the source of the infamous interview in 1873, claiming that Jefferson was his father). A major discrepancy exists with the correlation between Madison's conception date and Jefferson's physical presence. Madison was conceived on or about April 27, 1804. It is well known that Jefferson was at Monticello for some weeks before the death of his daughter Maria (Polly) on the morning of April 17. It is highly improbable that during Maria's final illness and funeral, with a number of people gathered at Monticello, that Jefferson summoned Sally for a sexual liaison. The record indicates that he left Monticello on May 11, shortly after Sally's alleged conception, and was not present for Madison's birth.

The circumstances—Maria's illness and death—raise serious doubts about Jefferson's likely behavior at this time. As historian Joyce Appleby commented in her book *Thomas Jefferson*: "Jefferson's heart lay elsewhere that year: his twenty-five year old daughter Maria Jefferson Eppes died on

April 17, thirteen days after he returned from Washington to Monticello." Polly, as Maria was called, was the fifth child Jefferson had buried, though the others had died in infancy. Now there was only his eldest daughter, Martha, with her seven children. In a letter to a friend, Jefferson's profound grief surfaced: "My evening prospects now hang on the slender thread of a single life."[18]

Over three years passed before Sally's last known child, Eston (the DNA match), was born on May 21, 1808. Once again, where is the ongoing sexual relationship between Jefferson and Sally?

Contrary to the official Monticello report accepting Jefferson's guilt, *it is highly doubtful that Jefferson was present when Sally conceived each child.* The birth dates are taken from entries in Jefferson's own *Farm Book*. Yet he was actually present for only two births. In some cases his notations are illegible or inexact, and recorded years later. Jefferson probably obtained this information from his overseer, Edmund Bacon, or from Sally. The entry for Sally's last child, Eston, is the only clear and precise notation. One birth was revealed in a letter, rather than a note in the *Farm Book*. Thus, the births of Beverly, Thena, Harriet (II), and Madison raise monumental doubts about Jefferson's presence at Monticello during the conception dates.

More telling is the fact that when Jefferson ended his second presidential term and returned to Monticello permanently, Sally had no more children (at least not recorded). Why? After all, Jefferson was allegedly present for Eston's conception in 1807 and returned to Monticello permanently on March 15, 1809. Sally would have been in her prime, at age thirty-five.

In fact, Sally's physical whereabouts cast further substantial doubt on any alleged affair. No one can prove or verify that Sally was simultaneously present at Monticello with Jefferson at the time of the alleged conceptions. Sally probably served elsewhere, other than Monticello. For example, when Martha Randolph reported the death of "poor little Harriot" to Jefferson, she wrote her letter from Bellmont.[19] Was Sally there as well, perhaps as Martha's maid? When Jefferson wrote in 1799 about the birth of a daughter to "Polly's maid," apparently meaning Sally, was Sally living with Polly? If so, where? Eppington?

In 1801, Polly wrote to her father reporting that she had "borrow'd Crita," the slave who was Sally's older sister.[20] Jefferson approved, noting there was not much for her to do in his absence. The same would apply to Sally. Thus, it cannot be assumed, as the paternity contenders allege, that Sally was consistently present at Monticello.

The late Eyler Coates, a Jefferson researcher and former assistant Librarian of Congress, found fundamental flaws in the assumption that Jefferson was present at Monticello when all of Sally's children were conceived. Jefferson arrived at Monticello on July 17, 1797, and Beverly Hemings was born on April 1, 1798. That is two days short of the minimum normal gestation period, which is forty weeks, plus or minus two weeks.

"And that's assuming they both jumped into bed the moment Jefferson got back," Coates said. "That doesn't absolutely rule it out, but it makes it very doubtful."[21]

NEIMAN'S FLAWED ANALYSIS

The most provocative finding in the official Monticello report accepting Jefferson's guilt, was a statistical analysis by Fraser Neiman (an archeologist, not a mathematician). According to Neiman's flawed mathematical analysis "the chance is just 1% that his [Jefferson's] presence was a coincidence" with Sally's pregnancies.[22]

Dr. Ken Wallenborn, a slight, bespectacled former Virginia medical school professor and tour guide at Monticello, vehemently disagrees. Wallenborn took Neiman's statistical report to the chief of the biostatistics department at the University of Virginia hospital, and to his assistant on biogenetics. After reviewing the report and Neiman's conclusions, both scientists were unable to form any conclusions from Neiman's report. Wallenborn pointed out that if Jefferson was truly not the father (or impotent at the time), Neiman's study would still implicate Jefferson as the most likely candidate for the father of Sally's children. Wallenborn told me that "there is an old saying about statistics: statistics are like a bikini bathing suit—what they reveal is interesting, but what they conceal is vital."[23]

Neiman ran four mathematical models, but all based on a *false supposition*: no documentary evidence to support that Sally was also present at the exact same times that Jefferson was present at Monticello. The record is absolutely silent. Moreover, the record reveals that Jefferson visited Monticello a total of twenty-two times during the periods of conception

in question. Yet for sixteen of those twenty-two times, no conceptions resulted for Sally. Why?[24]

Neiman's mathematical model cannot rule out the prospect that Jefferson's visits to Monticello co-occurred with some other event, such as a
visit by his brother Randolph. This is not idle speculation but documented evidence in Jefferson's letter (see original letter in chapter 3).
Moreover, Neiman's report does not document exactly where Sally was in
her conception periods, other than to conclude there is no "evidence suggesting Sally Hemings was away from Monticello when Thomas Jefferson
was present." Yet, there is no documentary evidence to say *she was not
away* from Monticello at the time Jefferson was there.

The paternity believers engage in a complete double standard of proof,
chaining uncertainties together. Moreover, according to Dr. Wallenborn,
a member of the original Monticello Committee who dissented from the
conclusion that Jefferson was Sally's lover, obstetrical calculations are notoriously fallible. Early or late deliveries throw substantial doubt on
Neiman's statistical study. His study, according to Wallenborn, cries out
for valid comparative studies of other Jefferson males who may have fathered Eston. In the absence of those comparisons, Neiman's results are
inconclusive at best. Since no accurate records were kept of these other
male Jefferson visits to Monticello, no accurate comparison can be performed.[25]

For Wallenborn and genealogist Cynthia Burton, "the Merck Manual
revealed Neiman's fatal flaw. By ignoring the fact that babies seldom arrive
when due, the study fails to account for Jefferson's absences during parts of
the times when four of Ms. Hemings's babies could have been conceived."[26]

According to Wallenborn, the article by Neiman rested on two unsupported assumptions: (1) that there was a single father for all of Sally's
children; and (2) that rival candidates to Jefferson would have had to arrive and depart on the exact same days he did. Here, the assumption of
random behavior makes little sense, because the visits to Monticello of
the other paternity candidates, Jefferson's friends and relatives (including
his brother Randolph, Randolph's sons, and the Carr brothers), were not
random occurrences. They would have been far more likely to occur
when Jefferson himself returned to Monticello from extended absences.
More importantly, Neiman's parameters were deliberately set to "get"
Thomas Jefferson as the father of Sally's children. In fact, Wallenborn re-

ports that when Neiman presented his study to the Committee, he stated gleefully: "*I've got him!*"[27]

One final, critical error, according to Wallenborn, made both in the Neiman study and in the Monticello report is the assumption that Sally continuously lived at Monticello. We simply do not know enough about Sally, even her duties at Monticello, to conclude that she would have remained at Monticello rather than travel to Poplar Forest (Jefferson's second home), at the probable times of her conceptions. In fact, Sally is documented to be living away from Monticello, at Eppington in 1787 (age fourteen) at the home of Elizabeth and Francis Eppes, Jefferson's brother-in-law.[28] The question is particularly important given biographer Henry Randall's reference to "well known circumstances" that Jefferson did not father Sally's children. As documented by Randall, Jefferson's daughter "directed her sons' attention to the fact that Mr. Jefferson and Sally Hemings could not have met—were a far distant from each other—for fifteen months prior to the birth" of the child who supposedly most resembled Jefferson. Everyone has assumed that Martha was referring to Jefferson's absence from Monticello at that time, but she was clearly referring to Sally.[29]

Science writer Steven Corneliussen also disputes Neiman's scientific methodology in an article for the *Richmond Times-Dispatch*. The fact that Jefferson was around for some of the days when each Hemings child was conceived is important qualitatively, but that is not what Neiman's statistical study claimed. Its claim invoked the full authority of science itself. It said that statistical science proved that Thomas Jefferson definitely fathered six children by Sally Hemings. Corneliussen argues that statistical science did not prove it, or even contribute to proving it. The fatal blunders, according to Corneliussen, of the statistical study are obvious.[30]

Corneliussen went on to state in a lengthier article[31] that Neiman's 2000 statistical study used an invalid scientific protocol that led to invalid findings.[32] Corneliussen consulted two scientific experts to review Neiman's analysis: William C. Blackwelder, a biostatistical consultant who completed a career at the National Institutes of Health and David R. Douglas, a physicist, fellow of the American Physical Society, and senior scientist at Jefferson Lab.[33]

Blackwelder condemned Neiman's scientific conclusion. A scientifically unsupportable leap from association to causation invalidates Neiman's

claim that "[s]erious doubt about the existence and duration of the relationship and about Jefferson's paternity of Sally's six children can no
longer be reasonably sustained." Neiman's assumptions are faulty, according to Blackwelder. It is a basic tenet of studies of statistical association
that association does not imply causation. Thus, Neiman is certainly not
entitled to say, no matter how strong he believes the association to be, that
he has proven Jefferson's paternity. According to Blackwelder, Neiman is
not even entitled to state that he has shown that the probability is high that
Jefferson was the father of any of the six children, much less all six.

Concerning the study overall, Blackwelder concluded: "To me this
seems a clear case of 'guilt by association,' and the association is itself less
strong than claimed. In my opinion, Neiman's conclusion . . . is, on the
basis of the data he presents, a gross misinterpretation."[34]

Corneliussen declares that Neiman's study has other problems, too.
The fundamental failure lies in the handling of conception dates. In five
of the six cases, Neiman estimated the dates simply by counting back
from each recorded or estimated birth date 267 days, a misused number
from the medical literature. In the sixth case, because Jefferson had arrived
at Monticello after the conception date that Neiman computed, Neiman
simply assumed a three-day fudge factor.

In what Corneliussen calls a "back-of-the-envelope calculation"—a
simple estimate—Blackwelder did note one inevitable implication of any
valid distribution. He wrote that it "would result in a probability less than
50 percent that Jefferson was present at Monticello at the time the second
child was conceived, and thus an overall probability for his *presence at all
six conceptions of less than 50%*."[35]

The combined data show Jefferson absent for a day or so at the window's very end for both Eston and his brother Madison, absent for a week
from the alleged unnamed third child's window, and absent for more
than half the window for Beverly. Concerning the crucial case of Eston,
however, there is more. Neiman himself cites an article that concludes
modern-era black mothers have comparatively short pregnancies. So
what about the gestation lengths in the eighteenth century of the partly
white Sally Hemings? If Jefferson's absence from the end of Eston's conception window lasted not just a day or so, but longer, the window itself
would be shifted closer to the date of birth. Such a shift would increase
the appreciable chance that Jefferson *was not present* at Monticello at the

time of conception of Eston, the only child linked to Jefferson by the DNA marker.[36]

In essence, Corneliussen destroys Neiman's analysis:

At what point does carelessness with scientific arguments become disrespect? At what point does carelessness with the authority of science become science abuse? Before science entered the Hemings-Jefferson paternity debate, [historian] Annette Gordon-Reed criticized a pervasive disrespect for historical evidence that had originated mainly in disrespect for owned humans and their descendants. Now that science has entered the debate, what explains the ways in which some scientists, editors, scholars, commentators, and journalists have mishandled science's part in the debate, in the process disrespecting both science and history?[37]

6

CARR BROTHERS AND
OTHER MALE JEFFERSONS

The almost white children born to Sally Hemings were probably fathered by Peter Carr, Jefferson's wayward nephew who enjoyed free rein at Monticello, including the slave quarters.
—John C. Miller, "Slavery," in *Thomas Jefferson: A Reference Biography*, (Merrill Peterson, ed.)[1]

The Carr brothers, Peter and Samuel, were the young sons of Jefferson's sister and her husband, Dabney Carr. Dabney was a close friend of Jefferson's from boyhood, but died tragically when he was thirty years old. Thereafter, Jefferson acted as guardian and helped raise Samuel and Peter. They often visited Monticello and remain major suspects for fathering Sally's, and her sister Mary's, children, other than Eston.

In fact, they stood accused by Jefferson's grandson and, according to his account, they virtually admitted their sexual complicity with Sally. Thomas Jefferson Randolph wrote: "To my knowledge and the statements of other gentlemen made to me 60 years ago the paternity of these parties was admitted by two other persons."[2]

The recorded evidence shows that the Carrs were present at Monticello during Harriet's conception in 1795, when the second Harriet was conceived in 1800 and when Eston was conceived in 1807. Contradicting historian Fawn Brodie's claim that the Carr brothers had left the Monticello area when Sally became pregnant is Jefferson's own account book, made early in the year (1795) when Harriet was conceived:

Feb. 11 Gave S. Carr to Pay Clarkson&c.

Knitting 2 pr stockgs., 2 Dollars.

Mar 2. Gave P.Carr to send by S. Carr to

Dabney Carr 8 Dollars.[3]

According to Ellen (Jefferson's granddaughter), there was a distinct impression that Sally's children were fathered by Colonel Carr (Samuel). He was the "most notorious good-natured Turk that was ever master of a black seraglio kept at other men's expense." The Carr brothers admitted their paternity of Sally's children, according to Ellen.[4]

Jefferson Randolph ("Jeff"), Thomas Jefferson's grandson, related these admissions to the historian and biographer Henry S. Randall. Randolph would testify that he knew firsthand that the Carr brothers were responsible for Sally's children because they admitted it to him. This version was told to Randall in the late 1850s, and he repeated it in 1868 to Jefferson's new biographer, James Parton:

> Col. Randolph informed me that there was not a shadow of suspicion that Mr. Jefferson in this or any other instance ever had commerce with female slaves. . . . He said he had never seen a motion, or a look, or a circumstance which led him to suspect for an instant that there was a particle more of familiarity between Mr. Jefferson and Sally Hemings than between him and the most repulsive servant in the establishment, . . . no person ever living at Monticello dreamed of such a thing.[5]

Henry Randall himself, commenting on Randolph's interview, proclaimed that he could "give fifty more facts were there time and were there any need of it, to show Mr. Jefferson's innocence of this and all similar offenses against propriety."[6]

According to Randall, he did not include the allegation against the Carr brothers in his biography, *Life of Thomas Jefferson*, because Jeff Randolph prohibited him from doing so, warning: "You are not bound to prove a negative. If I should allow you to take Peter Carr's corpse into Court and plead guilty over it to shelter Mr. Jefferson, I should not dare again to walk by his grave: he would rise and spurn me." Randall added, again citing Jeff Randolph, that Jefferson was "deeply attached to the

Carrs—especially to Peter. He was extremely indulgent to them and the idea of watching them for faults or vices probably never occurred to him."[7] Jefferson had always loved Peter as the son he never had, and had great hopes for him. This was one instance in which Peter disappointed his uncle. But Jefferson, a man of character and honor, would never attempt to absolve himself by implicating his sister's son.

The Hemings historians derisively label this testimony the "Family Denial." Yet, this is further proof that they cannot prove their case by the "greater weight of the evidence."[8] The confusion about the Carr brothers is just one example of the inconsistencies and contradictions of the evidence. Ellen accuses Samuel of paternity, but Jeff Randolph names Peter as well. Historian Frank Berkeley, the curator of historical manuscripts for twenty-nine years at the University of Virginia and former Monticello Board Member, agrees with Randolph's indictment:

> . . . [the nephews] were very much involved in this . . . I don't think Samuel had too much to do with Sally, but Peter did . . . Everybody knew she [Sally] was living with Peter . . . and Samuel had a mistress at Monticello too . . . the reason I am so persuaded of that relationship . . . that Peter being seen daily at [Sally's cabin] . . . what was he doing there? I think he had a long time love affair with her . . . I think it was a genuine love affair. . . .[9]

OTHER MALE JEFFERSONS

Jefferson's younger brother, Randolph, also had teenage sons who visited Monticello when their uncle arrived, and would certainly be candidates for Sally's paternity. Some scholars have absurdly argued that Randolph's sons were too young to have fathered children with Sally. Research reveals four of Randolph's sons were single and between eighteen and twenty-six years of age when Eston Hemings was conceived. Thomas Jefferson, Jr., was only eight or nine years younger than Sally. Medical studies suggest these ages represent sexual peaks for their respective genders. They were sixteen or seventeen years old at the time. Sally would have been twenty-seven.[10]

When considering Randolph's sons, a statement concerning the Hemings children made by Jefferson's granddaughter, Ellen, is vital: "There were dissipated young men in the neighborhood who sought the society of the mulatresses and they in like manner were not anxious to establish any claim of paternity in the results of such associations."[11]

In fact, according to genealogist Cynthia Burton, Thomas Jefferson, Jr. (hereinafter TJjr.), Randolph's oldest son, was schooled near Monticello both in 1799 and from 1800 to 1801. Those dates coincide with one of Sally's pregnancies.[12] TJjr. was the eldest son of Randolph and Anne Lewis Jefferson and approximately twenty-five to twenty-six years old when Eston Hemings was conceived. Beginning in 1799, there are notations in Jefferson's *Memorandum Books* for two years of various payments for TJjr.'s clothing, boots, schooling, and dance lessons. One payment was to nearby Mrs. Snead for six months of schooling. This would place the eighteen- to nineteen-year-old TJjr. in the neighborhood about the time Harriet II was conceived, when Sally Hemings was twenty-seven years old.

TJjr. would have been in the Monticello neighborhood in late summer of 1807 for many of the same reasons as his father, Randolph. He would have desired to say good-bye to his aunt, uncle, and cousins who were about to move west. He also had friends living nearby in the Milton area. TJjr. married Mary "Polly" Randolph Lewis, his double first cousin who lived down the road from Monticello on October 3, 1808—just four and one half months after Eston Hemings was born.[13] Thus, TJjr. could easily have fathered Sally's last four children, and evidence suggests he was probably at Monticello during the conception periods of Harriet II and Eston.

As discussed briefly, Randolph's other son, Isham, was about twenty-three or twenty-four years old when Eston Hemings was conceived. Isham lived in Buckingham, Fluvanna, and Albemarle Counties and was also a slave owner. Jefferson helped educate and clothe his brother's eldest and youngest sons, so it is likely Isham was treated likewise. Notations in Jefferson's *Memorandum Books* mention R. Jefferson, Rand. Jefferson, and Randolph Jefferson probably refer to Isham since Jefferson called him "Randolph." Some references in these accounts specifically identify "my brother," but others do not.[14]

There is an interesting entry in the 1805 Monticello household accounts kept by Jefferson's granddaughter, Anne Cary Randolph, that probably refers to Isham Jefferson. The household accounts were records of purchases from slaves and neighbors. Usually listed in these accounts were the year, month, day, seller's name, item bought, and amount paid. The relevant entry was dated Sunday, September 1805. The seller was "Isham" providing "1 doz. eggs." There is an erasure mark in the space provided for amount paid, so apparently Isham was not paid for the eggs. It is probable Isham was living inside the house at Monticello in September 1805, which disqualified him from being paid for the eggs and explains the erasure mark, but does qualify him as Sally's sexual partner.[15]

In short, other male Jefferson family members, most notably Randolph and the Carr brothers, were much stronger candidates for the paternity of Sally's children, rather than Thomas Jefferson.

7

JEFFERSON'S DECLINING HEALTH

My health has entirely broken down in the last eight months.
—Jefferson at age fifty-two, to John Adams (1795)[1]

Thomas Jefferson died from a wasting, internal infection. For the last two decades of his life, his health had declined at an accelerated pace, and affected two of his physical passions: a fondness for hunting and his skill as a daring horseman. In fact, he was a frail sixty-four years old, suffering from excruciating migraine headaches, debilitating rheumatoid arthritis, diarrhea, and numerous intestinal infections when he was supposedly having vibrant sex with a twenty-two-year-old Sally.[2]

In May 1808, (when Eston was born) Jefferson had lived to an age that was double the life expectancy for men born in 1743. *He was the oldest of all the probable paternity candidates.* His age, illnesses, prescribed treatments, stress level, habits, and lifestyle certainly had an adverse impact on his fertility and potency.[3] And although Jefferson did not *seem* to suffer any life-threatening illnesses, he continued to suffer from chronic migraine headaches during the conception periods of Sally, which confined him to darkened rooms for weeks at a time. This was coupled with chronic diarrhea and intestinal disorders, prostrate problems, and what he referred to as "rheumatism" most of the second half of his life.[4]

"Jefferson's health has been completely overlooked," historian and

Jefferson researcher Cynthia Burton explained. "His fertility had been waning for over 30 years at this time."[5] In 1793, at age fifty, Jefferson wrote to James Madison: "My health is entirely broken down and my age requires that I should place my affairs in a clear state." He wrote this a few months after Sally's first confirmed child, Harriet I, was conceived in January 1795. In 1796, he noted to a friend: "I begin to feel the effects of age. My health has suddenly broken down, with symptoms which give me to believe I shall not have much to encounter of the *tedium vitae.*"[6]

Although he lived thirty-three more years, he felt that he had only a few years remaining.

It is against this framework that one must examine Jefferson's health during the conception period of Sally's children. In short, his decrepit health would not permit a sexual relationship with a healthy Sally.

EMOTIONAL HEALTH

Before we discuss Jefferson's deteriorating physical health, it is important to note his emotional health during the conception years. Jefferson's psyche, in fact, had been declining since his days as secretary of state, and he was worried about his family's well-being and finances. His thoughts were *not* on a second family or a reinvigorating love affair.

Jefferson, who worried about his physical health, also fretted about his mental deterioration. He had "forgotten much" of his mathematical knowledge, Jefferson complained to Dr. Rush. He found that he could regain what he had lost, but with difficulty. He also feared that his mental capacity would force him to retire from public life: ". . . the fear of becoming a dotard, and of being insensible of it, would of itself have resisted all solicitations to remain."[7] Author Gore Vidal notes that, "in old age he said he read only one newspaper and promptly forgot what he had just read."[8]

Mentally, Jefferson also suffered from profound grief and depression over his daughter's (Polly) death when Madison Hemings was conceived in March 1804. His emotional state certainly exacerbated his rheumatism pain. Jefferson continued to suffer from periodic bouts of dejection and despair, during which he was full of "gloomy forebodings" about his future. Not long before he composed the Declaration of Independence, the young Jefferson lay for six weeks in ill health at Monticello, paralyzed by a mysterious "malady." Similar emotional and physical lapses were to recur during anxious periods in his life, often accompanied by violent headaches. The worst of these moments came after his wife, Martha, died in 1782. But two years later, after being dispatched to Europe, Jefferson recovered nerve and spirit in the salons of Paris, where he became smitten with the beautiful young artist, Maria Cosway. When their relationship ended, Jefferson's health again broke down.

By 1815, when his brother Randolph died, Jefferson had suffered the emotional loss of his wife, five of their children, two of their grandchildren, and the deaths of five siblings and numerous friends.[9] This emotional distress certainly played an adverse role affecting his health during this time. As discussed earlier, August 1807 was an intensely anxious time for Jefferson—one of the busiest and most stressful periods of his political career. This was not his usual summer visit to Monticello—it was a working vacation. Government crises loomed, as well as major problems to deal with regarding his properties.

Jefferson was also in a constant state of emotional distress over his financial situation. Deep in debt when he left the presidency, he teetered on the edge of bankruptcy. He worried about leaving his family bankrupt. In fact, six months after his death, his family sold much of their furniture (and almost all of the slaves) at public auction to pay debts. Until the family sold the mansion in 1831, they lived in a comfortless shell of a dwelling that was not only drafty but also leaked.[10]

The stress of financial problems made it impossible for Jefferson to keep his cherished Monticello in proper repair. The mansion began to show signs of decay long before his death. During this same period, one in which Jefferson's physical health rapidly deteriorated, he proposed a lottery to benefit his survivors. Under the plan, citizens across the country could buy chances to win a prize consisting, originally, of acreage Jefferson owned in Bedford County. He hoped to raise $60,000 this way. Unfortunately, before the Virginia legislature approved the plan, Jefferson would have to offer Monticello itself as the ultimate prize. When he heard this news, he "turned quite white," a relative recalled, but he agreed nonetheless.[11]

After his presidency, Jefferson discovered that private life could be more distressing than public life. His daughter, Martha, had married an abusive, wife-beating alcoholic, the future Governor Thomas Mann Randolph.

Martha's eldest daughter, Anne Cary Randolph, also had married an abusive drunk, Charles Bankhead of Caroline County. In February 1819, ten years after Jefferson's return to Virginia, Anne Cary's brother, Thomas Jefferson Randolph, came to blows with Bankhead in the streets of Charlottesville, nearly bleeding to death after his brother-in-law stabbed him.[12]

While in Paris, Jefferson took ill, both emotionally and physically. He was confined to his house for six weeks. Sunshine was his great personal physician, he liked to say, and there was too little of it in Paris. Then in the last week of January, came devastating news from Virginia. His two-year-old daughter, Lucy, had died of whooping cough. Of six children, now only two survived. According to historian David McCullough, "the shadow of his unspeakable sorrow fell on everyone around him."[13]

MIGRAINE HEADACHES

Jefferson was plagued by vicious migraine headaches for much of his adult life. The "periodical head ach," as he called it, was the major illness of his life. Jefferson's headaches were so severe they incapacitated him for days and even weeks at critical times in American history.

In 1794, at age fifty-one, Jefferson wrote that he was worn down "with labours from morning to night." While visiting John and Abigail Adams, Jefferson told Abigail that "he expects not to live a Dozen[more] years." In 1804, four years before he supposedly fathered Sally's children, he wrote to James Madison that "the motion of my blood no longer keeps time with the tumult of the world. It leads me to seek for happiness in the lap and love of my family. . . ."[14]

Preeminent history professor and Jefferson scholar Forrest McDonald emphasizes Jefferson's fragile age: in his mid-sixties when he allegedly fathered Eston Hemings. Jefferson suffered severe migraine headaches and was undergoing a foreign policy crisis in the midst of his second, less-successful presidential term. "You can cut the mustard when you're sixty-five, but you can't do it when you're 65 and have migraines," McDonald added. "It just doesn't happen." McDonald also argues that Hemings would have been pregnant far more often through the years had she and Jefferson had a long-standing relationship. "Jefferson's wife, who died fairly young, had two children who lived, but she was pregnant six or seven times," McDonald said. "She got pregnant all the damn time. This was the norm in the 18th century . . . There was no contraception in those days."[15]

Jefferson, mostly a vegetarian his whole life, lived to a remarkable age of eighty-three years old, but suffered numerous maladies over his lifetime. His exercise regimen, begun as a student at William & Mary, running at twilight a mile out of Williamsburg and back again, had been affected by the brutal headaches.[16] In 1776, Jefferson was thirty-one when his mother's death precipitated another bout of crippling headaches that confined him to bed for almost two months. Jefferson noted his mother's death in one brief sentence, indicating his extreme subconscious emotional distress: "My mother died at 8 o'clock this morning in the 57th year of her age." The death of his mother and his emotional distress over his wife's health (complications from a previous pregnancy), spun him into a health collapse. In fact, he was so sick both physically and mentally that he did not return to Congress for six weeks.[17]

One historian dates his migraine problems to Jefferson's awkward, quivering marriage proposal to his first love, Rebecca Burwell, when he was only twenty years old. Her rejection and subsequent engagement to a rival, Jacquelin (Jack) Ambler, triggered the onset of Jefferson's headaches. He recorded a "violent head-ach" that he suffered for days. He also described another headache at Natural Bridge, the famous rock formation in southwest Virginia: "Looking down from this height about a minute gave me a violent head ach."[18] As one historian wrote: "In the clinical literature of our own time one reads that migraine sufferers . . . are generally 'anxious, striving, perfectionist, order-loving, rigid persons, who, during periods of threat or conflict, become progressively more tense, resentful, and fatigued.' "[19]

This is a perfect description of Jefferson.

Another example of his debilitating headaches occurred in 1808, the same year as Eston's birth. For nearly three weeks, Jefferson wrote, he was "obliged to be shut up in a dark room from early in the forenoon till night, with a periodical head ach." This time coincided with the collapse of the pivotal treaty negotiations with Great Britain, a life-threatening illness to his son-in-law, and the impending treason trial of Aaron Burr.[20]

In their article "Thomas Jefferson's Headaches: Were They Migraines?" Gary L. Cohen, M.D., and Loren A. Rolak, M.D., corroborate Jefferson's first recorded headache after his failed courtship with Rebecca Burwell.

As one historian recorded: "At eleven o'clock at night on March 20, 1764, racked by 'a violent head ache' with which he had been afflicted for two days, Jefferson wrote of the finality of his loss."[21]

Dr. Cohen verifies the second headache with the death of Jefferson's mother, in the spring of 1776. This was a time of emotional distress and personal loss as described by historian Dumas Malone: "This was just about the time that he had expected to return to Congress, but in the meantime he himself fell ill and was incapacitated for some five weeks longer. The report got around that he was suffering from an inveterate headache which had a hard name; probably it was what we now call migraine. By early May he was over it, and in the fullness of time he descended from the mountain . . . duty called him to Philadelphia and he was ready."

A third documented headache noted by Dr. Cohen occurred at the end of his years in Paris, serving as American minister to France. In Paris, Jefferson became infatuated with the beautiful painter Maria Cosway. Maria was described as "a wisp of a woman, soft and delicate with deep blue eyes set in an oval face, with a head of frothy golden curls."[22] Jefferson was literally "head over heels" for her, and allegedly jumped over a fence or a fountain while strolling with her along the Seine. He broke his right wrist, which caused a lifetime of suffering in his writing hand. French doctors bungled setting the fracture, and negligently recommended mere soakings in warm springs. Jefferson's hand developed atrophic changes and was a source of intermittent pain, "rheumatism," for the rest of his life.

When Maria Cosway chose to return to her husband in England, Jefferson suffered another prolonged, excruciating headache. One historian defined the onset of this headache, "On September 2 he said goodbye to John Trumbull, whom he had asked to become his secretary. . . . One hour after Trumbull left for London Jefferson was in bed seriously ill. The old migraine was back for the first time since he had set foot on French soil. It lasted six days."[23]

Jefferson's fourth known episode of prolonged headaches occurred in the spring of 1790, when he returned to America to become secretary of state. The fifth recorded time of severe headache, according to Doctors Cohen and Rolak, occurred during the winter of 1790–1791, as Jefferson continued to have personal and political differences with Alexander

Hamilton. His headache seemed to blind him during the day, forcing him to do his reading and writing exclusively at night, by soft candlelight. After leaving Washington's Cabinet in 1793, claiming a permanent retirement, he had no more headaches for a decade, until after his election as president.

Jefferson's headaches became severe again while he was president, from 1801 to 1809. Some have suggested that these headaches were not migraines, but rather "tension" headaches (TTHs) triggered by stress.[24] Doctors Cohen and Rolak note that Jefferson's headaches meet most of the formal requirements of the International Headache Society's criteria for "migraine without aura" (also known as a common migraine with no warning signs).[25] Jefferson's further description of his headaches as "violent" and "blinding" is more suggestive of migraines instead of the less severe TTHs that most patients describe. His eldest daughter, Martha, also had migraine headaches, suggesting a hereditary component found in the majority of migraine patients. On balance, the doctors conclude, the diagnosis of migraines fits Jefferson best.

RHEUMATOID ARTHRITIS

Both Jefferson and George Washington suffered from debilitating rheumatoid arthritis. Washington's case was so severe that he could not roll over in bed without pain, and resorted to sleeping with one arm in a sling.[26]

According to historian Cynthia Burton in her book, *Jefferson Vindicated*, at fifty-one years old, Jefferson had severe soreness in his joints, which progressed to a debilitating case of chronic rheumatism and kept him bedridden for weeks. "I begin to feel the effects of age," he noted the following year, adding that his body was sending him signals "which give me to believe I shall not have much to encounter of the *tedium vitae.*"

Jefferson complained of debilitating rheumatism as early as 1785 (age forty-two), and expressed his dislike for cold, damp weather because of the suffering it inflicted upon his joints. From Paris he wrote to James Monroe that:

I have, had a very bad winter, having been confined the greatest part of it . . . The air is extremely damp and the waters very unwholesome. We

had for three weeks past a warm visit by the sun (my almighty physician) and I find myself almost reestablished.[27]

Burton's research uncovered this Jefferson letter to William Dunbar in
1801, describing his declining health:

> ... that cold is the source of more sufferance to all animal nature than
> hunger, thirst, sickness, & all the other pains of life & of death itself put
> together ... when I recollect on one hand all the sufferings I have had
> from cold, & on the other all my other pains, the former preponderate
> greatly.[28]

At Monticello, Jefferson would frequently travel to a friend's home to
dine in the afternoon, then spend the evening at their home to avoid the
night air on his arthritis. While in Washington, he declined a dinner invitation from Dr. William Thornton in February 1801 stating it had been
his practice for the past ten years to avoid evening engagements due to
health considerations.[29]

According to Burton's detailed research, Jefferson probably suffered
from severe degenerative joint disease such as rheumatoid arthritis, sciatica, osteoarthritis, or a combination of these ailments about the time Eston was conceived in 1807. Approximately one month before Eston was
conceived, Dr. Robert Patterson wrote to Jefferson prescribing a remedy
for his leg by wrapping it with flannel. Jefferson wrote to his granddaughter, Ellen Wayles Randolph on October 25, 1808, that he had been
kept from the races by "an attack of rheumatism." He wrote: "It is precisely the same as that which I had at Monticello ... I keep up but can
scarcely walk, and that with pain. I suppose it will take the same course as
it did at Monticello, and that I shall be well at the meeting of Congress."
His daughter wrote two days later, "I am truly concerned to hear that
your rheumatism has fixed in so dreadful a part of the back. You will be
obliged to try flannel next to the skin in which I have a very great confidence, particularly as you never abused the use of it."[30]

As we know from modern medicine, rheumatoid arthritis is a type of
chronic arthritis that typically occurs in joints on both sides of the body
(such as hands, wrists, or knees). In addition to affecting the joints,
rheumatoid arthritis may occasionally affect the skin, eyes, lungs, heart,

blood, or nerves. Symptoms of rheumatoid arthritis include: joint pain and swelling, stiffness, especially in the morning or after sitting for long periods and fatigue. While it is two to three times more common in women than in men, men tend to be more severely affected when they contract arthritis, which usually occurs in middle age.[31]

Considering Jefferson made a payment to Dr. Patterson and received a prescribed remedy, it is probable Jefferson was experiencing rheumatism or sciatica during the summer of 1807, when Eston was conceived. Burton's book concluded that Jefferson's arthritis was also aggravated by a drop in barometric pressure and rising humidity preceding stormy weather at Monticello. Evidence indicates there was significant rainfall in that summer of 1807, as in other summers. Even George Washington commented on the storms and rain during the August summers: "The Rains have been very general, and more abundant since the first of August than ever happened in a summer within the memory of man."[32] In fact, Burton notes that there was extensive flooding damage to Jefferson's mills shortly after his arrival at Monticello that year. Humid August evenings on the mountain aggravated Jefferson's musculoskeletal pain, what modern medicine terms "atmospheric pressure changes that alter the pressure within a person's joints."[33]

According to Burton, Jefferson:

> . . . experienced his debilitating rheumatism, especially during the warm months at Monticello. This coincides with four of the five conception dates for Sally. He was also confined with rheumatism during August and September 1794. Other significant bouts of rheumatism mentioned in Jefferson's correspondence were in spring 1797, summers of 1802 and 1806, August 1811, August 1813, August 1818, and August 1819. He wrote that these attacks affected his back, hips, and thighs, and kept him from walking. He was certainly ailing during the probable 1807 conception period for Eston.[34]

PROSTATITIS AND OTHER DISEASES

One medical expert, an anesthesiologist reviewing Jefferson's medical history, concluded that Jefferson "might have had an autoimmune disease, possibly Crohn's disease as this involves colitis and arthritis, possibly reflex sympathetic dystrophy from the fracture of his wrist and certainly prostatitis."[35]

According to medical experts, Crohn's disease fits some of Jefferson's symptoms. For example, the disease is a chronic inflammatory disease of the intestines. It primarily causes ulcerations (breaks in the lining) of the small and large intestines, but can affect the digestive system. Crohn's disease is related closely to another chronic inflammatory condition that involves only the colon called ulcerative colitis. Together, Crohn's disease and ulcerative colitis are frequently referred to as inflammatory bowel disease. Ulcerative colitis and Crohn's disease have no medical cure. Once the diseases begin, they tend to fluctuate between periods of inactivity (remission) and activity (relapse).[36]

Specifically, during his presidency, Jefferson was once weakened by diarrhea so severe that he had to solicit Dr. Benjamin Rush for relief.[37] In January 1812, Jefferson revealed in a letter to his brother that on the advice of a doctor, he had brought home from Philadelphia some "lunar caustic" (bougies) that were commonly used for urinary strictures. He expressed knowledge of their discomfort when he told his brother "the pain will be great . . ." Dr. Robley Dunglison had to use bougies to dilate Jefferson's urethra in 1825–1826 during his last, fatal illness. It is quite probable Jefferson had a history of urological problems for which he was first treated in Philadelphia. More importantly as to the paternity issue, modern medicine has confirmed that trauma to the urethra causes chronic problems affecting potency.[38]

The third president suffered chronic intestinal disorders through most of his life. According to his doctor, Benjamin Rush, the reason that Jefferson suffered in silence without consulting doctors was because he saw no immediate need for professional counsel. Once, he had suffered from diarrhea after eating fish. Yet, Jefferson himself described his intestinal condition as chronic, and doubted if medicine could help at this age. He continued to experiment with home remedies such as cinnamon, brandy, and sugar. Dr. Rush prescribed other medicines for his patient including laudanum, and a radical experiment of mercury to be used internally in combination with opium or externally as an ointment.[39]

In a letter of 1819, Jefferson described in detail his dietary regimen: He preferred to eat "little animal food, and that not as an aliment so much as a condiment for the vegetables, which constitute my principal diet." He enjoyed a moderate amount of "weak wine" daily and drank little water. Jefferson also liked to conduct his own experiments on his health and diet.

Certain doctors speculate that Jefferson also suffered from chronic prostititis that led to benign prostatic hyperplasia (BPH). Chronic prostatitis is "an inflammation of the prostate gland that develops gradually" with subtle symptoms such as low back pain, painful urination, and *painful ejaculation*. Some degree of BPH is thought to occur in 80 percent of all men over forty years old.

According to Burton, Jefferson also suffered from chronic urological problems during Hemings's childbearing years. A February 1799 entry in Jefferson's *Memorandum Book* records a payment to a surgeon, Dr. Philip Physick, in Philadelphia. Jefferson's family begged the former president to consult Dr. Physick during his last illness when he suffered from urological and prostate problems. Jefferson probably saw Dr. Physick for urological problems in 1799 while in Philadelphia. There are no published letters from Jefferson to his daughters from February 7 to March 8, 1799, when he returned home to Monticello.[40]

Jefferson's health was so bad, at times, that it stirred rumors of his impending death. Once when he arrived at Monticello in late summer 1802, it was reported that Jefferson was so sick that he required the constant attention of half a dozen doctors.[41] Jefferson was often ill during his stay in France. In fact, Jefferson's health was of great concern to both John and Abigail Adams, though Jefferson himself dismissed it as no more than "seasoning" required of all newly arrived strangers. Privately, Jefferson at age forty-one, confided to Abigail that he did not expect to live more than a dozen years longer.[42]

As historian Burton concludes from her extensive research of Jefferson's letters, when he described his health as good, he judged it according to his age. With undue optimism, he wrote to Abigail Adams in 1813 about suffering from "rheumatism" and "excepting for this I have enjoyed general good health; for I do not consider as a want of health the gradual decline and increasing debility which is a natural diatheses of age."[43]

IMPOTENCE

By the time of Eston's conception, Jefferson was, "within a reasonable degree of medical certainty," impotent. His laudanum related drugs caused reduced libido and decreased potency. So did Jefferson's prolonged horse riding. He was an avid horseman, and continued riding until age eighty-three when he "was so weak that he could only get into the saddle by stepping down from the terrace."[44] Saddle pressure causes impotence in horsemen. Jefferson made many long trips on horseback (i.e., Philadelphia to Georgetown prior to Beverly Hemings's conception), and he generally rode his horse a minimum of three to four hours a day, as he felt it was therapeutic. One historian concludes:

> that medical studies of the last thirty years link impotency, infertility, and erectile dysfunction to bicycling and horseback riding caused by saddle compression to arteries and nerves. Jefferson's medical history and lifestyle would indicate he probably had significant sexual loss as early as the 1790's, when he began complaining regularly about his symptoms associated with aging.[45]

During the conception years, according to a professor and male reproduction expert in the Department of Urology at the University of Virginia Medical Center, "a 50–60 year old male in the late 1700's and early 1800's was likely a much 'older' male than is presently the case, much more worn down by the salts of disease, the stresses of lifestyle, and the inadequacy of medical care."[46] In short, male fertility starts to decline after age thirty-five, so Jefferson's fertility had been waning for thirty years by 1808.[47]

FINAL DAYS

For most of his life, Jefferson was keenly interested in his own health and holistic cures. The gardens at Monticello allowed him to combine his interests in botany and self-care. In 1794, for instance, he listed sixteen medicinal herbs in his gardening journal, including peppermint, lavender, chamomile, thyme, and rue.

Yet, from 1816 until his death in 1826, his health declined rapidly. His disabilities made rising from a chair or walking through his garden more difficult. In 1822, he broke his arm falling off the back steps of Monticello.[48] He also complained that the arthritis in his wrists and fingers worsened with age, and complained that "the unceasing drudgery of writing keeps me in unceasing pain and peevishness." A few months before his death he lamented that "those who have no claims upon me, will at length advert to the circumstances of my age and ill health."[49]

His final years were a series of maladies. On August 7 through 21, 1818, Jefferson visited Warm Springs and left seriously ill. Jefferson's self-treatment for the body abscesses he caught at the springs almost killed him—an oral mercury compound. In 1825, Dr. Dunglison, his English doctor, made his first professional visit to Monticello as Jefferson's health declined.[50] As his health grew worse, Jefferson turned his thoughts to death. He wrote how he wished to be buried. He wanted a simple grave on the mountainside below his house. He even sketched an obelisk headstone that he wanted at his gravesite.

Jefferson's health had suffered during his years of work for the University of Virginia. He was eighty-two-years-old and feeling his age. Yet, he still enjoyed riding his reliable horse, Eagle, his steadfast companion with a white spot on his nose. Jefferson also found his memory was failing, and sensed he did not have much longer to live. He told a friend: "When I look back over the ranks of those with whom I have lived and loved, it is like looking over a field of battle. All fallen."[51]

In 1826, the Bursar of the University of Virginia wrote that: "Mr. J's health is rather better than it has been for some weeks past. Yet his spirits are much worse than I have ever known them. Indeed, it is wonderful that he retains any under the many distressing circumstances under which he now labors."[52] Jefferson wrote many times that his health had never been the same since his time in Warm Springs. He recorded that his hearing had become too dull for him to take in the chatter at the dinner table, and when he reached eighty-three he declined gravely.[53]

On May 11, 1825, Jefferson received a memorandum from his physician advising him that he was suffering from dysuria, a stricture and inflammation of the urinary canal apparently brought on by the enlargement. Dr. Dunglison rode scores of times from the University of Virginia to Monticello. In the summer of 1825 Jefferson had commented with grim humor that he had one foot in the grave and the other uplifted to follow.[54]

The date that marked the beginning of his last illness was June 24, 1826, when he summoned his trusted physician, Dr. Dunglison, who had visited him a month earlier for troubled diarrhea. His small reserve of strength was being depleted and his doctor saw no hope of recovery. In fact, Dr. Dunglison remained on call at Monticello during the last week of Jefferson's life.[55]

As historian Dumas Malone describes, Jefferson lapsed into unconsciousness the night of July 2 and he awakened only a few times thereafter: "On one or more of those occasions he inquired if it was the fourth of July. Dr. Dunglison's response was that it soon would be . . . When the hands reached twelve they knew that the old patriot's wish to live until the day he had done so much to make glorious had been granted. The end came at fifty minutes past noon. It was remarked afterwards that the Declaration of Independence was presented to the Continental Congress at approximately that time."[56]

CONCLUSION

Based on Jefferson's health records, it is beyond common sense to believe he was having a sexual affair with Sally during the last two decades of his life. From an objective review of the most credible medical records, it is virtually impossible for Jefferson to have conducted an ongoing sexual relationship with Sally, not only based on his enfeebled physical health, but also his emotional state of mind caused by the death of his beloved daughter, compounded by personal financial woes. This evidence has been all but ignored by the Hemings historians.

Linking Jefferson's health to the specific conception periods we observe the following pattern: Sally's first child, Harriet I, was conceived on or about January 1795. Jefferson wrote to James Madison on April 27, 1795 (three months after Harriet I's conception): "My health is entirely broken down within the last eight months, my age requires that I should place my affairs in a clear state; these are sound if taken care of, but capable of considerable danger if longer neglected." Jefferson further wrote to secretary of state, Edmund Randolph, on September 4, 1794: "Your favour of August the 28th finds me in bed, under a parozysm of the rheumatism which has kept me for 10 days in constant torment, and presents no hope of abatement."[57] Jefferson again writes to George Divers on September 28, 1794: "I have no prospect of getting on a horse for a month to come." Jefferson to Benjamin Waller October 9, 1794: ". . . but about beginning of September I was attacked by violent rheumatism, which after keeping me so long in constant agony, leaves me no prospect of release from my con-

finement within any given term of time."[58] And on October 23, 1794, Jefferson writes George Wythe: "I have had a painful and tedious rheumatism complaint. It has now nearly left me . . . We are now living in a brick
kiln, for my house in its present state is nothing better." Thomas Jefferson
to Edmund Randolph, November 6, 1794: "I am still confined in a great
measure by the remains of my rheumatism, being unable to go out, either
on horseback or in a carriage." Jefferson to James Madison, September 13,
1795, (less than one month before Harriet I's birth, explaining his bad
health): "I would have been with you before this, but I have had almost
constant threats of rheumatism obstinately fixed in its part as to render it
imprudent for me to move much."[59]

When we add these risk factors such as Jefferson's age, stress level,
rheumatoid arthritis, severe migraine headaches, eighteenth-century
lifestyle, laudanum use, and urological issues in August 1807, Jefferson
would have been impotent and/or infertile when Eston was conceived.

Jefferson once wrote that "the most undesirable of all things is long
life; and there is nothing I have ever so much dreaded."[60] A marshaling of
the facts leads to one conclusion: It defies both medical and common
sense that Jefferson, at the frail "undesirable" age of sixty-four, would be
engaging in vibrant sexual activity with a woman who was forty years his
junior. His health would simply not support such a relationship.

8

THE SCHOLARS COMMISSION AND
THE CHARACTER ISSUE

But in the end, the idea is to get your history right. And that means trying to put your arms around all of the evidence and evaluate the evidence in a critical manner.

—Daniel P. Jordan, former Monticello President[1]

In 2000, after a year of investigating American history's most famous paternity case, a panel of independent scholars concluded that the historical and scientific evidence does not come close to proving Thomas Jefferson fathered Eston, or any slave child for that matter. Panel members included historians, law professors, political scientists, a biochemist, and a doctor.[2]

After weighing the evidence, both scientific and historical, a commission of thirteen professors led by Professor Robert F. Turner, a law and national security professor at the University of Virginia, announced in April 2000 that, given the two dozen-plus Jefferson males (with DNA markers in common) roaming Virginia at the time in question, there simply can be no grounds for certainty. "The commission agrees unanimously that the allegation is by no means proven," the summary of the report reads, "and we find it regrettable that public confusion about the 1998 DNA testing and other evidence has misled many people." With the exception of one low-key dissent, the scholars' conclusions "range from serious skepticism about the charge to a conviction that it is almost certainly false."[3]

"Thomas Jefferson was simply not guilty of the charge," said Forrest McDonald, professor of history at the University of Alabama. McDonald, and other panel members, point to another suspect—Jefferson's brother, Randolph.[4] One of the historians was Alf J. Mapp, author of two books about Jefferson that discounted the possibility of Jefferson having had a sexual relationship with Hemings. Previously, McDonald and at least three other panel members had believed the story was true, said esteemed panel chair Robert F. Turner.[5] Turner also noted that none of the scholars was paid for investigating the controversy.

"Regarding the relations that existed between Thomas Jefferson and his slave Sally Hemings, lies were told long ago, and today, even with the help of DNA analysis, we still cannot be certain as to who told the truth," Professor Paul Rahe, the lone dissenter, said in the report.[6]

Turner, the Scholars Commission's chairman, said he believes it would have been out of character for Jefferson to have risked entering into a sexual relationship with Sally, who was thirty years younger and served as maid to one of his daughters. Randolph Jefferson, according to Turner and most of the other panel members, is a far more likely suspect. He apparently visited Monticello often, and his years as a widower corresponded with the years in which Hemings had children, Turner said. "We know that Randolph had a habit of socializing at night with the slaves," he added.[7]

Alabama history professor Forrest McDonald, eighty-three, is widely regarded as a leading American historian, having written acclaimed books on the Constitution, the American presidency, and the Founding Fathers, including a study of Jefferson's presidency. Though respectful of younger scholars like that of his colleague at Alabama, Professor Joshua D. Rothman (a paternity believer),[8] McDonald has concluded from his own look at the DNA evidence and his knowledge of Jefferson that the father had to be someone else, most probably Randolph. "Randolph had all male children. Thomas Jefferson had all female children [—except for a nonviable infant]. The DNA matched a male child," he said. So convinced was McDonald that he joined the panel of scholars drafting a rebuttal to "Rothman's crowd."[9]

"It's going to be as devastating a critique as you're likely to see," McDonald said prior to the release of the report. "I'm a Hamiltonian," referring to Alexander Hamilton, with whom Jefferson was at odds politically.

"I'm always delighted to hear the worst about Thomas Jefferson. It's just that this particular thing won't wash."[10]

Comparatively little press attention followed the release of the Scholars Commission report that exhaustively reexamined all the evidence and came to the following conclusion: There is no proof that Thomas Jefferson was the father of any of Sally Hemings's children or even slept with his slave.[11] The DNA evidence gathered by Dr. Foster established only one thing with reasonable certainty: that Eston Hemings's male descendants carried a Jefferson Y chromosome. According to the panel, this means in all probability he was fathered by one of twenty-five men alive in Virginia at the time who were descended from Thomas Jefferson's grandfather. President Jefferson was one of the twenty-five, of course. But at age sixty-four, he was a man keenly conscious of his reputation in history. Other Jeffersons had as much opportunity to sleep with Sally and far less to lose. The scholars' report concludes that the most likely candidate was the president's younger brother, Randolph, who was mentioned in a slave's memoirs as frequently socializing with the slaves at Monticello. He was the uncle of Jefferson's daughter and quite probably the "Jefferson uncle" of Hemings family legend.[12]

One of the original scholars' members was Professor Willard Sterne Randall.[13] Randall read the official Monticello report, which accepted Jefferson's guilt. Not so fast, says Randall, whose 708-page biography, *Thomas Jefferson: A Life*, was published in 1993 and nominated for a Pulitzer Prize. Randall, a visiting professor of humanities at Champlain College in Burlington, and twelve other scholars on the commission were dissatisfied with the popular conclusion on Jefferson and Hemings.[14]

"I don't think we can put any old thing down and call it history," said Randall. "If we just suck stuff off Oprah and put it in the history books, then we're going to have crappy history. Disney would come off as a responsible historian compared to how this was handled. They're now rewriting the encyclopedias on Thomas Jefferson, and we've got to straighten it out. . . . To turn it into a mock O. J. Simpson trial of a dead president to me is a bit bizarre."[15]

McDonald agreed, and concluded that his year of study on the commission had changed his long-held conviction. Now, "I just don't believe it."[16]

After more than a year of independent research, it is worth noting the commission's verbatim conclusions, which follow:[17]

> . . . the question of whether Thomas Jefferson fathered one or more children by his slave Sally Hemings is an issue about which honorable people can and do disagree. After a careful review of all of the evidence, the commission agrees unanimously that the allegation is by no means proven; and we find it regrettable that public confusion about the 1998 DNA testing and other evidence has misled many people.

OTHER CANDIDATES FOR THE PATERNITY OF ESTON HEMINGS

"If Thomas Jefferson was not the father of Eston Hemings, the obvious question arises: "Who was?" Jefferson scholars for nearly two centuries have until very recently dismissed the Callender allegations, and without a great deal of apparent thought simply accepted the various reports that Thomas Jefferson Randolph had overheard Peter and Samuel Carr confessing to the paternity of Sally Hemings's children. But the 1998 DNA tests clearly ruled out any member of the Carr family as a possible father of Eston Hemings.

Candidly, we don't know who fathered Eston Hemings. The DNA tests narrowed the possible fathers down to a group of about two-dozen known Jefferson males in Virginia at the time, and there is at least a theoretical possibility that there may have been illegitimate sons carrying the Jefferson Y chromosome among the slaves passed down from Thomas Jefferson's grandfather, through his father, to the president. But when we consider things like the geographic location of many of these Jefferson men, the list of "most likely suspects" narrows quickly to Thomas Jefferson and perhaps half a dozen of his relatives. We know almost nothing about many of them.

Emphasizing again that we are not reaching a finding that Randolph Jefferson was Eston's father, it does appear that the circumstantial case that Eston Hemings was fathered by the president's younger brother is many times stronger than the case against the president himself. Among the considerations that might point to Randolph are:

- In *Memoirs of a Monticello Slave*, former slave Isaac Jefferson asserts that when Randolph Jefferson visited Monticello, he "used to come out among black people, play the fiddle and dance half the night. . . ." In contrast, we have not a single account of Thomas Jefferson spending his nights socializing with the slaves in such a manner. As already noted, we have Jefferson's letter inviting Randolph (and presumably his sons as well) to come to Monticello shortly before Sally became pregnant with Eston. It was common for such visits to last for weeks.

- Pearl Graham, who did original research among the Hemings descendants in the 1940s and believed the story that Thomas Jefferson fathered Sally Hemings's children, wrote in a 1958 letter to a leading Jefferson scholar at Princeton University that a granddaughter of one of Sally Hemings's children had told her that Randolph Jefferson "had colored children" of his own. Until Professor Fawn Brodie persuaded the descendants of Eston Hemings that President Jefferson was his father, their family oral history had passed down that Eston was fathered by "Thomas Jefferson's uncle." That is not possible, as both of his paternal uncles died decades before Eston was conceived. But to Martha Jefferson Randolph, who was generally in charge of Monticello during Eston Hemings's entire memory there, her father's younger brother was "Uncle Randolph"—and he was referred to as such in family letters.

- We don't know exactly when Randolph's first wife died, but we do know that he remarried—to a very controlling woman— shortly after Eston Hemings was born. About the same time, Thomas Jefferson retired from public office and spent the rest of his life at Monticello, where he could presumably have had access to Sally Hemings any night he wished. But Sally, although only in her midthirties, gave birth to no known children after Eston was born in 1808. Even the Thomas Jefferson Memorial Foundation report acknowledges that Sally's childbearing years may have corresponded to the years in which Randolph Jefferson was a widower.

- Randolph Jefferson had at least four sons between the ages of seventeen and twenty-seven when Eston was conceived, and if one accepts the data relied upon in the Monticello report, the number was five. One might expect the sex drives of young men in this age bracket to be greater than that of the sixty-four-year-old president, and with their father's reported example there is no reason to assume they were under strong social pressure at home to refrain from sexual relations with female slaves. Again, we have not the slightest bit of direct evidence that any of them ever fathered a child by Sally Hemings; but that puts them in essentially the same category as Thomas Jefferson as possible suspects.

SCHOLARS REPORT

We do not pretend that this is the final word on the issue, and it is possible that future developments in science or newly discovered evidence will warrant a reconsideration of our conclusions. We understand that useable DNA might be obtained from the grave of William Beverly Hemings, son of Madison Hemings, which could provide new information of relevance to this inquiry. If his Y chromosome did not match that of Eston Hemings and the descendants of Field Jefferson, that would confirm that Sally Hemings could not have been monogamous. A match with the Carr family would also be significant. A match with Eston might strengthen the case for Sally's monogamy, but would not conclusively establish even which Jefferson male was the father of either child. Our thoughts here are further tempered by our concerns about the ethical propriety of disturbing the remains of the dead in the interest of historical curiosity. It may also prove useful to search for evidence concerning the whereabouts of Sally Hemings over the years. This could prove decisive, but we are not optimistic about the existence of additional records of this nature at this point in history.

In the end, after roughly one year of examining the issues, we find the question of whether Thomas Jefferson fathered one or more children by his slave Sally Hemings to be one about which honorable people can and do disagree. . . . With the exception of one member . . . our individual conclusions range from serious skepticism about the charge to a conviction that it is almost certainly untrue."[18]

CHARACTER ISSUE

There exists "but one system of ethics for men and for nations."
—Thomas Jefferson[19]

The Scholars Commission also advanced a fundamental reason why this allegation is a complete falsehood: Jefferson's impeccable character. As one historian correctly wrote, the allegations of an affair with Sally were "distinctly out of character, being virtually unthinkable in a man of Jefferson's moral standards and habitual conduct."[20]

One specific incident illustrates this point: The evening of March 3, 1801, was the last day of John Adams's presidency. Yet Adams remained busy making last-minute, spurious judicial appointments, hastily sending them to his secretary of state, John Marshall, to quickly sign the commissions. Having learned of this Jefferson gave specific instructions to Levi Lincoln, his designated attorney general, and forcefully placed a pocket watch in Lincoln's quivering hand. When the hour of midnight fell, Lincoln strode into Marshall's office, snapped open Jefferson's watch and placed it in front of Marshall. At precisely 12:01, he demanded the secretary of state stop signing, though many unfinished documents lay on Marshall's table.[21]

Jefferson's fundamental sense of right and wrong, as well as his sense of morality, would have prevented him from engaging in any type of sexual liaison with a teen slave. Historian Douglass Adair has written that the professional historian is taught to be skeptical of any alleged episode in a person's career that contradicts the *entire* tenor of his life and requires belief in a reversal of character.[22]

The most reasonable argument to a jury would be the simplest: Thomas Jefferson's impeccable character would prevent him from conducting an affair, especially with a house servant, virtually in front of his two devoted daughters. The purported affair does not ring true in the context of his life and character. Historian Frank Berkeley adds: "Of all the presidents, I think he was probably the most rigidly self controlling and self disciplined."[23]

One can easily document Jefferson's extensive correspondence with his beloved daughters, Polly and Martha. These documents are living proof to Jefferson's propriety, love, and character, demonstrating that he would never be so insensitive to consummate an affair with Sally in their presence. Neither daughter ever acknowledged the possibility of his affair with Sally, although both were in a unique position to know and personally observe it. In fact, Martha vehemently denied it. Martha's daughter, Ellen, echoed this denial.

Martha visited Monticello, with her children, quite often. The same was true for Polly, until she was married in 1797. No doubt they would have confronted their father with the embarrassing rumor, who would have explained his long record of silent attitude toward "calumnies."[24] He explained his refusal to dignify the charges with denials: "Many of the [federal lies] would have required only a simple denial, but I saw that even that would have led to the infallible inference, that whatever I had not denied was to be presumed to be true."[25]

The incongruity between Jefferson's honorable character and a long, illicit affair with a servant is easily established. Although Jefferson was no saint, his reputation for veracity and integrity would be verified by two former presidents: James Madison and James Monroe. The former was a close friend and colleague of Jefferson's throughout his political life. Madison visited Monticello many times. But there is no evidence that he ever believed the Hemings affair, though he undoubtedly was aware of the charges made by Callender. Indeed, both Madison and Monroe met with Callender before the infamous article. Monroe was not as close to Jefferson as Madison, yet never commented on the Hemings allegation. He lived nearby and certainly heard the rumors circulating in Albemarle County. In fact, he purchased a slave from Jefferson, a seventeen-year-old who was a daughter of Betty Hemings. He even advised Jefferson on how to rebut Callender's accusations.[26]

Some historians soon forget Jefferson's pedigree: He was the son of wealthy, high-born, landed parents, and trained as a lawyer when this meant memorizing and analyzing centuries worth of British common law. Along the way, he mastered Latin, Greek, French, Spanish, and enough philosophy that lead to his choice as President of the American Philosophical Society, a position he held for seventeen years. It was to this group that Jefferson, a self-trained paleontologist, presented one of his prize possessions: the fossilized bones of a prehistoric creature he called Megalonyx.[27]

What Ellen Coolidge, his granddaughter, meant by "moral impossibility" is clear from the context of the statement in her letter: that it is highly unlikely that Jefferson would begin a sexual relationship with Sally in France, where she was a "lady's maid" to his daughters. This would require one to imagine "so fond, so anxious a father, whose letters to his daughters were so replete with tenderness, and with good counsels for their conduct, should . . . have selected the female attendant of his own pure children to become his paramour."[28] Similarly, the likelihood of such a relationship existing at Monticello during Jefferson's presidency, given not only Jefferson's undoubted love for his children and grandchildren but also the logistical difficulties entailed in keeping secret a sexual liaison, seals the "impossibility" of such an affair.

Another sense in which a sexual relationship with Sally would have been doubtful focuses on Jefferson's own moral code: "[T]he summum bonum is not to be pained in body, nor troubled in mind" and that "the indulgence which prevents a greater pleasure, or produces a greater pain is to be avoided." This adherence gave Jefferson ample reason to remain celibate.[29]

Moreover, according to historian Frank Berkeley, sex with a slave was at total odds with everything Jefferson believed:

> Jefferson thought, and he was passionate in his belief, that the worse evils of slavery was that unprincipled masters would have what he termed "sexual commerce" with women who were helpless to defend themselves because they were slaves . . . he repeatedly said that was the worse of all evils of slavery . . . he would have been a total hypocrite because he expressed himself many times with a real passion. I don't think he was hypocrite. I don't think he was liar . . . he was very open about his affair with Mrs. Walker.[30]

As Adair comments in his famous essay, such an affair with a slave is at complete variance with Jefferson's known character, revealing gross insensitivity and a callousness that he lacked. The Hemingses would ask us to believe that Jefferson's physical desire for Sally approached the compulsive. That his obsession was the passion of his life: first consummated when the she was fourteen, and he forty-five, resulting in one child when Jefferson was fifty-two, a second when he was fifty-five, another when he was fifty-nine, a fourth when he was sixty-two, and a fifth child born in his sixty-fifth year. This portrayal of Jefferson requires a literal reversal of his character as a decent family man, attested to by a myriad of scholars who have studied every facet of his life and career.

THE EXPERT WITNESSES AND JEFFERSON'S CHARACTER

In a mock civil trial, Jefferson's lawyers would call several leading historians to lend their expert opinions as to the lack of credibility of the Hemingses accusation, and to attest to Jefferson's impeccable character.

The first great landmark of Jeffersonian historiography was the three-volume biography by Henry S. Randall. His first volume was published in 1858 and the last in 1871. He enjoyed the confidence of Jefferson's surviving grandchildren, especially Jeff and his sister, Ellen. They supplied him with their reminiscences, through letters and conversations. He also enjoyed extensive access to Jefferson's correspondence and papers. Some years later, when the historian James Parton wrote his biography of Jefferson, Randall summarized what he had learned from "Jeff": "[T]here was not a shadow of suspicion that Mr. Jefferson, in this or any other instance, had any such intimacy with his female slaves."[31]

Both Randall and Parton attacked Callender as a vicious scandalmonger. Parton, armed with Randall's letter claiming the Carr brothers as Sally's sexual culprits, went further than Randall and chose to offer his crisp rebuttal to Madison Hemings's interview: "Mr. Hemings has been misinformed. The record of Mr. Jefferson's every day and hour, contained in his pocket memorandum books, compared with the records of his slaves' birth, proves the impossibility of his having been the father of Madison Hemings. So I am informed by Mr. Randall, who examined the records in the possession of the family. The father of these children was a near relation of the Jeffersons, who need not be named."[32]

Near the end of the century another biography was published by John T. Morse, Jr., in the American Statesmen Series. Morse ripped into Callender for pouring "bucketful after bucketful from [his] foul reservoir."[33] He also defended Jefferson's silence in the face of "gossip about Jefferson's graceless debaucheries."[34] The President of the United States "could hardly stoop to give the lie to a fellow like Callender."[35]

Henry Adams, in his monumental volumes dealing with Jefferson's

administration, *History of the United States*, joined the detractors of Callender, the critic of his great-grandfather, John Adams. This was the same
complaint of Adams's great-grandmother, Abigail, in her letters of repri-
mand to Jefferson. The only result, Henry Adams concluded, was to leave
a "fixed prejudice in the New England mind."[36]

Thus, the most eminent historians of the nineteenth century completely exonerated Jefferson. Specifically, Parton based his defense on the
"indecent" vituperations of Callender. Randall cited the "offensive imputations against [Jefferson] by the opposition press; and which has since
been the subject of a good many historical misstatements."[37]

For most of the twentieth century, historians agreed with Randall and
Parton, though they adopted a more sophisticated analysis. Two major
historians wrote political biographies of the Jefferson era. The best known
has been Professor Dumas Malone's magisterial, six-volume biography of
Jefferson, considered a monument of historical scholarship.[38] His final
volume of Jefferson's life, *The Sage of Monticello*, was hailed as one of the
towering achievements in the annals of American biography. Malone was
awarded the Pulitzer Prize in 1975. A companion to Malone is Merrill Peterson's one-volume biography, as well as his review of Jefferson's "image"
over the centuries. In *The Jefferson Image in the American Mind*, Peterson
succinctly concluded: "The legend survives, although no serious student
of Jefferson has ever declared his belief in it."[39]

Both scholars dismiss the sexual accusations against Jefferson. Malone,
in his volume dealing with Jefferson's first presidential term (1970), devoted a separate Appendix refuting "The Miscegenation Legend."[40] Malone
also coauthored a scholarly monograph in the *Journal of Southern History*.
Quoting from contemporary commentary of other competitive journalists, he too dismissed Madison Hemings's interview as "solicited and published for a propagandist purpose."[41] Willard S. Randall also brushes off
Madison Hemings. Hemings's account "resembles many uncorroborated
slave narratives and cannot be credited. It is full of hearsay."[42]

Two well-known biographers, Saul Padover and Nathan Schachner
(1942 and 1951, respectively), give the Hemings story little credence.
Padover's abridged paperback biography ignores it altogether, and
Schachner devotes his attention to the Betsey Walker affair. Later, many
historians relied on the analytical 1960 essay of historian Douglass Adair.
Adair found Sally's story, as related by Madison, had internal inconsisten-

cies that "shake our faith in [her] statement."[43] In particular, Adair cites the memoirs of Edmund Bacon, Jefferson's overseer, and concludes: "No matter how sympathetic one is to Sally, one must conclude that she is not trustworthy about Jefferson's relations with her."[44]

John Chester Miller wrote extensively about Jefferson's attitudes toward slavery, including a separate chapter on "The Sally Hemings Story." In his expert opinion, there was no proof of the accusation that Sally was Jefferson's "concubine."[45] As for Madison Hemings's claims, Miller also dismissed him: "His unsupported undocumented testimony conveyed in a politically suspect vehicle, the *Pike County Republican* would certainly not carry conviction" in a court of law.[46] Historian Winthrop Jordan published his profound work *White Over Black: American Attitudes Toward the Negro*, in 1968, and concluded that miscegenation would have been a "gross lapse of character" for Jefferson in the eighteenth century. Jordan explained that Jefferson "recognized these slaves as a necessary support for his manner of living. But his interest in them was always more theoretical and programmatic than personal. . . . He described their condition in America as 'miserable,' but he thought of them as a category of people rather than as individual persons."[47]

9

Madison Hemings: Gossip and Hearsay

All Hemings family authors, when it suits their cause, rely heavily on Madison's "Reminiscences" for much of the family history.
—Judith Justus, *Down from the Mountain*[1]

Cross examination is beyond any doubt the greatest legal engine ever intended for the discovery of truth.
—5 Wigmore on Evidence 1362 (1940)

Madison Hemings was Sally's second son, born in 1805 at Monticello.[2] He lived there until Jefferson's death in 1826. Both Madison and his younger brother, Eston, were freed by Jefferson's will. According to the terms of the will, both were apprenticed to their uncle, John Hemings, as cabinetmakers until they reached age twenty-one.

The freeing of the Hemings, as previously discussed, was nothing out of the ordinary as some historians have claimed. Rather Jefferson provided for their release because he believed they could maintain themselves as freed men by their carpentry skills. He also freed Bob and James Hemings because he was confident they could take care of themselves as freed men. This action was in line with the policy Jefferson followed with respect to other male slaves he had freed.[3]

Madison's hearsay testimony would be derived from his "interview" in the *Pike County* (Ohio) *Republican* on March 13, 1873, under the title "Life Among the Lowly, No.1.," (Harriet Beecher Stowe's subtitle to her book, *Uncle Tom's Cabin*), in which Madison declared that he was Jefferson's son.[4]

Madison's recollection, at age sixty-eight when he was interviewed, reflects a defective memory. Betty Hemings, his grandmother, died when

Madison was quite young. Moreover, Madison said that during Sally's stay in Paris she became Jefferson's "concubine"—the very same word used by Callender seventy years earlier. Madison declared that when Jefferson returned to Virginia from Paris, Sally was "enceinte" (French, for pregnant). "Soon after their arrival, she gave birth to a child, of whom Thomas Jefferson was the father. It lived but a short time. She gave birth to four others, and Jefferson was the father of all of them."[5]

Madison's testimony strains common sense. For example, there is no evidence in the interview that Sally herself claimed Jefferson as the father of any of her children. In fact, Madison Hemings's statements so closely resemble the original Callender allegations from 1802 (for example, in their identical misspellings of John Wayles's name), it seems obvious that he (or the editor, Wetmore) based his story on Callender's version of events.

Madison's account also revealed a new tangent—Sally refused to return with Jefferson from Paris without some quid pro quo. When Jefferson returned to the United States and brought Sally (and her brother, James Hemings) back to Monticello, she "demurred" according to Madison. He recalled that Sally began to learn the French language and in Paris she was free (slavery, for all intents and purposes, was outlawed in France, and a slave could sue for freedom), while in Virginia she would be "re-enslaved." According to Madison, to "induce" Sally to return, Jefferson promised her "extraordinary privileges" and made a "solemn pledge" that her children would be freed at the age of twenty-one. "In consequence of his promises, on which she implicitly relied, she returned with Jefferson to Virginia."[6]

Madison was very young at the time period he described, and probably heard this secondhand version from his older siblings, Beverly and Harriet. Madison was only seventeen when Harriet and Beverly "ran away," implying they were freed with Jefferson's acquiescence. More telling is the fact that Madison is *the only one* of Sally's children to commit his accusations to record. None of Madison's brothers or sisters ever made *any* claim against Jefferson. Indeed, none spoke or wrote for the record. In fact, Eston's family claimed descent from a "Jefferson Uncle" (as noted previously Randolph, Jefferson's younger brother, was known at Monticello as "Uncle Randolph"). Eston himself was asked about his possible lineage to Jefferson, while he lived in Ohio. Apparently the interviewer thought

Eston resembled a statue of Jefferson that he had seen in Washington. Strangely, Eston replied: "My mother was never married." He could have easily replied "yes" if he had believed he was Jefferson's son, but he did not.[7]

Madison's interview was heavily edited, if not written altogether, by the editor, S. F. Wetmore, an abolitionist from New England who had a bias against Jeffersonian Democrats. For example, notice the extraordinary vocabulary used by a former slave who "induc[ed]" the white children to teach him his "letters." The interview included specific words such as "demurred," "compunctions of conscience," "aristocratic," "interment," as well as the punctuation "viz."

Following the gains made by Jeffersonian Democrats in the elections of November 1872, S. F. Wetmore published a series of reminiscences, reminding his readers of the shame of slavery as practiced by Jefferson. Madison Hemings was ideal for Wetmore's purpose. In fact, Wetmore may have known about Madison, since Wetmore was a census taker. In the 1870 census there is a notation (not by Wetmore) opposite Madison's name: "This man is the son of Thomas Jefferson." It is clear that Wetmore sought out Madison, to make a political case against Jefferson, the slave owner—clear evidence of bias and motive.[8]

Wetmore's suggestive editing is exemplified by sophisticated, specific phraseology, not likely to be used by the semiliterate Madison. For instance, Madison's sister married a white man, but she was never suspected of being "tainted with African blood." Beverly's daughter was never suspected of having any "colored blood coursing in her veins." In fact, Madison's interview is laced with racial commentary. He asserted that white slave masters had no "compunctions of conscience [against] parting mother and child." He asserted that "like many [false] promises of white folks to the slaves," his alleged namesake, Dolley Madison, promised but never gave his mother any gift. Finally, his use of the French phrase "enceinte," or pregnant, raises red flags: Is this the editor's sophisticated word or Madison's, a poorly educated ex-slave?[9]

Preeminent historian Julian Boyd notes that Madison's testimony "was obviously prompted by someone . . . shaped and perhaps even written and embellished by the prompter." Dumas Malone assigns it a place in "the tradition of political enmity and abolitionist propaganda."[10] Biographer Willard S. Randall agrees:

I wish I knew what Madison Hemings said. The piece was written, and rewritten and rewritten by an abolitionist journalist after the civil war when Jefferson and the south were in disrepute . . . we don't have Madison Hemings words. We have a doctored version by a disreputable journalist. The problem is that this is oral tradition, it is not written history.[11]

In his interview, Madison alleged that, "[u]nlike Washington [Jefferson] had but little taste or care for agricultural pursuits."[12] This is monumentally wrong, as Jefferson's voluminous *Garden Book* would attest.[13] Jefferson wrote that "the greatest service which can be rendered any country" is to "add a useful plant to its culture." Farmers, he believed, were the "chosen people of God."[14] The Virginian was a skilled botanist, farmer, and inventor. He mastered many elements of horticulture and applied the best techniques to the raising of crops. His "plants gracefully curved away, in keeping with the undulating horizons beyond" Monticello.[15] In 1778, Jefferson placed orders for ninety thousand bricks, and oversaw the first planting of peas and several varieties of fruit trees.[16]

According to Madison, another of Martha's (Jefferson's daughter) sons, George Wythe Randolph, was "Jeff Davis," first secretary of war in the late "unpleasantness." This is also wrong. In fact, Leroy Pope Walker was the first Confederate secretary of war.[17]

The most credible evidence proves the following: Madison never claimed that he learned the identity of his father from Sally. In fact, Sally is virtually absent from his interview. Madison's brother, Eston (DNA match), never spoke of his relationship with Jefferson, perhaps, because when he settled in Wisconsin he and his family were regarded as "white." Eston's oral tradition suggested his family was related to one of Jefferson's uncles, but they "never heard of Sally Hemings."[18] Jefferson's younger brother, Randolph, was known as "Uncle Randolph" for obvious reasons. This oral tradition is highly probative as to Eston's likely father: Randolph Jefferson. Moreover, Eston is a Randolph family name, not common among the Jeffersons.

Madison also states he was named by Dolley Madison herself when she visited Monticello at his birth on January 19, 1805. This is flat-out wrong, and strains common sense. In fact, Dolley was serving as assistant to her husband, James Madison, then secretary of state. She also served as Jefferson's hostess in the White House in his second term. It is ludicrous

to suppose Dolley informed Madison and Jefferson that she had to travel
to Monticello because a male slave was to be born to Sally Hemings, and
Dolley must be present to name him after her husband. Of course, this
was well before science made it possible to determine the sex of a child
before birth. The Madison Papers and correspondence indicate that the
Madisons *never* visited Virginia from Washington during that winter.[19]

Traditionally, historians long have recognized the unreliability of oral
tradition as evidence, as Law Professor Robert Turner pointed out as chair
of the independent Scholars Commission. These include the high probability of errors creeping into stories that are told and retold from one generation to the next, as well as the tendency "to embellish the family legacy
to instill pride and confidence in the next generation." Indeed, family oral
traditions should not be called "history" at all, for they are rather, quite
literally, myth.[20]

In a court of law, there is good reason why hearsay is, generally, not ad-
missible. First, the person is not testifying under oath. Second, the speaker
is not in court for the jury to observe his or her demeanor. And third, and
of prime importance, the declarant is not subjected to cross-examination
in order to test the truth of the statement.

In short, Madison's testimony lacks certainty and veracity. It is utter
hearsay and amounts to little more than third-hand gossip. His lack of
credibility, bias of the editor, and faulty memory would be evident to a
modern-day, impartial jury.

ISRAEL JEFFERSON

A few scholars have relied on another slave at Monticello, Israel Jefferson,
who also resided in Ohio and supported Madison's claim of paternity. Israel's interview was the second installment of a partisan, abolitionist series published in the *Pike County* (Ohio) *Republican*.[21] But his support of
Madison is oddly phrased:

> I also know that [Jefferson's] servant, Sally Hemings, (mother to my old
> friend and former companion at Monticello, Madison Hemings) was
> employed as his chamber-maid, and that Mr. Jefferson was on the most
> intimate terms: that, in fact, she was his concubine. This I know from
> my intimacy with both parties, and when Madison Hemings declares he

is a natural son of Thomas Jefferson, the author of the Declaration of Independence, and that his brothers Beverly and Eston and sister Harriet are of the same parentage, I can conscientiously confirm his statement as any other fact which I believe from circumstances *but do not positively know*. [emphasis added][22]

His testimony is easily impeached for its many errors. Israel's own testimony—"do not positively know," is telling. His phraseology was suspiciously similar to Madison's interview—"concubine," "demurred," "piercing eye," "balancing in his mind,"—strongly suggests the hand of the biased, abolitionist editor, S. F. Wetmore. Israel had no firsthand knowledge or observation of the relationship between Jefferson and Sally, and, once again, provides only gossip, speculation, and hearsay.[23]

Israel claimed he was born in 1797 and was only eight years old when Madison, his "old friend and former companion, was born."[24] Israel said that he remembered the "exciting" preparations for Jefferson's departure to assume the presidency. Yet, for this to be true Israel would have been a child prodigy. The *Farm Book* shows that he was born on Christmas day 1800, not 1797 as he claimed. Thus, either he was not born yet or only a few weeks old when his "earliest recollections" occurred when Jefferson moved to the White House in December 1800.[25]

Israel's interview also includes bitter remarks about Jefferson's grandson, Jeff Randolph, who he claims to have encountered after the Civil War. He found the "proud and haughty Randolph in poverty, at Edge Hill, . . ." in 1868.[26] This is the same Jeff Randolph that Madison mentioned presided over the Republican convention of 1872. Jeff Randolph learned of Israel's interview and was incensed. He wrote a stinging rebuttal to the newspaper—"Israel is made to revive and confirm of his own knowledge a calumny generated in the hot bed of party malice."[27] Randolph also declared that the other slaves were bitterly jealous of the Hemings and sought to explain their privileged position—that being "very superior intelligence capacity and fidelity to trusts." In his rebuttal, Jeff explained that the purpose of reviving the calumnies against his family was motivated by "pondering [*sic*] to a ferocious hate of the southern white man."[28]

10

JEFFERSON ON TRIAL

It is not often that a principal character in history throws so much light on his rivals that, in the process, he himself is illuminated; shadowed, too.
—Gore Vidal, *Inventing a Nation*[1]

WITNESS FOR THE PROSECUTION

In a civil trial, one of the principal witnesses against Jefferson would be James Callender. Through cross-examination, it could be proven that Callender had both a bias and motive against Jefferson, and his testimony amounts to little more than scurrilous, political hearsay. Callender, perhaps, would defend himself by claiming that the charge (sexual relationship with Sally) was well known among "Virginia gentry."[2]

"Light-Horse Harry" Lee

One of these gentlemen was probably Henry Lee (nicknamed "Light-Horse Harry" Lee), a Federalist and dedicated opponent of Jefferson. Lee was a friend to John and Betsey Walker, and the assumed source of Callender's accusations against Jefferson in the "Walker affair."[3] A genuine Revolutionary War hero, Lee would be an impressive witness. But he would not have firsthand knowledge of the Jefferson-Hemings relationship, and his testimony would be excludable hearsay. In fact, some time later, at

General Bloomfield's table at Trenton, Lee declared "that there is no foundation whatever for that story."[4]

John Hartwell Cocke

John Hartwell Cocke was another Virginia gentleman aware of the Hemings-Jefferson allegation. Cocke served on the Board of Visitors of the University of Virginia, and was a well-respected, wealthy Virginian residing at Bremo in Fluvanna County. He became a general in the War of 1812 and, in his later years, was a radical antislavery agitator.

Cocke would testify, from his diary entries recorded in 1853, that Jefferson was a "notorious" example of white masters cohabiting with slaves. In 1859, he wrote that Jefferson was an "example" of the "damnable practice" of keeping a slave as a "substitute for a wife."[5] Cocke's testimony, however, can be discredited on several grounds: (1) he did not have first-hand information or observations, other than inadmissible hearsay; (2) his diary entry was unreliable, recorded more than thirty years after his relationship with Jefferson; and (3) by this time, he had become a radical abolitionist like S. F. Wetmore, the editor of Madison's so-called "interview." (see Appendix H—Rebuttal of the John Hartwell Cocke Letters).

After he remarried, Cocke became a rabid abolitionist and a strong supporter of the Christian temperance movement. Most of this activity was long after Jefferson's death. In their earlier days together, when Cocke helped Jefferson found the University of Virginia, there was evidence that Cocke was jealous of the credit Jefferson received for starting the University, while Cocke received little or no credit.[6]

Betsey Walker

Some scholars suggest that two women could testify as to Jefferson's pattern of sexual behavior: Mrs. John Walker, known as Betsey, and Maria Cosway, who he met in Paris.

Betsey Walker would testify that young Jefferson, before he was married, made advances to her when her husband, John Walker, was absent. Callender revealed this story, a tangled and complicated situation.

John Walker and Jefferson were boyhood schoolmates and friends at William & Mary. Walker married Betsey in 1764. A few years later,

Jefferson made "improper" advances toward Betsey. According to a document dictated by Walker to General Henry "Light-Horse Harry" Lee in 1805, Jefferson's advances continued, but Betsey remained silent and did not inform her husband for over a decade.[7] She finally confessed to Walker when Jefferson was away in France. When Jefferson returned, Walker demanded satisfaction. Harry Lee acted as mediator, and Jefferson offered to settle the affair by publicly exonerating Betsey from any blame.

The Walker affair is the *one charge* that, after it became public, Jefferson admitted was a youthful indiscretion. He never admitted, either directly or indirectly, the Sally accusation and in fact denied it in multiple private correspondences.

Maria Cosway

Jefferson met Maria in Paris in 1786, and instantly became attracted to her. In all probability, she reminded Jefferson of his late wife, for they shared many of the same traits: both were petite, pretty (both were blonde and blue eyed), vivacious, and unusually accomplished in the fine arts such as music and painting.[8]

They spent time together exploring the environs of Paris. Dumas Malone wrote that Jefferson "was quite swept off his supposedly well-planted feet."[9] How far this romantic relationship progressed is unknown, but it seems to have stopped short of a sexual affair. Although he sensed that Maria was "a chapter apart" from other women, Jefferson was ambivalent when he wrote his famous letter to her, "A Dialogue Between My Head and My Heart," in the form of a popular eighteenth-century literary genre, the dramatic dialogue.

Historian Julian Boyd, editor of the authoritative edition of Jefferson's writings, concluded that this letter is "one of the most revealing in the entire body of TJ's correspondence, and one of the most notable love letters in the English language."[10] Jefferson spent days drafting the letter, which he had to write left-handed since his writing hand was broken. He then meticulously copied the small tome onto three sheets of paper, all with his left hand. Jefferson described Maria as a lady who had "qualities and accomplishments, belonging to her sex, which might form a chapter for her: such as music, modesty, beauty, and that softens of disposition which is the ornament of her sex and charm of ours."[11]

Malone believes that Jefferson was "deeply in love" with Maria, and the historian goes one step further: If the widower ever made love to another woman, "this was the time."[12] Yet ultimately Malone believed their relationship was merely a flirtatious friendship. For whatever reason, however, their passion receded and the relationship wound down. By the winter of 1787 it was over. In fact, Jefferson formed another companionship with Alexander Hamilton's sister-in-law, Angelica Church, (another married woman) but that too seems to have remained platonic.

Jefferson's customary discretion makes it impossible to know whether the affair with Maria had an active sexual, or merely suggestive, component. It seems that the character of their correspondence suggests that Jefferson preferred an emotional relationship, rather than a physical one.[13] Paternity believers contend that his relationship with Maria proves that Jefferson, the man, was not immune to sexual attraction. Some have suggested that Sally's arrival in Paris coincided with Jefferson's termination of relations with Maria. These arguments fail. What deterred Jefferson and limited these romantic forays was the shadow, perhaps guilt, of his beloved wife, Martha, who had died two years earlier. As to Jefferson's alleged vulnerability to Sally, the opposite was closer to the truth. The restraints on his relationships with Maria and Angelica would apply more strictly to any temptation for Sally, barely out of puberty. Maria stimulated Jefferson, and most probably helped him to "move on" with his emotional life, but he commanded self-restraint, and it does not appear to have lead to sexual consummation.

When Jefferson returned to the United States, he corresponded with Maria. Early in 1795, he received two letters from her, the woman historian Donald Jackson said "ranked first after his daughters on the limited roster of women who held a firm place in his heart." Jefferson, his ardor dimmed by this time, managed to reply that "you have the power of making fair weather wherever you go."[14] Historian Dumas Malone comments about his romance with Maria: "Like other deep intimacies of his life, this one remains obscure and mysterious. Not the least significant aspect of it is the beauty with which he garbed the relationship in his own memory."[15]

In short, all the evidence we have about Jefferson suggests that, despite a short-lived romance with Maria, he remained celibate following the death of his beloved wife, Martha. Since her death, although Maria rekindled some lost emotions, he remained "impervious to the feeble attractions of common society" and "dead to the world."[16] The intensity with which Jefferson involved himself in politics during the period 1789–1809 fits the pattern of a man who obsessively pursued his career as a substitute for an intimate, sexual relationship. And after his retirement from the presidency, Jefferson just as passionately pursued the three obsessions of his life—his family, his farm, and his books.

JEFFERSON'S DEFENSE: "A MORAL IMPOSSIBILITY"

Some historians indict Jefferson because he did not publicly deny the Sally accusation. Jefferson had a long history of refusing to dignify salacious charges in public forums, rather he preferred private denials to his friends and colleagues. For example, in a letter he wrote to Edmund Randolph in 1792, he alludes to an anonymous newspaper attack, signed by "an American":

> Every fact alleged under the signature of "An American" as to myself is false, and can be proved so, and perhaps will be one day. But for the present lying and scribbling must be free to those mean enough to deal in them, and in the dark. . . .[17]

Jefferson never denied Callender's charges in public, but he did so in private correspondence. He stated that there was "not a truth existing which I fear or would wish unknown to the whole world." On one specific occasion, in private correspondence, he denied the paternity charge, among other allegations.[18] In a cover letter dated July 1, 1805, and written to Secretary of the Navy Robert Smith, Jefferson denied the "charges" made against him, admitting that he was guilty only of one—"that when young and single [he] offered love to a handsome lady" [the Walker affair]—which he maintained was "the only one founded in truth among all their allegations against me." Jefferson's letter to Smith referenced an enclosed letter written to Attorney General Levi Lincoln that fully responded to the charges but which, unfortunately, has not survived. From Jefferson's cover letter it is clear that he desired both Smith and Lincoln to read the enclosed letter as "particular friends" of Jefferson with whom he "wish[ed] to stand . . . on the ground of truth."[19]

According to historian Willard Sterne Randall this denial has a crucial subtext of importance:

> That admission [of the Walker affair] was in writing to the Secretary of Navy [Robert Smith]. The secretary of Navy's sister was married to Peter Carr and it was quite pointed and advised what Jefferson meant. *You* [emphasis added] know that that I am not the father of this child . . . that is the reading of that I have to take out of it.[20]

Some critics have assumed that Jefferson's *public* silence is a tacit admission of guilt. This is a canard. If we accept the Hemings oral tradition that John Wayles (Jefferson's father-in-law) was Sally's father, and by association Martha's (Jefferson's wife) half sister, Jefferson's silence takes on fresh poignancy. If this hearsay is correct (again this point is highly debatable), Jefferson bore quietly for half a century a burden of responsibility for the illegitimate half brothers and sisters of his own adored wife. As Dumas Malone wrote: "There is material here for the tragedian, but the historian must recognize that oral tradition is not established fact. Jefferson himself would have been the last person to mention such a relationship . . . it was quite in his character as a private man." In fact, silence appeared to be the wiser course to Jefferson and was wholly in character for family matters.[21]

Yet, the misguided Monticello report dismissed Jefferson's letter as "ambiguous," referring only to the charge of Jefferson's affair with Mrs. John Walker. It is clear to a reasonable person from the full context that Jefferson was *denying all* the charges made against him by his political enemies, including the Hemings allegation. The significance of Jefferson's denial in this letter to a friend, who was also a member of his administration and a political confidant, should be obvious: It is the *only direct evidence* left by Jefferson in his own words and handwriting that bears on the Sally question.

The Monticello Committee report also notes, without any analysis, the only known account of the paternity allegation being raised in Jefferson's presence. According to nineteenth-century biographer Henry S. Randall when confronted by his daughter, Martha, with an offending poem (a couplet by Irish poet Thomas Moore linking Jefferson with a slave), the president's only response was a "hearty, clear laugh," hardly the response of a man filled with shame in front of his beloved daughter. Taken together, Jefferson's denials are consistent with the testimony of many family members, friends, and acquaintances who similarly denied the Sally paternity allegation.

Scant evidence exists that the paternity allegation survived, even among Jefferson's political enemies, much past the 1802 elections. Randall reported that Dr. Robley Dunglison, Jefferson's doctor in 1825 and 1826, did not believe the story and that both Dr. Dunglison and Professor George Tucker, "who lived years near Mr. Jefferson in the University, and were often at Monticello," never heard the subject mentioned in Virginia. Significantly, after his retirement from the presidency, not even Jefferson's political enemies took the Sally allegation seriously enough to press it.[22]

Weary of office and longing for the tranquility of private life amid the hills of Monticello, Jefferson was ready to retire after his first term in office in 1804. His friends, however, urged his continuance. Yet, other reasons persuaded Jefferson to run for reelection: vindication of his good name against salacious allegations. For example, note his letter to Philip Mazzei on July 18, 1804:

> I should have retired at the end of the first four years, but the immense load of Tory calumnies which have been manufactured respecting me, and have filled the Europe market, have obliged me to appeal once more to my country for justification. I have no fear but that I shall receive honorable testimony by their verdict on these calumnies.[23]

Edmund Bacon

Captain Edmund Bacon was an overseer at Monticello. As an eyewitness to the Jefferson-Hemings relationship, he would completely exonerate Jefferson of the sexual accusation. His recollections and eyewitness testimony, recorded by the Rev. Hamilton Pierson in 1862, were published and they destroy this sexual allegation.

Bacon never hinted at a relationship between Sally and Jefferson. Indeed, he directly refuted it. Recalling Sally's daughter, Harriet, Bacon testified that "[s]he was nearly as white as anybody and very beautiful." As to claims that Jefferson freed her because he was her father, Bacon said, "She was not his daughter; she was ___'s [omitted] daughter."[24] Rev. Pierson, in the preface, alludes to the omitted name because "he did not like to publish facts that would give pain to any that might now be living." This probably refers to names omitted in various stories throughout the volume. As noted by author Cynthia Burton in her book *Jefferson Vindicated*, "some of Randolph Jefferson's descendants lived in the county adjacent to Edmund Bacon."[25]

Some Monticello researchers have suggested that Bacon's remarks could not be accurate because he was not working at Monticello at the time. Once again, this is proven false by historian James Parton's July 1873 article, "The Presidential Election of 1800." Jefferson's April 1801 instruction to Bacon covers one month *prior* to Harriet II's birth:

> Take this brief passage of his last orders in April, 1801, as a specimen of the kind of directions he frequently gave while he was apparently absorbed in affairs of state:—. . . . The nails are to be sold by Mr. Bacon, and the accounts to be kept by him; and he is to direct at all times what nails are to be made. The toll of the mill is to be put away in the two garners made, which are to have secure locks, and Mr. Bacon is to keep the keys.[26]

This clearly indicates that Bacon was present at Monticello, and knew Harriet from birth. Bacon would also testify that he was born and raised a few miles from Monticello. His family knew Jefferson before he was employed there and Bacon's older brother had worked at Monticello as well. Bacon visited often, but did not start his official duties as overseer until late 1806. Employed at Monticello on an informal basis, Bacon visited Jefferson in Washington on three different occasions, shortly after his inauguration in March 1801.

In his memoirs, Bacon commented on interracial relations at Monticello. For example, he related a story about a fight that involved a schoolmate of Jeff Randolph's, William Rives. Bacon added that Rives would spend the night at Bacon's house, but thought the other boys were too "intimate with the Negro women."[27]

> Speaking about a young man (Wm. C. Rives), that used to hang around Monticello a great deal with the other boys, but very often he did not like the doings of the other boys, when I (Edmund Bacon, overseer),

gave them the keys to stay up there alone, and he would come down and
stay all night at my house. He has stayed there many a night. The other
boys were too intimate with the negro women to suit him.[28]

This was a clear reference to the Carr brothers, or Randolph Jefferson's sons.

It has been argued by some paternity believers that Bacon was only at
Monticello for twenty years, and could not have known firsthand who
Harriet II's father was. This is false. Bacon lived nearby. His father and
brother had previously acted as overseer and, as a young boy, Bacon had
frequented Monticello. He related in his memoirs that:

I am now seventy-six years old, I was born March 28, 1785 [for reference Harriet II was born May 1801], within two or three miles of Monticello, so that I recollect Mr. Jefferson as far back as I can remember
anybody. My father and he were raised together, and went to school together. My oldest brother, William Bacon, had charge of his estate during the four years he was Minister to France. After Jefferson became
President he wanted to again hire William, but by then he was quite an
old man and well off and turned the job down so Edmund, too young
according to his father, Edmund being not of age yet, however he went
to live with Mr. Jefferson the 27 of December before the President was
inaugurated and if I had remained with him from the 8th of October to
the 27th of December, the year that I left him, I should have been with
him precisely twenty years.[29]

As genealogist Herbert Barger confirmed: "I have spoken with a former caretaker of Mr. Bacon's grave in Trigg County Kentucky for many
years and know exactly where he is buried. You can see that Edmund Bacon was always around Monticello long before he became overseer."[30]

Historian Douglass Adair explains the significance of Bacon's testimony: "Here, at last, not on the basis of Randolph's testimony alone or of
Bacon's alone, but on the joint corroboration that each of these witnesses
speaking independently give to the other, we have positive evidence . . .
for declaring Thomas Jefferson innocent of the charge that he fathered a
mulatto by his slave Sally Hemings."[31]

Abigail Adams

At 4:00 A.M. on March 4, 1801, a pudgy figure waddled through a wintry cold to his waiting stagecoach. He hoisted his aching bones into the carriage, and bounced in the predawn for the next fourteen hours to Baltimore, enroute to Quincy, Massachusetts. Officially, he was still the President of the United States and would be until Thomas Jefferson was sworn in later that afternoon. And so ended John Adams's presidency, "in gloom, chill and apparent stealth."[32]

In contrast to Adams's sullen departure, days before, Jefferson had bid a fond good-bye to his dear friend Abigail Adams, as they nibbled cake and sipped tea. Abigail and Jefferson shared a deep, honest, and affectionate friendship for almost forty years. They enjoyed a trust so deep that she was the one woman, besides Jefferson's wife, that he literally entrusted with his children's lives. Abigail was charmed by Jefferson's perfect manners, his variety of interests, and depth of reading. And though she did not ever record it, she was flattered by the engaging attention he paid to her. Knowledge of the repeated tragedies that had been inflicted on Jefferson strongly affected Abigail. She admired his stoicism, as Jefferson had described to "keep what I feel to myself." Abigail had known heartbreak herself.[33]

She could testify to direct, personal observations of Sally. Abigail, already in London, received Jefferson's daughter Polly and Sally, on their way to Paris. Abigail was in a unique position to observe Sally. In fact, she would record in a letter to Jefferson that Sally was quite immature, and "wholly incapable" of looking after Polly:[34]

> ... the girl [Sally]. ... is quite a child, and Captain Ramsey is of opinion will be of so little Service that he had better carry her back with him.[35]

This is a unique, firsthand observation of young Sally. A jury would find Abigail a persuasive witness for Jefferson, altogether an intelligent, shrewd observer. Her personal observations and opinions would carry great weight. Abigail's testimony does not suggest the alluring young "wench," as Callender charged, or the portrait of a sultry Sally in the movie, *Jefferson in*

Paris. Nor does her direct testimony bear out the absurd theory that she seduced Jefferson or provoked his carnal lust in Paris.

To Abigail, Sally seemed as much as a child as Polly. In the opinion of Captain Ramsey, as Abigail related, she would be of "so little Service" that he recommended taking her back to Virginia. Abigail told Jefferson he would have to be the judge. "She seems fond of the child and appears good natured." Abigail concluded that Sally, without supervision, would be incapable of her responsibilities.[36]

Robert Smith

Robert Smith was secretary of the navy under President Jefferson. Jefferson wrote to Smith in 1805, in response to a letter from a Virginia "gentleman" of "respectable character" named "Thomas Turner," a pseudonym.[37] This letter revived the charge that Jefferson had made improper advances to Betsey Walker, and continued after Jefferson was married. The letter was published in Boston and taken over by a Washington Federalist newspaper in June 1805. As a footnote to his letter, "Turner" also revived the accusation that Jefferson had a slave mistress named Sally—"the affair of black (or rather mulatto) Sally is unquestionably true."[38]

The true author of the Turner letter was most probably "Light-Horse Harry" Lee, a Federalist and close friend of Walker's. When the affair resurfaced, via publication of the so-called "Turner" letter, Jefferson confronted the issue. He wrote to his attorney general, Levi Lincoln, by way of a covering letter to Robert Smith. In the Smith letter, however, Jefferson acknowledged the allegations about his conduct toward Betsey Walker, but insisted that it was the only accusation "founded in truth."[39]

In other words, this letter constituted a complete denial of the accusations concerning Sally.

Martha ("Patsy") Jefferson

Jefferson's daughter, Patsy, was an abused wife, both physically and emotionally. She and her children suffered in her marriage to Tom Randolph, who proved to be an impulsive, bullying man consumed with self-doubt. Tom was also physically abusive to Patsy, an indifferent father, an inept plantation manager, and a burdensome son-in law to Jefferson.[40] It is no wonder she, with her children, fled to the safe confines of her father and Monticello. After Jefferson's death, Martha formally left Tom, who had been beating her and escaped to Boston with their two youngest children. She returned to Monticello only when Tom was on his deathbed. He died in June 1828.[41]

Martha was one of three family members who denied emphatically any secret or open relationship between Sally and Jefferson based on her personal observations—a relationship she was in a unique position to witness. Martha Jefferson would be an impressive witness to a jury. John Randolph, a sharp opponent of Jefferson, described her as the "noblest" of women. A family friend testified that she was "the most accomplished woman I have ever known."[42] Martha was extremely close to her father, especially after her sister Mary died. Gradually, she took over as mistress of Monticello, inheriting the estate when Jefferson died.

In her waning years, Martha summoned her son "Jeff" (Col. Jefferson Randolph) and his younger brother, George, and urged them to "defend" their grandfather's reputation. She insisted that prior to the birth of one of Sally's children, Jefferson and Sally were apart for fifteen months:

> She asked the Colonel if he remembered when "—Henings (the slave who most resembled Mr. Jefferson) was born . . ." She then directed her sons attention to the fact that Mr. Jefferson and Sally Henings could not have met—were far distant from each other—for fifteen months prior to such birth. She bade her sons remembers this fact, and always to defend the character of their grandfather.[43]

She urged Jeff to find the precise dates in Jefferson's account books. He did so and verified Martha's claim (this was later disputed). Biographer Henry Randall told subsequent biographer Parton that he had been able to confirm this fifteen-month separation in Jefferson's account book, but nobody else since has found this information.

Jefferson molded Martha into a strong and reliable woman, who knew her lofty place among Jefferson's affections. As an eleven-year-old staying in Philadelphia while Jefferson attended congress in Annapolis, Martha received a reminder from her father: "I have placed my happiness on seeing you good and accomplished, and no distress which this world can now bring on me could equal that of your disappointing my hopes."[44]

Martha always went to Monticello days before her father's arrival from Washington. Throughout his presidency she had made it a practice to be there, along with her children, whenever Jefferson was home. Previously, she had returned to Edgehill after his departure but apparently she did not go back, except for brief visits, after her father came home to stay after his presidency. As historian and author Elizabeth Langhorne notes:

> From this time forward, in fact, on his return to Virginia from public business Jefferson always stopped first at Martha's home. Insisting that she leave husband and children and accompany him to Monticello before he himself would set foot there. In the light of suppositions concerning Sally Hemings this is an interesting point. Would a lover rushing to the arms of his mistress wish always to be accompanied by his highly moral and shrewdly observant daughter?[45]

Martha's persuasive testimony is an eyewitness account. She had extensive, firsthand knowledge of life at Monticello and knew Sally both in Paris and in Virginia. Of all the witnesses, she would be in the best position to know the truth. She is the missing witness in all the scholarly research on "Jefferson's women." She was the one constant in Jefferson's life. Martha became her father's sole companion in the long rides through the Blue Ridge Mountains as Jefferson grieved over his wife's death. Several years later, she accompanied him to Paris. After Jefferson's presidency ended, she and her seven children came to live at Monticello permanently.

Martha Jefferson is the forgotten witness in history. She must be heard.

Ellen Coolidge

Jefferson's granddaughter, Ellen Wayles Randolph Coolidge (1796–1876) lived, intermittently, at Monticello. She was close to Sally before she married Joseph Coolidge and moved to Boston in 1825. In a letter written to her husband on October 24, 1858, she related that she had talked to her brother Jeff on the subject of the "yellow children."[46] Ellen would testify that the father of Sally's children was "Col. Carr" (meaning Samuel Carr, Jefferson's nephew). She noted that Jefferson was surrounded by his grandchildren and enjoyed the most affectionate relationship with them: "How comes it that his immoralities were never suspected by his own family—that his daughter and her children rejected with horror and contempt the charges brought against him?"[47]

Ellen recalled:

> That my brother, then a young man certain to know all that was going on behind the scenes, positively declares his indignant disbelief in the imputations and solemnly affirms that he never saw or heard the smallest thing which could lead him to suspect that his grandfather's life was other than perfectly pure. His apartment had no private entrance not perfectly accessible and visible to all the household. No female domestic ever entered his chambers except at hours when he was known not to be there and none could have entered without being exposed to the public gaze.[48]

The phrase "none could have entered without being exposed to the public gaze" is crucial testimony.[49] Ellen's testimony that her family never suspected nor witnessed any clandestine romance—"rejected with horror and contempt the charges brought against him" is essential.[50] Defending her grandfather, she asked how could a man of his character be likely to have sexual relations "under [his family's] eyes and carry on his low amours in the circle of his family"? She singled out Sally and asked why Jefferson "should . . . have selected the female attendant of his own pure children to become his paramour! The thing will not bear telling. There are such things, after all, as moral impossibilities."[51]

According to Ellen's letter, there was a general impression that Sally's children were fathered by Col. Samuel Carr. He was the "most notorious good-natured Turk that was ever master of a black seraglio kept at other men's expense."[52]

Thomas Jefferson ("Jeff") Randolph

Jeff Randolph (1792–1875), Thomas Jefferson's trusted grandson, was described as six foot four (an inch and a half taller than Jefferson) who towered over most men. A model son and grandson, Jeff was hardworking, conscientious, and each year assumed more responsibility for managing Jefferson's plantations. Jeff married in 1815, and three years later had small children of his own.[53]

Jefferson's widowed sister, Martha Carr, lived on and off at Monticello, bringing her three sons, Peter, Samuel, and Dabney with her until her death in 1811. Jeff related the Carrs' admissions of intimacy with Sally to historian and biographer Henry S. Randall. Jeff told Randall that he knew firsthand that the Carr brothers were responsible for Sally's children because they admitted it to him. This version was told to Randall in the late 1850s, and he repeated it to Jefferson's new biographer, James Parton, in 1868:

> Col. Randolph informed me that there was not a shadow of suspicion that Mr. Jefferson in this or any other instance ever had commerce with female slaves. . . . He said he had never seen a motion, or a look, or a circumstance which led him to suspect for an instant that there was a particle more of familiarity between Mr. Jefferson and Sally Hemings than between him and the most repulsive servant in the establishment—and that no person ever at Monticello dreamed of such a thing.[54]

According to Jeff, Thomas Jefferson was "chaste and pure" in all sexual circumstances, indeed as "immaculate a man as God ever created."[55]

Other Slave Witnesses

The lack of corroboration of the Hemings allegation from other Monticello slaves is significant. With the exception of Israel Jefferson, not a single one ever spoke or wrote about a relationship between Jefferson and Sally.

Isaac Jefferson, a slave at Monticello, set down his recorded recollections in 1847 at Petersburg, Virginia. He provides considerable detail about Jefferson, life at Monticello, the slaves, their families, and Sally. Isaac would testify that he was deeded to Polly (Jefferson's daughter) when she was married in 1797, but he apparently worked for Martha and Tom Randolph. He claimed that he worked at Monticello until four years before Jefferson's death (Jefferson died in 1826, so this would have been 1822). After Jefferson's death, he owned his own blacksmith shop and eventually dictated his own recollections, which were not rediscovered until 1951. Isaac's memoirs are important because he never alluded nor hinted at *any* relationship between Sally and Jefferson.[56]

According to historian and curator Frank Berkeley, Isaac's memoirs are crucial, proving Jefferson's innocence:

> ... we came upon a manuscript ... Isaac Jefferson, son of Ursula the cook. Isaac comes through as the most honest man as you can imagine ... transparently honest ... one of the questions asked was "who were the Hemings?" He replied, without reflection, in a courteous way ... there was not one mention about Sally. Why? Why didn't Campbell ask him about Sally's children. I think the answer is perfectly obvious when you think about it. Everybody knew who they were. Everybody knew she [Sally] was living with Peter [Carr]. . . . [57]

Another slave, Robert Hemings, was Jefferson's personal aide, who was eventually freed. Martha saw Robert occasionally in Richmond prior to Jefferson's death, yet he never mentioned or alluded to the Jefferson-Hemings connection. James Hemings, who lived with the Jeffersons and Sally in Paris, was also freed and traveled for some years, including a probable return to Paris. He, too, was silent concerning the relationship, and eventually committed suicide. So, too, were John Hemings, as well as Burwell and Joe Fossett, Betty Hemings's grandsons.

Thus, no Hemings, except Madison, ever hinted at or addressed a relationship between Sally and Jefferson.

II

SECRET ROOMS AND
OTHER HOLLYWOOD FANTASIES

Over three decades their passionate, complex love affair endured and flowered ... Barbara Chase-Riboud has fashioned a dramatic—and unashamedly romantic—novel.
—Viking Press, promotional blurb to the 1979 novel *Sally Hemings*[1]

MONTICELLO

Monticello has been described as Jefferson's "essay in architecture." It was the one place beyond all other venues that he could enjoy supreme peace with his family. He once said that "all my wishes end, where I hope my days will end, at Monticello." Designing the great house was Jefferson's "delight, and putting up and pulling down one of my favorite amusements."[2]

Retirement at his mountain retreat also meant happy days for his daughter Martha and her children. They were particularly established under Jefferson's benevolent influence, especially since Martha's moody husband had prolonged absences, and an apparent lack of interest in his own family. Jefferson wrote that it was the "ineffable pleasures ... of family society" which always came first in his affections.[3]

However, some paternity crusaders have claimed, through novels and movies, that Jefferson transformed his cherished family home into a maze of secret rooms and staircases for a sexual rendezvous with Sally. Again, this is a complete fabrication. A simple review of his letters, architectural plans of Monticello, and a personal tour of the home discredits this myth.

A thirty-minute tour of Monticello took me into some of Jefferson's most intimate spaces, including his private library and the bedroom where he died. Most days during his retirement, Jefferson was alone, pen in hand, in an office dubbed his "cabinet," adjacent to his bedroom. During his lifetime, he produced some twenty thousand letters. In 1817, he penned to John Adams: "From sun-rise to one or two o'clock, and often from dinner to dark, I am drudging at the writing table." To relieve the pressure on his aching wrist, Jefferson used a swivel chair and an armless, backless sofa straddled by his writing table, his eighteenth-century attempt at ergonomics.[4]

As you tour Monticello, one can imagine Jefferson taking a break from his correspondence by walking through the glass doors of his office (cabinet) into the exterior room, called his "Venetian" porticle (porch), a welcome respite of solitude. The adjoining piazza (greenhouse) has an airy motif with windows covered by green Venetian blinds ("porticles"), leading into his green house.

Author Alan Pell Crawford suggests in his book *Twilight at Monticello*, that Jefferson had some sort of secret room, blinds, or a staircase installed so "Sally . . . could easily have entered Jefferson's private chambers at any time of day or night, without being seen or heard." Crawford probably based this assumption on an article written by Helen Leary in the *National Genealogical Society Quarterly* that speculated: "These porticles may not have been built specifically to facilitate Sally's nocturnal visits, but they certainly would have concealed them."[5]

This is not factual. There are only two ways to gain access to Jefferson's bedroom. Through the side door, off the main entrance, which would be clearly visible to everyone in the house. Or two, a circuitous route up from the slave quarters, over the south pavilion, through the green house window, through another window to Jefferson's summer study (southwest porticle), through the French doors and into his bedroom. All of which could have been heard throughout the house. Moreover, Crawford writes that the "porticles" (blinds) and staircase were added at the same time. This is not accurate. They were built at two different times—porticles in 1805 and the staircase in 1796. The staircase he refers to leads into a hallway, not directly into Jefferson's library.[6] Another stairway in his bedroom leads to a narrow storage closet over his bed, used for out-of-season clothes and legal papers. This was reached by a ladder in an alcove near the head of Jefferson's bed, and there was no other entrance to this closet.

Some have speculated that Jefferson had the green, louvered shutters put over his windows to hide his sexual liaisons with Sally. Once again, this is patently false. Early in the 1800s Jefferson modified the greenhouse outside of his bedroom chamber with louvered green verandas, which he called "porticles" on the windows. Even though they permitted air and light, he erected them to shield his privacy from a variety of inquisitive strangers, who would wander up to Monticello to glimpse the famous man. The eastern portico, near Jefferson's bedroom, faced the entrance road to Monticello and it was there that "parties of men and women would sometimes approach within a dozen yards and gaze at him point-blank until they had looked their fill, as they would have gazed at a lion in a menagerie."[7]

The wooden shutters, as author Jack McLaughlin explains in his book *Jefferson and Monticello*, coincided with "the addition of the terrace walk [that created] a public promenade directly in front of [Jefferson's] bedroom-library suite."[8] The louvered porticles did not exist when Sally was conceiving her children. In fact, Jefferson's history of collecting shutters over thirty years indicates he placed them on the windows of virtually every house he lived in, even temporary residences.

McLaughlin notes in detail that:

> There are those who will view Jefferson's porticles as yet another strand in the web of circumstantial evidence linking him to Sally Hemings: the porticles were constructed to conceal her presence in his bedroom and to allow her to slip more easily in and out of his sleeping quarters . . . A much more likely explanation for the timing, however, is the addition of the terrace walk outside of his bedroom. With the construction of the promenade, he realized the full impact of what he had inadvertently wrought—an orchestra seat to his private life for anyone who cared to view it . . . The only solution to the problem of privacy in his personal quarters was the kind of architecturally unsatisfactory one he arrived at.[9]

The article in the *National Genealogical Society Quarterly* also intimated that a "secret" passageway was built in 1802–1803. This was actually a planned stairway, and was not available for the earlier Hemings births in 1795, 1798, and 1801.[10] In actuality, there are no "circular" stairways or hidden entrances to Jefferson's suite. He opposed such large staircases because he thought they wasted space. He designed his stairways, architecturally, after those he had seen in Paris. The very narrow and steep stairways to the underground passageway were not hidden entrances, but one of convenience and practicality for use by the servants and guests. These slightly winding staircases also lead to the upstairs bedrooms. More importantly, as it relates to the privacy issue, the door from the hallway to Jefferson's cabinet is see-through glass from midway up, allowing light from the greenhouse into the hallway. Thus, even if a servant was to ascend that way, there was no allowance for privacy. More to the point, the doors at the bottom of the stairs that lead to the underground passage were locked at night preventing intrusions to the family quarters.[11]

Long before Sally Hemings was born, Jefferson's first version of Monticello was designed for privacy. When married, Jefferson's bedroom/dressing room wing was isolated, and his second floor library/study over the parlor could be closed off to intruders. The outside blinds, which some scholars infer were installed to shield Jefferson's sexual trysts, were referred by Jefferson as louvered shutters. They were placed on all the ground-floor windows, long before Sally. Jefferson's infatuation with these louvered shutters went back as early as 1770 (pre-Sally) when he ordered six pairs for the first house, all facing southwest. In Paris, he bought five more pair, then five more in Philadelphia, and six in New York. All of these were installed in Monticello.[12]

In addition, the design of the "dependencies" (stables, kitchens, slave quarters, etc., below the house) functioned as two sides of an open-ended rectangle, turned to the outside, decidedly *away* from the house. Jefferson's design effectively screened the service areas from contact with the great house and west lawn.[13]

A public perception that Sally either lived in the space over Jefferson's bed or used it for access to an upstairs room appears to derive from pure fiction. The space, not a bed but an out-of-season storage closet, varies in width from 2'6" to 2'9". According to architectural historians, who removed a modern staircase in 1979, the space was reached either by a ladder or a steep ladder-like stair.[14]

Moreover, in 1795 Jefferson plunged into the greatest and most costly construction project of his life. He had decided to transform Monticello—to tear off the entire second floor and more than double the size of the house. He remodeled the design after an elegant residence he had seen in Paris, a palatial house with a dome called the Hotel de Salm, on the left bank of the Seine.[15]

Nothing has been found in the documentary record to indicate that Sally ever lived inside the Monticello house. On her return from Paris to Monticello in 1789, Sally most probably lived in the stone house on Mulberry Row (presently Weaver's Cottage), where her sister Critta was known to have lived. Thus, in 1793, she would have moved, as did Critta, into one of the three new, twelve-by-fourteen-foot, log cabins on Mulberry Row.[16] Some time between 1803 and 1808, she evidently moved into one of the "servant's rooms" in the South Dependencies between the South Pavilion and the dairy. In 1851, while walking around Monticello, Jefferson's grandson, Jeff Randolph, pointed out to biographer Henry S. Randall "a smoke blackened and sooty room in one of the collonades, and informed me it was Sally Henings' [sic] room."[17]

Historian and genealogist Cynthia Burton provided this emphatic appraisal:

> To suggest that Monticello was designed as a convenient love nest in which to carry on a clandestine liaison with a slave is preposterous. Even Thomas Jefferson could not have designed a totally private living space when he had such a large family living with him and so many staying there too.[18]

HOLLYWOOD

Unfortunately, the public's willingness to accept Jefferson's paternity guilt, secret sex rooms, hidden passageways, etc., has been spawned by various novels and movies. Despite its obvious aforementioned shortcomings, Fawn Brodie's account of a sexual liaison between Jefferson and Sally, beginning in France and continuing at Monticello, captured the lurid imagination of a reading public, and spawned both novels and movies. From imaginative (yet wholly outlandish) fictional re-creations such as Barbara Chase-Riboud's romance novel *Sally Hemings* (1979) or the Merchant-Ivory film *Jefferson in Paris* (1995), to *Sally Hemings: An American Scandal* (2000) (where Jefferson, Sam Neil, is depicted as fist-fighting with Peter Carr and physically assaulting Sally) to HBO's recent *John Adams*, the story of a Jefferson-Hemings relationship has become widely accepted in popular culture. For example, take this excerpt from a *Saturday Night Live* skit, with Robert De Niro playing Jefferson and Maya Rudolph as Sally Hemings:[19]

[JEFFERSON's *daughter* MARIA *enters, with her slave* SALLY HEMINGS]

MARIA: Gentlemen. If you'd like to adjourn to the dining room, dinner is nearly served.

THOMAS JEFFERSON: Maria.

MARIA: Yes, Father?

THOMAS JEFFERSON: Who is that? [*points to* SALLY]

MARIA: That's Sally Hemings, Father. The new slave you inherited.

[JEFFERSON *moves in for the kill*]

THOMAS JEFFERSON: Sally? I'm Thomas. Jefferson. The owner of this house.

SALLY HEMINGS: I know who you are.

THOMAS JEFFERSON: I just wanted to welcome you to Monticello. I hope you'll be very happy here with us.

SALLY HEMINGS: Well, I'm . . . I'm just happy to be indoors.

THOMAS JEFFERSON: [*chuckles*] That's charming.

[*cut to*]

STATESMAN #1: Oh, brother, here he goes.

JAMES MADISON: [*sighs*] Like a bee to a blossom.

STATESMAN #2: What are you talking about?

STATESMAN #1: Don't you read the papers? Everyone knows it. Thomas Jefferson only dates black chicks.

Humorous as political satire, but one more example of the perpetuation of the myth in popular culture.

JEFFERSON IN PARIS (1995)

No other film has done more to spread the Jefferson-Hemings sexual relationship than the film *Jefferson in Paris*, starring Nick Nolte as Jefferson and Thandie Newton as Sally. With no documentary evidence whatsoever, the film's implicit message is telegraphed to the audience: Jefferson had a sexual relationship with the fourteen-year-old Sally, leading to her pregnancy. For instance, the following excerpts are taken directly from Ruth Prawer Jhabvala's original screenplay:[20]

> JEFFERSON: [*indicating the dress she is wearing, which is the one he has given her*] What about that?
> SALLY: [*She makes a polite but not very convincing sound of appreciation, then continues with more enthusiasm*] I likes the bright colors best—pink I likes, and yellow.
> [JEFFERSON *takes something out of a drawer or box*—]
> JEFFERSON: . . . Now I wonder what you will think of this . . . Of course you may not care for it at all, in which case I might as well give it away to some other girl.

She becomes excited to see what he has—"Show, oh show, Master!"—but he teases her by hiding it behind his back. She goes behind his back to try and prize it away from him. He brings his hands forward, clenching them into fists. She taps one fist—he opens it and it is empty and she exclaims in disappointment. Then he opens his other hand and shows her a little locket on a chain. She picks it out of his palm—"Ain't that gay!"—She puts it around her neck but he has to help her with the clasp. She admires herself in the mirror "It plumb pretty"—then turns around to show him proudly, undoing the front of her dress so that he can see the chain better where it nestles in the cleft of her bosom. He traces his finger along the line of the chain.

In the middle of this, a shy tap on the door, and to his "Come in" SALLY enters and stands waiting for him to look up. When he does—

> SALLY: [*holding out poultice*] Master, let me lay it on your hand.
> [JEFFERSON *hesitates—then laughs and holds out his wrist. She kneels on the floor and gently applies the poultice, sometimes looking up at him to make sure she is not hurting him*]

———

GIRLS' BEDROOMS. NIGHT
[PATSY, *thinking she has heard some sound, goes to check up on* POLLY. *She finds her asleep, the space on the floor where Sally is supposed to sleep is empty*]

[PATSY *goes to* SALLY'*s closet—that too is empty. She stands on the stairs and looks toward the closed door of her father's bedroom. She returns to her own bed, looking stoically angry, her eyes dry and hard*]

SALLY: I go tell Old Master I wants my money.

JAMES: And if he says what for?

SALLY: I says for me and the little one what's coming. [*She bites at her corn, then laughs into his face at the expression on it*]

JAMES: You is scarcely 14.

SALLY: I is 15, and you knows it.

JAMES: You is glad to breed more little niggers to work in your master's fields.

SALLY: [*indignantly*] Won't be no field nigger when it's his own child I is carrying.

Thus, when some historians sought to vindicate Madison Hemings's claims, they found a ready audience, especially in the artistic community. British journalists and commentators used the story much as they had in the nineteenth century, to denigrate American Revolutionaries by associating them with slaveholding. For example, Christopher Hitchens suggested in the *Nation* that Jefferson henceforth be described as "the slave-owning serial flogger, sex addict, and kinsman to ax murderers." The reviews in the British newspaper the *Express* of the Mel Gibson movie, *The Patriot*, noted that the real Francis Marion, the "Swamp Fox" on whom Gibson's Benjamin Martin character was based, "raped his slaves and hunted Red Indians for sport."

These movies and books have distorted history with artistic license. Dumas Malone described it succinctly in a *Washington Post* interview: "Scandal and sex can be exploited to great financial advantage. The public will always believe the story. You can never get it back. You can never stop it." He went on to observe:

It is utterly impossible that Jefferson could have carried on in the presence of his own family in Monticello, being the kind of very moral and extraordinary devoted family man he was.[21]

Movies, television, novels, and stagecraft have had a dramatic effect on the public's perception of Jefferson's image. Psychologists have produced empirical research, terming this condition "the cultivation effect": that is, the influence of film on a viewer's information, beliefs, and attitudes. Cognitive psychologists conclude that there is a causal relationship, not merely a correlation, between film watching and belief formation. Their explanation is derived from what they term "heuristic processing": snap judgments based on rules of thumb, such as "Jefferson is guilty."[22]

The research concludes that people typically do not "discount" information derived from fictional sources such as movies even though they are aware that movies do not supply factual information. While most of the research on cultivation theory relates to television, the same conclusions attach to film. Thus, "Sally" films create and perpetuate negative impressions about Jefferson and life at Monticello. The empirical research bears this out. As professor George Comstock explains: "what is most striking about television is that its power is exercised almost beyond the control of anyone—viewer, writer, producer, actor, or network executive."[23]

Ironically, Jefferson feared his own history would become "fable." Jefferson wrote to William Wirt in 1814: "When writers are so indifferent as to the correctness of facts, the verification of which lies at their elbow, by what measure shall we estimate their relation of things distant, or of those given to us through the obliquities of their own vision." He added this prophetic statement to his own book agent in Philadelphia: "If [a] book be false in its facts, disprove them; if false in its reasoning, refute it."[24]

12

THE MONTICELLO REPORT: A "RUSH TO JUDGMENT"

They seem like they were rushing to judgment, and a preconceived judgment . . . it isn't the scholarly approach . . . it's sort of jumping to conclusions.

—Historian Frank Berkeley[1]

Following release of the DNA study in the fall of 1998, Daniel P. Jordan, then president of official Monticello (the Thomas Jefferson Memorial Foundation, or "TJMF")[2] appointed a nine-person in-house research committee that was charged, in Jordan's words, to "review, comprehensively and critically, all the evidence, scientific and otherwise, relating to the relationship of Thomas Jefferson and Sally Hemings." The TJMF consisted entirely of embedded Monticello researchers, two of whom, Lucia Cinder Stanton and Dianne Swann-Wright, had believed Jefferson's guilt at least three years *before the DNA study.*[3]

No scholar independent of Monticello took part in the report.

From the outset, the proverbial deck was stacked against Mr. Jefferson, as one of the committee members, Dr. White McKenzie (Ken) Wallenborn, concluded. Dr. Wallenborn agreed to share his experiences on that committee for the record and documents the bias and motive of the panel. In fact, Dr. Wallenborn authored the minority dissenting opinion of the report (see Appendix C), which argued that a stronger case could be made for Randolph Jefferson, Jefferson's younger brother, as Sally's sexual partner, rather than Jefferson. His critical report was initially suppressed by official Monticello.

The Monticello Committee essentially took the "family myths" of Madison Hemings's descendants and accepted them as sound-bite history. The committee was chaired by slave historian Dianne Swann-Wright, the African American Director of Special Programs at Monticello, including its "Getting Word" Oral History Project. The other members of the committee were all Monticello staff members, although the committee consulted with members of two other committees: the Advisory Committee for the International Center for Jefferson Studies and the Advisory Committee on African-American Interpretation.

Although the committee had concluded its work by spring 1999, its scripted report was not released until January 27, 2000. The report was immediately posted on the Internet, and Jordan noted that within a week the Monticello Web site received nearly sixty thousand "hits" a day, with some three thousand different individuals downloading the report. Two weeks later, after the television airing of the CBS miniseries *Sally Hemings: An American Scandal*,[4] Jordan noted that the hits "maxed out" Monticello's system, with as many as nine hundred thousand in one day. Although he dismissed the CBS miniseries as "ridiculous as history," "a soap opera," and "strictly Hollywood," Jordan acknowledged that "it certainly did encourage an interest in the story." He added, "Anything that encourages and raises the consciousness of the American people about history and race is a good thing."[5]

The Chairwoman of the committee, Dianne Swann-Wright, did not disclose that she was a good friend and colleague of author Annette Gordon-Reed (her sympathetic paternity book accepting Jefferson's guilt is discussed subsequently) before, during, and after the DNA study. In fact, she used Gordon-Reed's book as a blueprint for finding Jefferson guilty. Another member of the committee, Lucia Cinder Stanton, a senior research historian, is also a good friend of paternity believer Gordon-Reed's.

According to Wallenborn, the DNA Committee had finished its work in early April 1999. Cinder Stanton apparently wrote the final report and finished it by late April or early May 1999. After it was completed, the DNA study committee members did not discuss or see the final report until seventy-two hours before its release to the press. There was *no discussion* of the content, or any potential revisions. There were also some strange coincidences associated with the timing of the release, according to Dr. Wallenborn. Several members and its consultants were allowed to publish their work in the *William and Mary Quarterly*, which was also released about the same time as the official Monticello report. In fact, Martin Luther King's birthday celebration had been nine days before the TJMF media event. Black History Month was less than a week after the release of the report, and the CBS miniseries *Sally Hemings: An American Scandal* was aired a few days later. According to Wallenborn, the chair of the committee, Dianne Swann-Wright, did not share with the full committee his dissenting report (completed on April 1999) *until well after the release* of the final committee report on January 27, 2000.[6]

One of the glaring pieces of evidence the committee ignored, according to Wallenborn, was Edmund Bacon's (Jefferson's overseer) powerful exoneration of Jefferson, by witnessing another man come out of "[Sally's] room many a morning when I went up to Monticello very early."[7] The Monticello report, however, dismissed Bacon's account because he supposedly was not working for Jefferson at the time Harriet was conceived, and could not have known who Harriet's father was. Wallenborn suggested that it does not take much insight to understand what Bacon was saying. Just as the committee assumed (wrongly) Sally's children did not have multiple fathers, Bacon thought that whoever he saw coming out of Sally's room in the early morning hours was her lover, and therefore Harriet's father. In any case, what Bacon clearly stated was Thomas Jefferson was not Sally's sexual partner, or the father of her children.[8]

The committee concluded that "no one familiar with Monticello suggested that Sally Hemings was promiscuous or that her children had multiple fathers."[9] Wallenborn declares this is flatly wrong, again contradicted by Bacon, who was "familiar" with Monticello and wrote that he had personally witnessed someone else coming out of Sally's room on multiple mornings, and that man was not Jefferson.[10]

To Wallenborn, Bacon's account was the most important piece of evidence bearing on a relationship between Sally and Jefferson. Bacon was the only observer to express an opinion on Jefferson's paternity and then support it with eyewitness evidence. Bacon is the *only eyewitness* in the history of this scandal, and on record in this case. His testimony is compelling, overwhelming, and uncontradicted. Not hearsay, not second-hand gossip, but direct eyewitness testimony.

Dr. Wallenborn provided more insight into the background of the political climate in Charlottesville leading up to the DNA study in 1998, just as the impeachment of President Clinton was unfolding. Since 1993, the research department at Monticello, under Cinder Stanton, has launched "the most comprehensive black oral history project in the nation to recover the recollections from descendants of Monticello's slave population, with the primary focus on the descendants of the Hemings family." The title of the project is "Getting Word."[11] This socially conformed project not only guided the official Monticello report accepting Jefferson's guilt, according to Wallenborn, but was a full four years before Annette Gordon-Reed's book implicating Jefferson. Official Monticello also assisted and welcomed Annette Gordon-Reed, who provided the author with a public platform for her sympathetic, pro-Hemings's book.[12]

What was not mentioned in the official Monticello press conference and not acknowledged on its Web site until three months later (on March 23, 2000) was that one of the members of the Monticello Committee, Dr. Wallenborn had strongly dissented from the committee's report. Noting several areas of disagreement with the majority's report, Dr. Wallenborn concluded that "[t]here is historical evidence of more or less equal statu[r]e on both sides of this issue that prevent a definitive answer as to Thomas Jefferson's paternity of Sally Hemings's son Eston Hemings or for that matter the other four of her children."

Dr. Wallenborn urged official Monticello to continue to regard the paternity question as an open one. In an essay published subsequent to the release of his minority report, Dr. Wallenborn charged that the Monticello Committee, and particularly its chair, Dianne Swann-Wright and cochair Lucia Cinder Stanton "had already reached their conclusions" at the start of their deliberations. The committee ignored or dismissed as problematic "most of the evidence that would exonerate Mr. Jefferson."[13]

Equally troubling is Dr. Wallenborn's accusation that Dianne Swann-Wright failed to share his dissenting report with other members of the committee. Indeed, he notes that it was not shared with the "interpretive staff" (tour guides) at Monticello nor with the TJMF Board of Trustees until he personally began circulating it *after* the January 26, 2000, press conference.

This "Jeffersongate" atmosphere suggests Dr. Wallenborn's criticisms of the Monticello Committee were well founded, and further evidence of the predetermined conclusion to "get Jefferson." The final report is far from being the "scholarly, meticulous, and thorough" analysis that Jordan claims. Its general conclusion that Jefferson fathered one, and probably all, of Sally's children, fails to be adequately supported by the evidence gathered by the committee and summarized in its findings.

Dr. Wallenborn would testify that while the majority report "enhanced" the possibility that Jefferson was the father of one of Sally's children, "the findings do not prove that Thomas Jefferson was the father of Eston. This is a very important difference."[14] Dr. Wallenborn did not contest the statistical correlation (Neiman's study, discussed earlier) of Jefferson's presence and Sally's conception, but he emphasized that the vital third element of evidence was missing—Sally's presence at Monticello. Also missing was evidence concerning the presence of other males with the Jefferson haplotypes.

Dr. Wallenborn confronted then Monticello President Dan Jordan (who commissioned the report), and asked that his minority report be attached to the full report. Jordan flatly refused. When Wallenborn insisted that this would appear to be, in effect, suppressing a dissenting opinion to which the Board of Trustees had been denied access, Jordan reluctantly changed his mind and attached the report.[15]

The committee's report was a literal rush to judgment, according to Frank Berkeley,[16] curator of manuscripts at the University of Virginia for twenty-five years and Board of Trustee Member at Monticello. Allegedly completed in six months, in reality, the report was written and researched within three months. The Monticello Committee never consulted Berkeley, John Casteen (coresearcher with Berkeley, now President of the University of Virginia), or their extensive Sally Hemings file at the University. According to Berkeley:

> One thing we did . . . we looked and documented . . . any reference to the Hemingses, especially Sally . . . Well we found quite a few . . . especially among the Carr papers, who were very much humiliated by the behavior of their nephews. This committee didn't study that file . . . it was miserably written in a sweeping way . . . it contains statements that are entirely questionable . . . high in innuendo and low in fact . . . I'm afraid they were trying to rush toward a conclusion . . . [17]

According to history Professor David Mayer's brilliant analysis of the Monticello report, (Mayer served on the subsequent Scholars Commission debunking the report), a fundamental problem with the report is the lack of any objective standard for weighing evidence. When the report concludes that the "currently available documentary and statistical evidence, indicates a high probability that Thomas Jefferson fathered Eston Hemings," it offers no methodology by which the subjective terms "high probability" can be measured.

Another fundamental flaw in the committee's report, according to Mayer, is their blatant conflict of interest. The partiality in favor of oral tradition was compounded by the fact that the chair of the research committee was Dianne Swann-Wright, director of Special Programs at Monticello, who has had a vested interest in the "Getting Word" project since its inception in 1993. Given the intimate involvement of Dr. Swann-Wright with the witnesses interviewed for the "Getting Word" project, it is not surprising that the committee report relied on the 1873 Madison Hemings oral hearsay as the crux of Jefferson's guilt.

Dr. Mayer noted that oral hearsay evidence has a general problem of unreliability. The committee's report is flawed, in Mayer's opinion, not only because it relies almost exclusively on oral tradition, but it relies on it selectively, utilizing hearsay that fits with Jefferson's guilt. The committee noted, hypocritically, that the oral history of Eston's descendants (who claimed Sally's children were fathered by a Jefferson "uncle," i.e., Randolph) was dismissed as "altered to protect their passing into the white world."[18]

Mayer notes that there was one other oral tradition that was rejected by the committee: the direct testimony of Jefferson's grandchildren, Jeff Randolph and Ellen Coolidge. They identified one of the Carr brothers, Peter or Samuel (Jefferson's nephews by his sister Martha), as the father of Sally's children. That tradition was taken just as seriously as the tradition of Hemings descendants, and has the indicia of reliability based on eyewitness accounts. Yet, the official Monticello report dismissed the Carrs by the DNA, *assuming* that Sally's children were all fathered by the same man.

Both Professor Mayer and Dr. Wallenborn conclude that important pieces of evidence that question the Jefferson paternity claim were either ignored or dismissed by the committee. For example, Jefferson's own denial of the Callender allegations in an 1805 letter written to the secretary of the navy is dismissed as "ambiguous," a subjective judgment that fails to take into account its clear historical importance. The account of former household slave Isaac Jefferson, who mentioned and described Sally in his memoir, is omitted from the committee report, even though Isaac did not hint at any relationship between Jefferson and Sally—powerful evidence destroying the paternity myth.[19]

Other problems in the committee's report reveal that it was carelessly written. For example, although the report does include a facsimile of the 1858 Ellen Randolph Coolidge letter, it follows it with the flawed (or altered) transcription as found in Appendix E of Professor Gordon-Reed's book (discussed subsequently). The draft of committee member Fraser Neiman's article, "Coincidence or Causal Connection? The Relationship between Thomas Jefferson's Visits to Monticello and Sally Hemings's Conceptions" contains a typographical error that distorts the DNA study in a significant way. The article states that the molecular geneticists tested "male-line descendants of *Thomas Jefferson*," when of course it was not Thomas Jefferson, but Thomas Jefferson II, Jefferson's paternal grandfather, whose descendants were tested.[20] Thus, the report gave the false impression that Thomas Jefferson's, or his direct heirs', DNA had been tested, when, in fact, it had not.

Another Jefferson scholar faulted the report, as well as the committee that prepared it, for its unprofessional bias. "The DNA evidence by itself is straightforward, and can hardly be corrupted," said the late Eyler Robert Coates, Sr., a former librarian at the Library of Congress and compiler of the University of Virginia Web site, Thomas Jefferson on Politics and Government. "But the committee disregarded eyewitness testimony and confessions by one of the alleged perpetrators, and substituted . . . rumors and gossip that originated by unnamed persons. Much of this gossip came from Jefferson's neighbors. They could not possibly know who was the father of an unmarried woman's children."[21]

According to Coates, there is not a single piece of direct, eyewitness evidence that points to Jefferson as the father of Sally's children. "Jefferson denied it privately, his daughter and his grandson, both of whom lived in the same house with Jefferson, denied it. One of his nephews confessed to fathering the children himself, although the DNA indicates that he apparently was not the only father. Jefferson's overseer said he saw someone other than Jefferson many times coming out of Sally's room early in the morning. Yet all that testimony was disregarded, all those people were made out to be liars, and instead, credence was given to neighborhood gossip and the statements of people testifying to things that happened before they were even born! And that is the kind of stuff the committee called overwhelming evidence!"[22]

"The decisions made by the committee show incredible bias and poor judgment," Coates emphasized. "The committee engaged outside consultants, but this was for the DNA evidence, even though there was no controversy about the DNA science. In fact, one of the consultants told them the DNA study was so routine, it wasn't worth a scholarly conference. But on the real controversial parts of the study—the interpretation of the data—the committee did it all in-house, and did not consult with a single person who had a contrary view to the one they were obviously intent on adopting."[23]

The DNA evidence indicated that Tom Woodson was not a son of Thomas Jefferson, contrary to the very strong oral tradition held by Woodson descendants. "Isn't that curious," remarked Coates. "This whole mess of slanderous accusations started with James Callender writing in 1802 about Jefferson's 12-year old son, which he supposedly had by Sally, and who Callender said was living at Monticello at the time. No one contradicted him, but now that the DNA evidence shows that Tom Woodson could not have been Jefferson's son, suddenly there's no documentary evidence to support Tom Woodson's existence."[24]

"The ironic thing about all this," Coates added, "is that the very foundation established to honor and protect the name and contributions of Thomas Jefferson is the one to jump in on the side of Jefferson's enemies and calumniators. There is so much detail connected with this controversy, it is almost impossible to cover it all, even in a long article," Coates said. "And there's so much misinformation being put out by other people. The Foundation's report has good factual information in it. The travesty was in the way they interpreted it."[25]

Barger agrees and added, "To deny that there is a politically driven agenda in this controversy would be naïve in the least and border on blind ignorance at worse." An examination of the tax returns of Monticello corroborates Barger's point. Before the DNA controversy, public contributions to Monticello totaled a mere $2,380,743. After the DNA results and the official Monticello report finding Jefferson guilty, contributions climbed to $11,663,315 for the tax year 2001. In 2006, they reached $13,830,134. Apparently, sex, slavery, and controversy sell and official Monticello has embraced this.[26]

According to Barger, "the Gilder-Lehrman Foundation is a . . . major Monticello supporter and if I am not mistaken one is or was a member of the Thomas Jefferson Foundation."[27] In fact, Richard Gilder is a trustee, serving on the Board of Directors at Monticello. Lewis E. Lehrman, Gilder's partner and cofounder of the Gilder Lehrman Institute of American History, is a trustee of the Center for the Study of Slavery, Resistance, and Abolition at Yale University. Coincidentally, or perhaps conspiratorially, Professor Joseph Ellis and Monticello President Dan Jordan (both paternity advocates) serve on the advisory board of Gilder-Lehrman.

Finally, Barger points to the following material from the Gilder-Lehrman newsletter:

Scholarships Repairing Historical Wrongs: Reparations, Reconciliation and Intergenerational Injustice Applications are invited for a Ph.D. scholarship building upon the theme of "Repairing Historical Wrongs." This theme is chiefly concerned with the legal and political challenges arising from the recent growth of high-profile campaigns to redress serious historical injustices, such as enslavement, genocide and wartime atrocities . . . This is a joint offering from the Law School <http://www.hull.ac.uk/law/> and the Wilberforce Institute for the study of Slavery and Emancipation.[28]

Thus, in short, a distinct political agenda has been deeply involved in this entire controversy, and remains so today.

13

The Charlottesville Connection:
True Believers

I just can't imagine why anyone would bother to deny it at this point. The argument is so overwhelming that we need to move on to other more fruitful sites of inquiry.

—History Professor Peter Onuf, University of Virginia[1]

In the grave at Monticello lies the man whose fame is secure, no matter what slanderous allegations were advanced against him two centuries ago. However, the association tasked with preserving Jefferson's legacy, the Thomas Jefferson Foundation that operates official Monticello, has evolved into an embedded, cultural institution that has politicized Jeffersonian history. Consider the following items from their newsletter:

- "The Foundation also will restore Monticello's dependencies and documented structures on Mulberry Row [slave quarters]. These areas are 'crossroads' of the plantation, where Jefferson and his family interacted on a daily basis with the *enslaved African-Americans* [emphasis added] and paid laborers who lived and worked on the mountaintop. This restoration work will allow visitors to understand better the complex and dynamic worlds of *slavery* [emphasis added] and domestic life at Monticello."[2]
- "Restoration of Monticello's Dependencies Under Way. The rooms and spaces beneath the South Terrace will be returned to

their Historical appearance. When Daniel Webster dined at Monticello in 1824 he complimented the cuisine 'served in half Virginian style, half French style, in good taste and abundance.' His praise not only described the efforts of Martha Jefferson Randolph or one of her daughters, but those of *two enslaved women,* [emphasis added] Edith Fossett and Fanny Hern, who took over as Monticello's principal chefs, beginning with James Hemings."[3]

- The second paragraph in the official Monticello guidebook states that: "Monticello was home not only to Jefferson and his large family but also to as many as 135 *slaves* [emphasis added] who worked the plantations four farms. . . ." The guidebook declares to the world that: "Because of genetic testing in 1998 and an ensuing review of other kinds of evidence, most historians today accept the truth of Madison Hemings's statement and believe that he and his siblings were Thomas Jefferson's children."[4]

Since the early 1990s, a quiet revolution has been deepening the way the custodians of Monticello, curators, and historians, bring the estate to life for its visitors. "The Dependencies," including kitchen, stables, smokehouse, dairy, and Mulberry Row—what remains of the workshops and slave cabins—all figure prominently in the tour as much as Jefferson's alcoved bed and clever "polygraph" machine.[5]

The former head tour guide at Monticello, Elizabeth Dowling Taylor, instructed her last class of guides (before DNA results) to say that Thomas Jefferson *was* the father of Sally Hemings's children. She also asked the guides to dramatically increase their tour presentation of slavery throughout the house.[6]

In 1993, tours began to specifically focus on the slave community at Monticello. The same year marked the beginning of the "Getting Word" Oral History Project. Directed by senior research historian Cinder Stanton, the project "locates and records the descendants of Monticello's enslaved African-American community." Now, in addition to the house tour, visitors can take the "Plantation Community Tour," hearing an overview of African American life on the plantation.[7] While in the house, your guide will frequently refer to "enslaved men" or "enslaved children." According to Stanton, the understanding of Monticello's African American community "has been growing over the last 15 years," with this new focus on the Dependencies and exhibits exploring the lives of those enslaved individuals who made Monticello a "civilized" home.[8]

DIANNE SWANN-WRIGHT

Monticello's former special programs director, African American Dianne Swann-Wright (in 2000, she was the coauthor of the official Monticello report linking Jefferson to Sally), created programs that emphasized the legacy of slaves at Monticello. In remarks at Randolph Macon woman's college, Swann-Wright admitted that one of her goals was to document the journey of African Americans from slavery to freedom. She wished to "engage visitors in a conversation about the entire enslaved community at Monticello," instead of Jefferson as an icon. She wished to take historical interpretation of Jefferson and the enslaved community to a "new, deeper level."[9]

When Swann-Wright was hired as director of special programming at Monticello (as of this writing, the Monticello Board of Trustees now has among its more prominent members Julian Bond, the NAACP Chairman), she became the first African American in a senior staff position at Monticello.[10] Her hiring was arguably the most visible in nearly a decade of staffing and programming changes at Monticello that have signaled a shift in the foundation's attitude toward slavery.[11]

Following a stint as a historian at the Banneker-Douglass Museum in Baltimore, Swann-Wright came to Virginia ten years ago as the director of "multicultural" programs at Eastern Mennonite College in Harrisonburg.[12] Swann-Wright interviewed with Lucia Cinder Stanton, Monticello's then-director of research. The year was 1993, and a reunion of Woodson descendants the previous summer had taken place at Monticello. As Stanton notes: "All the oral history was from the slave-owning side," and she proposed to close the gap with an ambitious project: identifying and collecting oral histories from all the descendants of all the families enslaved at Monticello.[13]

Swann-Wright related in an interview: "And if you'd ever met Cinder, you'd know that she's not terribly persuasive. But it was almost as if someone had put the exact words into Cinder's mouth that would persuade me. She said, '*This won't be about Thomas Jefferson and Sally Hemings.*'" [emphasis added].[14]

Swann-Wright is also good friends with Annette Gordon-Reed and used her book as a guideline to write the Monticello report finding Jefferson guilty. As mentioned earlier, Swann-Wright should have disclosed that fact in the official report, to avoid the appearance of impropriety, yet she did not. In fact, Gordon-Reed thanks Swann-Wright in the acknowledgments sections of her 1997 book, as well as Monticello slave historian Cinder Stanton (another Monticello insider who found Jefferson guilty in the report). Their friendly, albeit conspiratorial relationship, obviously influenced the Monticello report.

PROFESSOR PETER ONUF, UNIVERSITY OF VIRGINIA

[H]e seems to think that history is what the historians say it is.
—Historian and Curator Frank Berkeley[15]

Onuf is a history professor at the University of Virginia, and an enthusiastic Hemings-paternity proponent. In his office he has the magnificent Houdon bust of Thomas Jefferson dressed in a reversed baseball cap, wearing sunglasses and a sign around its neck: MY MEAL TICKET.

This is the same new-age professor who, ironically, sits in the Thomas Jefferson Foundation seat at the University of Virginia history department, where such iconic Jefferson scholars spent their careers, including Dumas Malone and Merrill Peterson. In fact, Onuf took an active part in the official Monticello report accepting Jefferson's guilt. According to Dr. Wallenborn, when he pointed out to Onuf that you could not use evidence, if it was not reliable evidence, to accuse Jefferson of paternity, Onuf retorted: "We are historians. We do not need proof. We write history the way we want to." During a southern academic meeting at the Kenwood International Center for Jefferson Studies in Charlottesville, Wallenborn recalls Onuf saying in his presence: "Sometimes I hate Thomas Jefferson" and "We are going to have to knock Jefferson off his pedestal."[16]

Onuf authored a paper that appeared in the *William and Mary Quarterly* where he stated that Thomas Jefferson was a "monster of self-deception."[17] He concluded a conference at the University of Virginia with these words: "among professional historians, Jefferson's stock has sunk in the last generation, and it has a lot to do with race and slavery."[18] During one recent lecture, Professor Onuf told his students: "I would never be confused with an apologist for Jefferson. I don't defend the guy. I just make a living off him."[19]

Thus, it is against this political calculus that one must understand the climate in and around Monticello academia, and the Hemings-Jefferson controversy. A dramatic morphing has taken away from Jefferson, the man and accomplishments, and shifted on to slave life at Monticello.

ANNETTE GORDON-REED

I also think that the present author has permitted her . . . hostility to the regiment of Jefferson defenders to push her too far.
— Historian Winthrop Jordan, University of Mississippi[20]

The most high-profile historian influenced by the "Charlottesville connection" is Annette Gordon-Reed, a professor of law at New York Law School, who wrote *Thomas Jefferson and Sally Hemings: An American Controversy* in 1997, and the recent *The Hemingses of Monticello: An American Family*.[21]

Gordon-Reed, who is African American, is a close friend of Dianne Swann-Wright (also African American) and Cinder Stanton, both of whom wrote the official Monticello report accepting Jefferson's guilt. They also used Gordon-Reed's sympathetic 1997 book on the Hemingses as their blueprint for their official report released to the public. Among the courses Gordon-Reed teaches is one entitled Slavery and the Law.

Gordon-Reed followed Fawn Brodie's lead and centralized her case against Jefferson based on: (1) the dismissal of the Hemings myth by "white historians," and (2) the interview of Madison Hemings, which she accepted at full face value. She concludes: "[H]is mother, Sally Hemings, has come to be seen as a metaphor for the condition of blacks in American society."[22] For her, the antagonism between the oral history of one family (Hemings) against another (the Randolphs) was a racial issue, black against white. "On this score what Madison Hemings said and the way he said it establishes him as a more credible declarant than either T. J. Randolph or Ellen Randolph Coolidge."[23]

For Gordon-Reed, this issue boiled down to race, and in her own words: "What we are left with is a situation where the oral history of one family is pitted against the oral history of another family. It is black against white, under circumstances where whites for the most part have controlled the assemblage and dissemination of information."[24]

Through cross-examination, it can be established to an impartial jury that Gordon-Reed's opinions are marred by a cultural agenda against the "systematic dismissal" by white historians of the words of black slaves, such as Madison and Israel Jefferson.[25] She indicts the entire white community of historians because they "never made a serious and objective attempt to get at the truth of this matter." They ignored Madison Hemings because they had "no conception of slaves as human beings" and "doubted his words because he was a black man."[26] She admits that her "moral imperative" in writing about Jefferson and Hemings was to "recapture the humanity of the Hemings" and "the identity of African Americans at Monticello."[27]

According to Dr. Ken Wallenborn, a member of Monticello's official committee who filed a dissent casting doubt on the paternity myth, Dianne Swann-Wright, the chairman of the committee, asked him if he had read Gordon-Reed's book. According to Wallenborn:

> . . . it did not take me long to figure out . . . the committee's study outline seemed to be taken almost directly from Gordon-Reed's book. And by the way, Dianne Swann-Wright, Cinder Stanton, and Gordon-Reed *have been the closest of friends, both before and since the DNA Study Committee report was released.* [emphasis added][28]

According to Dr. Wallenborn, he took his concerns about Gordon-Reed's undue influence to Monticello's president, Dan Jordan, and declared that he sensed a "strong power play . . . to force them to accept something that was politically correct and not historically accurate . . . as the committee began to throw out most of the evidence that would exonerate Mr. Jefferson, it became even more obvious that they were following Gordon-Reed's lead, since this was the same tactic that she had used in her book."

Unfortunately, Gordon-Reed and others, have injected race into a debate that should be singularly about evidence. For example, she has written that "in the black community, the Jefferson-Hemings liaison stands along the Declaration of Independence as evidence of the deeply conflicted nature of American society. It is easy to understand why the story of a white founding father of America, his black mistress, and their black offspring would capture the imagination of black Americans."[29]

She added that "the knowledge that a group of blacks are closer genetically to Jefferson than all whites who are not Jeffersons is an irony too delicious to go unappreciated."[30] According to Gordon-Reed, "Black Americans have more than enough reason to mistrust the views of those who helped write the history of America, given the distortions of black life that regularly cropped up in such writings." She writes that "rational Jefferson scholarship seemed incredibly 'white oriented,'" and that "it has not escaped the notice of black Americans that since colonial times, race-mixing has provoked severe anxiety among many whites."[31] She declares that blacks and whites have been fighting a cold war over the Jefferson-Hemings scandal, and the DNA results have now given "vindication of blacks' view on this subject."[32]

Gordon-Reed uses the Jefferson-Hemings legend as a metaphor for race relations. In a letter to the *New York Times* published soon after the DNA tests, Gordon-Reed admitted quite directly the "silver lining" she had found in the controversy, and what it shows about "the history of racism in America . . . If people had accepted this story, he would never have become an icon. All these historians did him a favor until we could get past our primitive racism. I don't think he would have been on Mount Rushmore or on the nickel. The personification of America can't live 38 years with a black woman."[33]

Gordon-Reed has not only injected race into the controversy, but she has played the race card "from the bottom of the deck." Her debate on slavery and race has diverted the attention from the central question: reliable, credible evidence on whether or not Jefferson had sex with a fourteen-year-old Sally.

In both the preface and conclusion to her 1997 book, Gordon-Reed freely admits that her mission is to expose the "troubling" assumptions made by historians who have denied "the truth of a liaison between Thomas Jefferson and Sally Hemings." To sustain the denial, she argues, historians must "make Thomas Jefferson so high as to have been something more than human" and "make Sally Hemings so low as to have been something less than human."

Indeed, she regards Madison Hemings as "a metaphor for the condition of blacks in American society." Madison was, she notes, "a black man who watched his three siblings voluntarily disappear into the white world" and yet who "chose to remain black and to speak for himself," only to be "vilified and ridiculed in a vicious manner" and then be "forgotten." She freely admits that she wrote her 1997 book to vindicate Madison.[34]

Gordon-Reed vilifies virtually every historian who had chronicled Jefferson and Sally, before her book: these included prominent Jefferson scholars such as Merrill Peterson, Douglass Adair, Dumas Malone, John Chester Miller, and Virginius Dabney. Her initial treatment of historian Andrew Burstein is illustrative of her technique. In his 1995 book *The Inner Jefferson: Portrait of a Grieving Optimist*, Burstein briefly addressed Madison Hemings's 1873 newspaper interview, noting that it was "possible that his claim was contrived, by his mother or himself, to provide an otherwise undistinguished biracial carpenter a measure of social respect." Burstein added, "Would not his life have been made more charmed by being known as the son of Thomas Jefferson than the more obscure Peter or Samuel Carr?" Gordon-Reed answers this rhetorical question with an emphatic "no," in the process ridiculing Burstein's choice of words, particularly his reference to a "charmed" life.[35] Her criticism completely misses Burstein's point: Family genealogists are looking for ancestors of great distinction. If I were the Hemingses, I would much rather be descended from Thomas Jefferson than his obscure nephews, or brother.

In addition to ridiculing white male historians, Gordon-Reed carefully selects her evidence and presents it in the light most favorable to the Hemings. In the process, however, she breaks down most accepted standards for weighing evidence, particularly for weighing unreliable, hearsay evidence, creating a double standard that supports hearsay about Jefferson's guilt. Legitimate, reasonable doubts about Madison's contrived "interview" are ignored, as Gordon-Reed ignores whether a word like "enceinte" would have been used by a semiliterate black man. Her goal, as she admits, is to vindicate Madison Hemings and "present the strongest case to be made that the story might be true."[36]

Gordon-Reed has taken her racial rationalizations of the evidence too far. To paraphrase one historian, the story of Sally would be no more credible if the supposed object of Jefferson's affections had been white. As far as the factual evidence is concerned, the question of race is entirely irrelevant and clouds the issue of paternity. In Dumas Malone's words:

"From my understanding of his character, temperament and judgment, I do not believe that he would have done that with a woman of any sort. If I find the story unbelievable, it is not because of Sally's color."[37]

According to historian David Mayer's sharp critique of her book, Gordon-Reed ignores the possibility that Jefferson's brother Randolph or one of Randolph's five sons could have fathered one or more of Sally's children. Although she lists in her bibliography Bernard Mayo's *Thomas Jefferson and His Unknown Brother* (1942), she excludes Randolph and his sons from her genealogical table of "The Jeffersons" and "Randolphs," as well as from the nearly fifty "Important Names" listed in Appendix A to her 1997 book. Neither are Randolph Jefferson nor any of his children even referenced in her index.

Professor Mayer argues in his critique that "the flawed scholarship of the book is further epitomized by a significant transcription error which appears in Appendix E, the text of Ellen Randolph Coolidge's 1858 letter to Joseph Coolidge."[38] In relevant part, the original letter as found in the Coolidge Letterbook, University of Virginia Library, states the following about Jefferson's rooms at Monticello:

> His apartments had no private entrance not perfectly accessible and visible to all the household. No female domestic ever entered his chambers except at hours when he was known not to be there and none could have entered without being exposed to the public gaze.[39]

Gordon-Reed's altered version changes the entire meaning of the letter:

> His apartments had no private entrance not perfectly accessible and visible to all the household. No female domestic ever entered his chambers except at hours when he was *known not to be in the public gaze.* [emphasis added][40]

In fact, two other errors mar Gordon-Reed's transcription of Ellen's vital letter exonerating Jefferson: "indignant belief" should read "indignant disbelief" and "such things after" should read "such things, after all." Even if we give Gordon-Reed the benefit of the doubt and assume that omissions or alteration of these crucial words was not deliberate, such negligence casts doubt on the reliability of her conclusions.[41] Moreover, other studies in her bibliography are misidentified, raising questions about the author's knowledge of the era as well as the copyeditor's competence. Michael Durey's biography of Callender (*With the Hammer of Truth*) is identified as an autobiography, and Durey's entire subtitle is rewritten. Clifford Egan, who demonstrated Fawn Brodie's misinterpretations, has been renamed Clifford J. Hogan.[42]

Gordon-Reed was obviously influenced by several Charlottesville historians, who had already accepted Jefferson's guilt: namely history Professor Peter Onuf at the University of Virginia, the avatar of paternity proponents. Gordon-Reed writes in the acknowledgments section of her book: Professor Peter Onuf has been "a great supporter of my work, giving me invaluable comments, bolstering my confidence by making me feel at home in his own home."[43] To a fair jury this will be evidence of partiality and motive. Onuf clearly influenced her views, as evidenced by her own admission: "I look forward to continued associations with Peter, as well as more opportunities to spend evenings with him and his wife Kristin and their very handsome cats." She also describes the writing of her book as "my obsession." One can only assume her obsession is with the Hemings, not a fair and impartial weighing of the evidence for Jefferson.[44]

Gordon-Reed's newest book, *The Hemingses of Monticello*, is an acidic, eight hundred-page regurgitation of her flawed 1997 book with the Jefferson-Hemings sexual allegation at the center of her social commentary on slavery. Two tenets combine to make this highly speculative tome even more flawed—the author's techniques of "psychohistory" misinterpret clear evidence, and her speculation concerning Jefferson and Sally's "thoughts" ventures far beyond the demonstrable. Through her prism of race and slavery, Gordon-Reed attributes every motivation to Jefferson and his "white" family (compared to what she terms his "shadow" family) to race, sex, or slavery, culminating in her sullying Jefferson as a "rapist" of Sally. Although considerably researched, she fails to offer a shred of documentary evidence, eyewitness, footnote, or source to support her venal opinion, yet she makes the "rape" charge repeatedly throughout the book.

Gordon-Reed preaches that Sally "Hemings must be seen as a figure of historical importance."[45] Unfortunately, she offers no reasons for this bold assertion, other than Sally was at the epicenter of sordid gossip about the most famous Founding Father. She does not document any of Sally's "accomplishments" of historical importance, or her writings for that matter. Moreover, the author admits that no new documentary evidence exists, and "no contemporaneous evidence of what members of the family were thinking as the talk of the pair made its way through the country's newspapers and communities has come to light."[46]

Gordon-Reed hurls page after page, chapter after chapter of undocumented, unsourced psychological theory about Jefferson's sexual "thoughts" concerning "beautiful" Sally. She also crafts numerous narrative chapters based on Sally's "thoughts" of Jefferson, with no documentation, other than far-fetched sexual interpretations. Once again, there is not a scintilla of documented, eyewitnessed evidence to support Sally's "thoughts" about Jefferson. Gordon-Reed admits there has been no new documentary evidence left by either Jefferson or Sally—so she speculates with "total obsession," her own description of this slavery book.[47]

She concludes that "history is to a great degree an imaginative enterprise."[48] Unfortunately, it would take an entire book to detail Gordon-Reed's "imaginations" point by point (as did Virginius Dabney to Fawn Brodie's book). Thus, I will illustrate a few examples of the author's heroic feats of "imaginations":

- "Whether Jefferson used violence or employed his well-known charming manner with women to win Hemings over . . . Sally Hemings did not—because she could not—consent to sex with Thomas Jefferson."[49] "The questions are whether Jefferson's ability to rape Hemings means we are to assume that he did it, and whether we are to take his ability to do it as the strict measure of how he felt about her."[50]

This conjecture is so absurd it merits little reasoned dissent.

How would Gordon-Reed know this? There is no source, footnote, documentation in all of history for this outrageous charge. Does she really expect the public to believe Thomas Jefferson was a rapist? She concludes "for some, the reality that Jefferson 'could have' raped Hemings is the only reality that counts."[51] As noted historian Winthrop Jordan retorts, "such terms as *rape, concubinage,* and *marriage* . . . do little to help our understanding" of Jefferson or Hemings.[52]

This is one more example of her gross misinterpretations.

Unfairly, Gordon-Reed sanitizes Jefferson's benevolent attitude toward his slaves: Madison Hemings said that Jefferson "was uniformly kind to all about him."[53] Isaac Jefferson termed Jefferson "a mighty good master" and "very kind to servants."[54] Where are these statements in Gordon-Reed's book? Her preoccupation with "rape" and "forced sex" taints the entire book. Unlike her own inaccurate words, "as to Sally Hemings, there is no response to rape,"[55] there is a response dictated by the factual, historical record: The allegation is a complete falsehood, altogether invented.

- She criticizes Abigail Adams for labeling Sally as "immature" and incapable of helping Polly in her voyage to France. According to Gordon-Reed, Abigail, perhaps the most prolific and independent woman in colonial times, was "simply confounded by the surprising young girl in her midst . . . [it] requires keeping in mind that this was an encounter between a free adult white woman and an African American slave girl."[56]

Abigail may have been described with several adjectives, but the terms "confounded" and "racist" do not come to mind. Once again, this is a toxic "race" rationalization by the author to fit her thesis that Sally was an alluring woman, instead of the girl Abigail described: immature, bordering on incompetence as a nanny for young Polly.

- Gordon-Reed implies that Jefferson lived with Sally in some sort of quasi, common law marriage/concubinage for thirty-seven years.

Once again, not a scintilla of documentary or eyewitness evidence supports this claim. In fact, it is flatly refuted by James A. Bear, the former resident director of Monticello: "it is certain that she [Sally] was not housed in the main house."[57] Gordon-Reed does not, and in fact, cannot explain why Jefferson would not free his own slave "wife" in his will, or at the end of his life. Jefferson freed Sally's adult children (who had trades for their livelihood) but not Sally herself, his supposed lover of thirty-seven years and mother of his "shadow family?" Even if it meant that Sally would have to move out of Virginia within a year after his death (law at the time for freed adult slaves), would she not want her freedom from the bonds of "profane" slavery, as Hemings proponents claim happened at Monticello? Would she not have asked, or rather begged, her common law husband to do this for her? Once again, this entire line of argument defies common sense.

- "[O]nly recently have the Hemingses and other members of Monticello's enslaved community become the focus of scholarly attention."[58]

This is patently false. Sally has been the subject of attention for over two hundred years and more intensely since Fawn Brodie's book, thirty-five years ago.

- "Jefferson's white family, notably his grandchildren . . . fashioned an image of life at Monticello designed in part to obscure her relevance."[59]

Once again, the argument of the great family "cover-up" has no foundation, and was a commonsense approach to the defamations heaped upon Jefferson—an attempt to vindicate their grandfather's good name against a false and venal political rumor, knowing *absolutely* that the likely father *was someone other* than Jefferson. Gordon-Reed, and others, have implied that any "love letters" between Jefferson and Sally were destroyed by the family. Once again, she is masterful at using "negative evidence." There is another reasonable explanation: *There never were any letters.*

- Gordon-Reed tries to reconstruct a tender, sexual relationship in Jefferson's time of need, after the death of his daughter Polly.

This is strained speculation: that Jefferson would seek out Sally for sex mere days after the death of his beloved daughter. When Jefferson spoke of "happiness," he meant the pleasure of his own family, his daughters and his grandchildren. He never included Sally in this familial felicity, by name or reasonable inference. When Polly died in 1804, he wrote that "others may lose of their abundance, but I, of my want, have lost even the half of all I had. My evening prospects now hang on the slender thread of a single life." Gordon-Reed, and others, have implied that Jefferson was referring to Sally. It is beyond reason that he referred to Sally rather than his own surviving daughter, Martha.[60]

- "Hemings knew how Jefferson viewed women, and implicitly understood that if she were paired with an enslaved man she would have two men over her: her enslaved husband and Jefferson."[61]

And how would Sally know this? Did she read his letters? Could she read? Was she a psychiatrist? Once again, Gordon-Reed's bald-faced speculation, without support or evidence.

- She writes: "a teenage girl had been sent to live with a heterosexual middle-aged man who was not her blood relative. There was no counterpart to the man in the household. The dangers inherent to this situation are apparent and would be so apparent at any point in history"[62] "[I]n the almost unthinkable event that a pretty, free, white, sweet-natured and intelligent girl had been sent to live with Jefferson under the same circumstances, no one would have been surprised if the end result had been that he become infatuated with her and, perhaps, wanted to marry her."[63]

This is mastery of negative evidence, even if you do not consider the towering character of Jefferson. Gordon-Reed assumes that all eighteenth-century heterosexual, middle-aged males would have taken advantage of this situation, with not a shred of evidence, or eyewitness account to substantiate the statement. We are led to believe by Gordon-Reed that Jefferson would take advantage of a fourteen-year-old immature slave girl, who was nanny to his two daughters, in front of all who lived with him at his small Hotel in Paris, because he was such a lecherous person with women. Once again, monumental leaps and assumptions from historical accuracy.

- "[I]t made sense for Jefferson to have fixated on a young woman who knew and understood the universe, his place there, and how she would best fit into it."[64]

All at age fourteen? And why does it make sense for Jefferson to fixate on someone his daughter's age? His universe consisted of classic literature, law, politics, agriculture, astronomy, voluminous correspondence, and sophisticated social company. Which universe did Sally fit into? This statement makes sense only to revisionist, sound-bite historians trying to rationalize the "story" of Sally.

- Gordon-Reed repeatedly states that Sally's children were "white" under Virginia statute, and Jefferson may have considered Sally "white" as well.

This is not accurate. In fact, the law was perfectly clear on this point. If Gordon-Reed had read Jefferson's entire letter to Francis Gray, in which he discussed the difference between Virginia statute and his own biologically based interpretation of race, she would have known that children of slave women were slaves, regardless of the number of white male ancestors. As historian Douglas Egerton concludes: "Gordon-Reed writes, thus failing to grasp that for Jefferson race was based not upon appearance, but upon the percentage of 'pure negro blood' that one carried. Only octoroons had been purged of African blood; to employ Jefferson's terminology, Sally was but a 'quarteroon,' and therefore, still black."[65]

- And finally, Gordon-Reed on slavery and race: "[I]t is simply impossible to write slavery out of the life, personality and even the very existence of Thomas Jefferson."[66] "Hemings embodied the clash between the values of blood and family and racist views about blood and race, so that white supremacy and slavery complicated her connection to her sister Martha."[67]

Once again, Gordon-Reed has morphed the story of Jefferson and Sally into an agenda of victimized slavery, and away from the most credible, corroborative evidence proving Jefferson's innocence. *The Hemingses of Monticello* is creative historical imagination, but fails as biography and history in lieu of solid, documented material. In short, Gordon-Reed judges the past rather than entering into it.

As a final footnote, the *New York Review of Books* labeled Gordon-Reed's work "a brilliant book."[68] Unfortunately, the authors of the review, Edmund S. Morgan and Marie Morgan, failed to disclose that *they helped her write and edit the book*—a profound conflict of interest. Gordon-Reed, in the acknowledgments section of her book, thanks several people for line editing her book, including Morgan: "The same can be said of Edmund S. Morgan, Professor of History Emeritus at Yale, who read the first two sections of the manuscript. Like any great teacher, Ed asked questions that made me think more deeply about what I had written and immediately identified areas that needed further consideration. His encouraging words, and those of his wife, Marie, came at just the right time to spur me on to complete the last section of the book."[69]

14

The "Sally" Books

We believe you can't understand Jefferson . . . and you certainly can't understand Monticello without understanding slavery.
—Daniel P. Jordan, President, Monticello[1]

We not only played the race card. We played it from the bottom of the deck.
—Robert Shapiro, O. J. Simpson's lawyer to
Barbara Walters on *20/20* (1997)

In a real trial, lawyers are permitted to "impeach" a witness through evidence of bias, motive, prior inconsistent statements, or showing a defect in the witness's memory. In court, expert historians could give their opinion as to the Jefferson-Hemings question *only* if their opinion was based on a "reasonable degree of historical *certainty.*" This standard would apply to all the Hemings historians in the Jefferson controversy. If they could not couch their opinions in those terms, their opinions would be stricken in court. In my view, all of the books (and opinions) written subsequent to the DNA study would be excluded, or severely impeached, in a real court, as well as the court of public opinion. Their collective work is based on "possibilities" too speculative in nature. These historians have engaged in gross speculation and psychological analysis, certainly outside their field of expertise.

The paternity proponents have relied on a handful of authors to accuse Jefferson of a sexual liaison with Sally. Upon further investigation, all of these individuals have a shared, collegial bond, both in and outside of Charlottesville academia. Although I have the utmost personal respect for these individuals, in a court of law, through a rigorous cross-examination, all their opinions can be impugned, impeached, and ultimately shown to be flawed or colossal misinterpretations.

FAWN M. BRODIE: *THOMAS JEFFERSON: AN INTIMATE HISTORY* (1974)

In her psychoanalytical book *Thomas Jefferson: An Intimate History*, the late Fawn M. Brodie, a UCLA history professor, resurrected the story attributed to Madison Hemings that while in France, Jefferson took the teenaged Sally as his "concubine." Most Jefferson historians, at the time, rejected Ms. Brodie's flimsy "psychological evidence" of a Jefferson affair in France, and with good reason.[2]

Brodie's Rorschach history was not only implausible but also failed to fit the facts. According to Jefferson biographer Willard Sterne Randall:

> [Brodie] suggested that, when Jefferson traveled through France and Germany and eight times described soil as mulatto in his twenty-five sheets of notes, he was not referring, as he labeled the appropriate column of his charts, to yellowish soil in the hills and valleys he traveled through but was really thinking of the contours of Sally's body . . . But mulatto is a precise term describing yellowish-brown soil. And when Jefferson used the term mulatto to describe soil during his French travels, Sally was still on a ship with Polly, accompanying her to France. If he had ever noticed her or remembered her at all, Sally had been only ten years old when Jefferson last visited Monticello hurriedly in 1784 to pack [Sally's brother] James Hemings off to France with him. She was only eight when Jefferson last resided at Monticello and was mourning his wife's death. Unless Brodie was suggesting that Jefferson consoled himself by having an affair with an eight-year-old child, *the whole chain of suppositions is preposterous.* [emphasis added][3]

In a small volume devoted entirely to Brodie's book, the journalist-editor Virginius Dabney disputed Brodie point by point. Moreover, in the decades that followed, there was a proliferation of new biographers who did not follow Brodie's lead, including Alf J. Mapp,[4] Noble E. Cunningham,[5] and Willard Sterne Randall.[6] Cunningham writes: "The evidence indicates that any Paris romance between Jefferson and Sally

Hemings belongs in a work of fiction, not history."[7] Randall concludes much the same: Madison Hemings's account "resembles many uncorroborated slave narratives and cannot be credited[;] . . . [it] must be put down as mere gossip."[8] One historian concluded that Madison made up the bulk of his interview to give himself a more distinguished ancestor.[9]

In Brodie's enthusiasm to find a link between Jefferson and Hemings, she misread language and invoked pseudo-psychological explanations to over interpret unconscious patterns in Jefferson's writing. Brodie wove a tale of psychological interpretation based upon selected letters written by Jefferson. Though her book received poor reviews from historians for its eccentric psychological ruminations, its allegations of deceit of a Founding Father made it a bestseller.

According to historian Douglas Wilson, writing in the *Atlantic Monthly*, Brodie's thesis about Jefferson and Hemings is an embellished reading of the evidence, but what is more significant is that Brodie insisted that her objective was not to pillory Jefferson but merely to humanize him. If, as a widower, he fell in love with a beautiful slave girl and took her as a mistress, it was "not scandalous debauchery with an innocent slave victim," Brodie assured us, "but rather a serious passion that brought Jefferson and the slave woman much private happiness over a period lasting thirty-eight years."[10]

Wilson explains that if Jefferson did take advantage of Hemings, he was acting out of character and violating his own sense of decency. Jefferson took matters of honor seriously, and such a hypocritical liaison would have been a source of shame. For his close-knit family to have been ignorant of such an arrangement would defy common sense. Jefferson was haunted by other troubles and financial difficulties. There is no documented evidence of this sort of shame or guilt in Jefferson's life, according to Wilson. That is why Brodie must depict Jefferson and Sally as a loving couple.[11]

Brodie also rationalizes that the names of the fathers of Sally's children were conspicuously absent from Jefferson's *Farm Book*, implying a clandestine relationship with her, or family "cover-up." This is a complete falsehood. Instead, it reflects the reality that there was no "relationship" beyond that of master and servant. True believers like Brodie, and others, seem particularly frustrated by the lack of mention of Sally in any of Jefferson's correspondence. Thus, they conclude, this is evidence of a Jefferson family conspiracy.

As historian Forrest McDonald succinctly stated: "Ms. Brodie's description of the inner Jefferson bears little resemblance to the Jefferson I have come to know. Moreover, her account is woefully inadequate and often inaccurate as history."[12] Dumas Malone was less kind: "That any real scholar could give serious consideration to such a book is beyond my comprehension."[13]

JOSEPH ELLIS, *NATURE* ARTICLE LINKING JEFFERSON TO SALLY

I want to step forward and say this new evidence constitutes, well, evidence beyond any reasonable doubt that Jefferson had a longstanding sexual relationship with Sally Hemings.
—Joseph Ellis, PBS *NewsHour*, November 2, 1998

Historian Joseph Ellis wrote *Founding Brothers*, which became a massive bestseller. In his well-regarded 1996 biography, *American Sphinx: The Character of Thomas Jefferson*, Ellis dismissed Callender's accusations and listed reasons to doubt his claim. Ellis concluded that, "[A] long-term sexual relationship with one of his slaves was not in character for Jefferson . . . the accusations of sexual promiscuity defy most of the established patterns of Jefferson's emotional life."

But with the DNA result, Ellis executed a twenty-year, bald reversal of opinion. His prior inconsistent statements would impeach his entire credibility in a real court of law. The Eston DNA match, according to Ellis, "shifts the burden of proof toward the presumption that Jefferson was the father of each" of Sally's children.[14]

Professor Ellis wrote a two-page article in the November 9, 1998, issue of *U.S. News & World Report* in which he tried to link President Clinton's impeachment scandal with the purported problems of Jefferson. He stated that the, "Foster study seemed impeccably timed to arrive like a comet that had been winging through space for 200 years before landing squarely in the middle of the Clinton impeachment inquiry." The full *U.S. News* story on Jefferson and Hemings ran eight pages, plus a cover page announcing Jefferson's "secret life."

Herbert Barger related the following phone conversation with Ellis, after Ellis's DNA article: "I asked him what about Randolph Jefferson. Mr. Ellis said *that he knew nothing of the younger brother of Thomas Jefferson,*

Randolph, and his five sons, who could have fathered the Hemings children. He also asked why no one had pointed this out before."[15] Barger asked Ellis if he had read the book *Thomas Jefferson and His Unknown Brother*. Ellis replied *no*. Barger informed Ellis that this Monticello book was very informative, and "this historian [Ellis] is ignorant of it?"[16]

According to Barger:

> Just because Prof. Ellis and any other unknowledgeable persons choose to say, "why wasn't Randolph mentioned before now?" doesn't mean that he was suspected in a vacuum. Until this DNA study came before us, there was no need to pursue and challenge every statement made by persons claiming descent from a famous president rather than his not so important brother.[17]

Unfortunately, Ellis's credibility and veracity could be severely impeached in a courtroom setting. An impartial jury would learn that the once Pulitzer Prize–winning author resorted to fabricating his professional résumé.[18] This is in clear violation of the American historical standard, the official group that holds that:

> Historians are obligated to present their credentials accurately and honestly in all contexts. They should take care not to misrepresent their qualifications in resumes, applications, or the public record. They should apply the same rigor and integrity in describing their own accomplishments as their profession applies to the historical record itself.[19]

It is appropriate to note that Ellis authored the *U.S. News* commentary on the Jefferson-Hemings affair, with the headline: "When a saint becomes a sinner."[20] Two days before Clinton's impeachment trial, a full-page ad appeared in the *New York Times* opposing his impeachment. Among the signers: historian Joseph Ellis, on which he noted the Hemings report as "impeccable timing."[21]

Ellis has also, apparently, read and influenced the developing manuscript of Gordon-Reed's book, which was going to print just as his own book was published. Ellis declared in a "blurb" for its back cover: "Short of digging up Jefferson and doing DNA testing on him and Hemings' descendants, Gordon-Reed's account gets us as close to the truth as the available evidence allows."[22] In Gordon-Reed's latest book, Ellis also provided a publicity blurb on the book jacket: "Thomas Jefferson often described his slaves at Monticello as 'my family.' Annette Gordon-Reed has taken that description seriously. Surely more seriously than Jefferson ever intended! The result, the story of the Hemings family, is the most comprehensive account of one slave family ever written. It is not a pretty story, but it is poignant beyond belief. And it demonstrates conclusively that we must put aside *Gone With the Wind* forever."[23]

Ellis, in his book *American Sphinx*, gives a "special note of thanks to Daniel P. Jordan" and also thanks Lucia Cinder Stanton, Peter Onuf, and Andrew Burstein, all rigid paternity believers, for reading "chunks" of the manuscript.

ANDREW BURSTEIN, *JEFFERSON'S SECRETS: DEATH AND DESIRE AT MONTICELLO* (2005)

Author Andrew Burstein has also reversed his previously held opinion of the Sally myth, setting himself up for a forceful cross-examination. In his first book, *The Inner Jefferson*, he doubted the Sally story:

> Thomas Jefferson Randolph told biographer Henry Randall . . . that his grandfather had given no reason for any family to suspect intimacy with Sally Hemings. . . . Randolph confided to Randall that, in fact, Peter Carr was the culprit. Randolph's sister Ellen, however, fingered Peter's younger brother Samuel. Either explanation is plausible . . . it seems highly unlikely that because light-skinned Sally Hemings bore light-skinned children at Monticello, they necessarily were fathered by Monticello's master. Moreover, Jefferson would have been uncharacteristically imprudent to be responsible for giving Sally Hemings the two children that she bore in the years after the charges surfaced, while he remained president.[24]

Burstein explained that Madison's testimony was "contrived—by his mother or himself—to provide to an otherwise undistinguished biracial carpenter, a measure of social respect."[25]

In his second book about Jefferson (post DNA), *Jefferson's Secrets*, he adopted Ellis's appraisal and made a stunning reversal: "Since 1998 the burden of proof has most definitely shifted. Perhaps the DNA findings have not absolutely made Thomas Jefferson the father of his house servant's children, but mounting circumstantial evidence makes him by far the most plausible father of these children, as most would now agree."[26] Explaining his change of mind, Burstein devoted a long chapter to exploring the attitudes, motives, and rationalizations of Jefferson.

He argues that Jefferson had intimate relations with Sally not out of: (1) love or affection for her; or (2) sexual gratification, but rather; (3) for "medicinal" purposes, as a way of "medical conditioning, to preserve his health."[27] He devotes ten pages to a ludicrous rationalization that Jefferson had sex with Sally for his "medicalized sensibility." Burstein devotes another five pages to a French doctor's view of "masturbation" as being unhealthy, and why Jefferson thought this made sex with Sally acceptable. Burstein opines that Jefferson's taking of Sally would have fulfilled "Tissot's urgent call for accomplished, intellectual men to forgo the wasteful activity of masturbation" because "the spermatic fluid was as healthy for the female who received it as it was unhealthy for the man who wasted it through masturbation."[28]

What?! To say that the scholarly debate has reached an intellectual low would be kind. Burstein is grasping at historical straws. His strained, psychoanalytical theory defies good, common sense: that Jefferson would turn to sex with a fourteen-year-old, black slave as his holistic cure.

Burstein also argues that "no white Jefferson descendant . . . ever suggested Randolph's name" and "a new candidate suddenly had to be found" to match the DNA. This is misleading and fundamentally wrong. The oral tradition of a black family, Eston Hemings, claimed that an uncle was their father, a clear reference to Randolph who was known as "Uncle Randolph." Burstein also claims, through Gordon-Reed's obvious influence, that Madison's "testimony . . . tells us what his mother told him."[29] Again this is flat out wrong. Madison *never* states in the interview Sally told him this myth. In fact, Sally is virtually absent, as a source, from the interview.

Both Burstein and Ellis seemed to have adopted historian Gordon-Reeds's erroneous judgment: "Clearly the burden of proof has shifted: Until otherwise disproved, Jefferson is now presumed to have fathered one or more of Sally Hemings's children." Burstein chronically uses the term "possible" in describing the allegations of Sally: "it seems entirely possible that Jefferson was a man increasingly fixed in his habits who found self sufficiency preferable to having a partner whom he would feel obliged to consult. In his worlds, such a choice did not have to result in celibacy."[30]

In *Jefferson's Secrets*, Burstein's book jacket cover is praised by two of his colleagues in the cottage industry of paternity believers: Joseph Ellis and Annette Gordon-Reed. Ellis writes: "Burstein has become the premier student of Jefferson's distinctive remissibility." Gordon-Reed added that *"Jefferson's Secrets* is a masterful work. . . . Burstein has written an absolutely indispensable addition to Jefferson scholarship." And Burstein dedicated both of his books to none other than the masthead of slave historians, Professor Peter Onuf: "He has been a fabulous mentor and a thoughtful friend. . . . I leave for the ultimate acknowledgment my friend Peter Onuf, to whom I appreciatively dedicate this book. . . . This book is just part of what I owe, Big Guy."

In short, Burstein quotes Onuf's misguided rationalization of Jefferson's guilt: "to secure the sexual frontier between two nations."[31]

JON KUKLA, *MR. JEFFERSON'S WOMEN* (2007)

The author of the Declaration of Independence . . . was surprisingly hostile toward women . . . with predatory misogyny.
—Book jacket description of Thomas Jefferson in *Mr. Jefferson's Women*

Before the DNA study, author Jon Kukla disbelieved the paternity allegations, commenting in 1979:

> Misrepresentation of historical fact deludes both authors and readers, however, and impoverishes public debates. It is ironic in this instance that the calumnies had been promulgated by a notoriously unreliable, disappointed office seeker, whose revenge was to accuse Jefferson of the paternity of illegitimate children.[32]

Kukla explained that documents "point strongly toward the conclusion" that Jefferson had no liaison with Sally Hemings. In light of "overwhelming evidence" that Jefferson was a loving father, the claim that he seduced a fourteen-year-old Sally and traveled in the intimate company of his two young daughters with her in a state of pregnancy "cannot be believed." Madison's assertion that his mother first bore a child soon after she returned to Monticello from France is "untenable."[33]

Yet, after the misleading DNA study Kukla completely changed his entire twenty-year thought process, further evidence on cross-examination of "prior inconsistent statements." He devoted one entire chapter on Sally in his new book, *Mr. Jefferson's Women*, and confessed that: "Callender was essentially correct about Jefferson's relationship with Sally Hemings . . . Jefferson fathered six children born to his slave Sally . . . between 1795 and 1808."[34]

Yet, in that single chapter on Sally he uses the terms "possible," "perhaps," or "could have," over twenty-one times to speculate on Jefferson's affair with Sally. This fails as an expert opinion in a court of law ("within a reasonable degree of historical *certainty*"), and should fail in the court of public opinion, too. The same could be said of all the recent paternity books. They all employ the speculative terms, "possible," "perhaps," "likely" to describe the allegation. This is not historical interpretation of accepted facts, but pure conjecture that has no basis in the law or history.

Kukla describes Jefferson as "the author of the Declaration of Independence," who was "surprisingly hostile toward women." This flies in the face of a staggering amount of family letters, which attest to Jefferson's love for his dear wife and two devoted daughters. Kukla also concludes that in Jefferson's dealings with women from Rebecca Burwell to Maria Cosway, and even in the grief over his wife, he always "put himself and his needs first." This is a flagrant misinterpretation of the evidence. Jefferson placed the welfare (physical, emotional, intellectual) of his two daughters and seven grandchildren above all living creatures, including himself. To deny this would be to deny his entire life and an entire volume of endearing correspondence with his family.

Kukla follows Burstein's bizarre theories on Jefferson's masturbation and sexual habits, referencing both Burstein's book and the French doctor Tissot's inane book, *Treatise upon the Disorders Produced by Masturbation*. Kukla penned that Jefferson found this French book "especially pertinent." Why? Neither author offers a satisfactory answer. Jefferson owned this book, among his collection of nine thousand books over his life time (sixty-seven hundred of which he sold to the Library of Congress). The authors select this *single* book to ascribe all its medicinal cures

to Jefferson, including the far-fetched theory on masturbation as it relates
to Sally.

Kukla also states that Jefferson never explicitly acknowledged (or denied) any relationship with Sally. Again, this is a misinterpretation of the
clarity of Jefferson's words. Jefferson wrote to Dr. George Logan: "As to
Federal slanders, I never wished them to be answered, but by the tenor of
my life. . . . [T]he man who fears no truths has nothing to fear from lies."
In another letter to Dr. Benjamin Rush, Jefferson wrote: *The Morals of
Jesus*, with a Syllabus, Washington, April 21, 1803: "And in confiding it to
you, I know it will not be exposed to the malignant perversions of those
who make every word from me a text for new misrepresentations &
calumnies."[35]

By any fair and reasonable reading of these letters (just a few examples), they are firm denials to Callender's allegations.

Kukla takes authorial assumption and declares that "in many ways
Thomas Jefferson's relationship with Sally Hemings had always been ex-
ploitive and selfish." As to evidence of this, Kukla offers absolutely nothing at all. Not one hard piece of evidence, not one letter, not one witness
linking Jefferson to Sally (perhaps someone saw them kissing, holding
hands, embracing, a furtive, loving glance—not one witness in history!),
except for a slim vial of blood and tissue sample linked to "some" male
Jefferson. In the final analysis, Kukla has to admit that their relationship
remains "obscure" and is "a matter of sentimental speculation."[36]

Kukla also acknowledges his collegial friendship with the coven of
die-hard paternists, led by Professor Peter Onuf (who keeps appearing in
all of these pro-paternity books: ironically, Onuf is the Thomas Jefferson
Foundation–sponsored history professor at the University of Virginia),
Annette Gordon-Reed, and Andrew Burstein. They "commented on preliminary versions of the text on four occasions . . . and the invaluable
scholarship of Lucinda C. Stanton." Kukla cites "the major texts in the recent debate . . . include Annette Gordon-Reed . . . Thomas Jefferson Memorial Foundation Report . . . and Peter Onuf."[37] Kukla also consulted
Fraser Neiman on the conception dates, further evidence of his preconceived notion of the book. The author specially thanks Dan Jordan, the
originator of the Monticello report linking Jefferson to Sally. In fact, Kukla
goes further in his influence by Jordan, an enthusiastic supporter of Onuf's,
Dianne Swann-Wright, and Annette Gordon-Reed, all paternity believers,

and "recognize[s] the extraordinary courage and integrity of Dr. Daniel P. Jordan in his leadership at Monticello."[38]

It is clear that Kukla sought out the unyielding paternity believers to promulgate his theories on Jefferson and women. His reversed thought process was obviously influenced by paternity proponents. On the witness stand, Kukla's 1979 words not only impeach his entire book, but his historical opinions. Pre DNA, his own judicious words would come back to impugn him:

> The historian's task is only to establish facts on the basis of evidence. . . . It is here that the chasm between the historian's careful sifting of evidence distinctly contrasts with the use of the myth in the service of a cause. No matter how noble the cause, or how despicable the vice to be reformed, if a historian departs from the rigorous standards of the craft in order to bolster a particular thesis, the departure demeans present and past generations.[39]

HISTORICAL STANDARDS

Perhaps, most importantly, this entire debate surrounding Jefferson and Sally has violated some of the very tenants of the historians' creed. For example, paragraph three of The American Historical Association's Statement on Standards of Professional Conduct, *adopted by Council, January 6, 2005*, states:

> Scholarship likewise depends on the *open dissemination* of historical knowledge via many different channels of communication: books, articles, classrooms, exhibits, films, historic sites, museums, legal memoranda, testimony, and many other ways. The free exchange of information about the past is dear to historians. . . . Professional integrity in the practice of history requires awareness of one's own biases and a readiness to follow sound method and analysis wherever they may lead.

The blatant attempt to suppress Dr. Wallenborn's minority report violates this very precept:

While it is perfectly acceptable for historians to share their own perspectives with the public, they should also strive to demonstrate how the historical profession links evidence with arguments to *build fair-minded, nuanced, and responsible interpretations of the past.* [emphasis added] The desire to score points as an advocate should never tempt a historian to misrepresent the historical record or the critical methods that the profession uses to interpret that record.

15

JEFFERSON UNDER SIEGE: "PRESENTISM"

Thomas Jefferson . . . said that God would punish America for the sin of slavery. I guess that makes Thomas Jefferson unpatriotic . . . Jefferson had intelligence, but he also had babies by a 15 year-old slave girl. I think the judges call that pedophilia.

—Reverend Jeremiah Wright (2008)[1]

I think it is unfortunate that this had become blended with the Clinton affair. The only similarity between these two men is Clinton's middle name . . . Jefferson.

—Historian Willard Sterne Randall[2]

History has become politicized in America, as illustrated by the widespread acceptance of the Hemings legend as historical fact. It seems that a period of self-analysis for the history profession is in order—at least under the portico that shelters Jeffersonian scholars. As much as this controversy has been about DNA's attempt to solve a time-shrouded mystery, it should be an occasion for reflection on the all-too-human failings of a few historians.

For many scholars of race relations in America, the Jefferson-Hemings story provides further evidence of the racism they say permeates American society. Indeed, for many, acceptance of Jefferson's guilt has become a kind of litmus test for social conformity: Those of us who continue to question the paucity of facts supporting the Hemings allegation have been stigmatized as racially insensitive.[3] This is intellectually stultifying, dishonest, and misdirects the focus of the controversy from the most convincing evidence.

Gordon-Reed, Kukla, and Onuf, the Jeffersonian experts du jour, are exhibit one in how scholars have misdirected the Hemings debate.[4] The Jefferson controversy is no longer a scholarly investigation about a sexual affair, but a muscular, social analysis on slavery. That is fundamentally unfair to Jefferson's legacy, and to the specific facts challenging the allegation. Cultural agendas are, and should be, entirely irrelevant to the historical controversy.

This climate is not confined to the University of Virginia. Agenda-driven courses taught at Wesleyan University and Bridgewater College require students to accept as historical fact that Jefferson fathered children by Sally. At the University of Rochester, a writing class in the English department is entitled Slavery and Miscegenation in American Literature & History. This course description assumes as historical fact that Sally was Martha Jefferson's sister: "James Hemings, one of Thomas Jefferson's slaves, was the son of Jefferson's father-in-law, and thus the half-brother of Jefferson's wife. He was, in other words, Jefferson's brother-in-law, and yet in the United States in the eighteenth century, there was no law to name him as such. Instead, both James and his sister, Sally (also fathered by Jefferson's father-in-law) were identified as property, despite their close familial ties to Jefferson, his wife, and his daughters."

Canisius College has a senior seminar that is described as "a wide range of infamous scandals in American history, including sexual hijinks, shady financial practices, political corruption, and sports fixing. Among other episodes, we will read about Thomas Jefferson's relationship with his slave, Sally Hemings; . . . the alleged adultery of the Rev. Henry Ward Beecher; . . . the financial machinations of robber baron Jay Gould; the graft of Boss Tweed and Tammany Hall; the Clinton-Lewinsky affair. By examining such episodes, the course will reveal the seamy underside of American cultural, financial, and political values." That Jefferson had a "relationship" with Hemings is a prerequisite that the student must accept. The only issue is where that "relationship" ranks with the other examples of sexual misconduct and financial fraud.[5]

At Cornelia Strong College, The University of North Carolina at Greensboro, the following was posted on its Web site: "Dr. O'Hara's Book-of-the-Week this week is a copy autographed to Strong College of 'Thomas Jefferson and Sally Hemings: An American Controversy,' by Annette Gordon-Reed. Dr. Gordon-Reed spoke about her research last week in the EUC, and Dr. O'Hara picked up the book there and had it autographed for us. Sally Hemings was one of Jefferson's slaves and a half-sister of his wife. It has now been established almost certainly that

Jefferson was the father of some of her children, as well. Come down to the Office to give the book a browse today!"

Note that the student is not invited to address the paternity issue as an exercise in historical analysis. It is required that the student accept the academic's analysis.[6]

At the University of Virginia, the school founded by Thomas Jefferson, it is no longer a debated issue for the students whether Jefferson fathered children with Sally. It is accepted *fact* in the history department. *The Cavalier Daily*, the student newspaper, quoted the Chairman of the History Department, Professor Peter Onuf: "The argument is so overwhelming that we need to move on to other more fruitful sites of inquiry."[7]

The Jefferson-Hemings debate has been turned into cultural symbolism for people of various political persuasions: to those on the left, it serves as a metaphor for racism in America; to those on the right, a metaphor for immorality. Some have used the Hemings story to denigrate Jefferson and, with him, one of the cardinal values of his life: individual liberty. As Timothy Sandefur notes in his essay "Anti-Jefferson, Left and Right," "what damns Thomas Jefferson in conservative and multiculturalists eyes alike is his appeal 'to all men and at all times,' and not to the considerations of race, class, and sex, of which the left approves, or to the 'whispers of dead men' that the conservative hears."[8] The Hemings story permits some to see Jefferson's whole political life as "bound up in the sexual exploitation of a slave," Sandefur adds. "Jefferson's position as the Enlightenment figure in America can thus be seen as inseparable from his ownership and exploitation of slaves."[9]

Jefferson is not alone. Revisionists deprecate most of our Founding Fathers, attempting to tarnish their bronze statues. Consider the following historical "legacies":

- Christopher Columbus's once untarnished reputation was revised by some scholars, changing from courage and imagination, to an assortment of villainies including genocide, racism, and heedless ruin of the environment.[10] While traditional historians typically view Columbus's journey as opening up inroads between the Old and New Worlds, revisionists often say his voyage represents forced European colonization and the brutal treatment of American Indians. Three years ago, protesters dumped red paint on the Columbus statue, which was dedicated in 1912. "No amount of interpreting can wipe away [Columbus's] cruelties, and none can erase his achievements," said Irtefa Anwara Bibte-Farid, a tenth-grader from Charlottesville as she read from her essay "Christopher Columbus—Imperfect Hero." Irtefa's essay won first prize in an event-related contest.[11]

- George Washington's reputation has been stained by those "who have decided that because the father of our country owned slaves [he] is not fit to have his name on a grammar school," said Roger D. McGrath, who teaches at California State University-Northridge.[12] He cited a decision by school board officials in New Orleans to remove Washington's name from an elementary school and quoted the board president: "The idea of kids going to a school named after a slave owner was demeaning. We wanted the kids to identify with role models from their own heritage."[13]

Take, for example, this pugilistic exchange between a prominent author and genealogist Herbert Barger, that exemplifies this cultural battleground:

Mr. Barger . . . I must tell you that I find it difficult to understand your utter and complete contempt for the history of the slaves at Monticello . . . I am fully aware that the Monticello Association, along with historians friendly to their point of view, has spent the last 100 years or so putting the blame for the fatherhood of Sally Hemings' children on one or the other of the Carr brothers. Now that the DNA results have effectively ruled out the Carr brothers as possible fathers of Sally's children, you are going about the despicable business of trying to place the blame elsewhere . . . In addition, I found your entire efforts to exonerate Mr. Jefferson from any potential fatherhood of Sally's children, while at the same time seeking to place the blame elsewhere—indeed, anywhere but upon Jefferson himself—to be absurd and racist and beneath contempt. Do not look to me for support for your pathetic efforts in this regard . . . My advice to you, Mr. Barger, is to get a grip.[14]

History Professor David Mayer gives a tangible name to this heated Jefferson-Hemings debate: "Presentism." The term presumes that the

historical past can be judged by the contemporary standards of the present.[15] Presentism, Mayer argues, plagues historical discussions of the past
by its inability to make allowances for prevailing historical conditions,
and none more so than in the Jefferson-Hemings controversy.

Emily Dickinson once said that "today, makes yesterday mean."[16] Her
statement contains truth—the perspectives of the present color the mean-
ings we ascribe to the past. This is readily apparent in the changing reputation of Jefferson, whose status often appears pinned to modern-day
standards. According to Professor Mayer, the patriotic teaching approach
of American history in public schools has been replaced by an emphasis
on the failures of the Founding Fathers (i.e., slavery and race relations).
Most revisionist news, at least where traditional American heroes are concerned, is bad. It is an instance of what historian Henry Adams termed the
law of acceleration—the tendency of change to come faster and faster.[17]

Mayer argues that: "The rise of three related phenomena in higher education, the 'political correctness' movement, multiculturalism, and post-
modernism explain why the Jefferson-Hemings myth has become so
readily accepted today, not only by the American general public but also
by scholars who should know better."[18] What began on behalf of diversity, Mayer opines, has devolved into a social movement merged with disturbing distortions in scholarship and public discourse.[19]

In recent years, according to Mayer, many historians have concerns
about the degree of culturalism dominating the leading organizations of historians: the American History Association (AHA) and the Organization of
American Historians (OAH). Some historians have resigned their membership in one or both groups. A politically diverse coalition of historians, rang-
ing in their political views from conservative to liberal, who share a concern
for the profession, have formed a new organization to compete with the
AHA and the OAH, called The Historical Society (THS).[20]

According to Mayer, the historical profession today has lost much of
the standards by which evidence can be objectively weighed and evaluated in the search for historical facts. Taken together, political and cultural agendas, have created an environment in the academic arena in
which scholars feel pressured to accept the Jefferson-Hemings myth.
White scholars in particular fear that by challenging the dubious Hemings hearsay, they will be called racists. Questioning the Hemings allegation has been equated with the denigration of African Americans and

their place in American history. This argument is intellectually dishonest, unfair, and morally bankrupt.[21]

He concludes that:

> ... some historians in the debate have ceased to function as an historian and instead have manipulated history, carefully marshaling every piece of evidence in favor of the desired interpretation. As to the evidence against the allegation, some scholars have carefully doctored all the evidence to the contrary, either by suppressing it when that seemed plausible, or by distorting it when suppression was not possible. It is far more likely that some historians involved in this debate are engaged in revisionism at its best—that is to say, the prostitution of scholarship for political ends. Some historians have turned this entire issue from one of scholarly evidence and interpretation, to a discussion on slavery and Jefferson's racial views.

Julian Boyd, the renowned editor of the multivolume *Papers of Thomas Jefferson*, seems to agree and summed up the revisionist movement:

> ... [the] despairing, ambivalent, indecisive and guilt-ridden Jefferson may be soothing to those who eagerly embrace the concept of collective guilt, who project our views of the rights of women and blacks into the past ... but it is assuredly not scholarship, and the resultant Jefferson—unless I have wasted thirty of the best years of my life in studying all his recorded actions—is only an imaginative creature and, in my view, a rather repulsive one.[22]

16

FINAL ARGUMENT: AN INNOCENT MAN

Delay is preferable to error.
—Thomas Jefferson, 1743[1]

"Reputation is worthless, trial is best."

The words of Theognis of Megara are applicable to the two-hundred-year-old Jefferson-Hemings controversy. I have tried to present the most persuasive evidence proving Jefferson's innocence. If this were a real trial, now would be the time for the judge to give you, the jury, some preliminary instructions before my final argument:

Members of the jury, I shall now instruct you on the law that you must follow in reaching your verdict. It is your duty as jurors to decide the issues, and only those issues, that I submit for determination by your verdict. In reaching your verdict, you should consider and weigh the evidence, decide the disputed issues of fact, and apply the law on which I shall instruct you, to facts as you find them from the evidence.

The evidence in this case consists of the sworn testimony of the witnesses, and all exhibits received in evidence. In determining the facts, you may draw reasonable inferences from the evidence. You may make deductions and reach conclusions which reason and common sense lead you to draw from the facts shown by the evidence in this case. But you should not speculate on any matters outside the evidence.

In determining the believability of any witness and the weight to be given the testimony of any witness, you may properly consider the demeanor of the witness while testifying; the frankness or lack of frankness of the witness; the intelligence of the witness; any interest the witness may have in the outcome of the case; the means and opportunity the witness had to know the facts about which the witness testified; the ability of the witness to remember the matters about which the witness testified; and the reasonableness of the testimony of the witness, considered in the light of all the evidence in the case and in the light of your own experience and common sense.

You have heard opinion testimony on certain subjects from persons referred to as expert witnesses. You may accept such opinion testimony, reject it, or give it the weight you think it deserves, considering the knowledge, skill, experience, training, or education of the witness, the reasons given by the witness for the opinion expressed, and all the other evidence in the case.[2]

A brief summary of *Sally's case* to the jury would be as follows:

The case for Sally Hemings is not complicated. It rests on two sets of facts.

First, the birth of her children taken directly from the records of the defendant Thomas Jefferson. From these records it is easy to work back in time to her probable conceptions. In each period, Thomas Jefferson was present at Monticello. Sally did not conceive any children in a period when Jefferson was not present. The conclusion is inescapable and not mere coincidence.

Second, there is hard scientific evidence: the DNA. The results are irrefutable and prove beyond any doubt that a Jefferson male was the father of Eston Hemings. In addition there is testimony of a witness who lived with Sally, her son Madison Hemings, who claimed in a written interview that Jefferson was his father.

Taken together these facts present persuasive evidence that Jefferson is guilty of fathering Eston Hemings.

———

My defense argument to the jury would be something similar to this:

On the occasion of a state dinner honoring the Nobel Laureates of the Americas, President John F. Kennedy called his assembled guests "the most extraordinary collection of talents that has ever been gathered together at the white House, with the possible exception of when Thomas Jefferson dined alone."[3]

Ladies and Gentlemen of the jury, on behalf of my client, Thomas Jefferson, I want to thank you for your attention in this trial. Today, the reputations of America's Founding Fathers seem to be in disrepair. Twenty-first-century Americans are skeptical of greatness. "Belittling arguments always have a force of their own," Justice Oliver Wendell Holmes observed, "but you and I believe that high-mindedness is not impossible in man."[4] Jefferson's biographer, James Parton, once said that "if Jefferson was wrong, America is wrong. If America is right, Jefferson is right."

Quite obviously, the controversy and debate over Jefferson-Hemings will continue beyond this trial. But today is Mr. Jefferson's day in court. His fate is now in your hands. I ask only one thing: Please use your common sense. The word "*verdict*" is a Latin word, and it literally means to speak the truth. And I am confident that when you weigh all the evidence, and apply your good common sense, your verdict will speak the truth: and that truth is that Mr. Jefferson is innocent of this slander and libel. Thomas Jefferson's reputation has lived with this damnable lie for over two hundred years. It is up to you, Ladies and Gentlemen, to vindicate his good name.

As we discussed at the beginning of this trial, the evidence in this case proves one of two things: Thomas Jefferson is either the most hypocritical liar in American history or the victim of the most scurrilous, two-hundred-year-old defamation of character allegation in legal annals. There is no middle ground. There is no compromise.

You must ask why some historians feel compelled to use so much frenetic energy to tarnish the reputation of one of our Founding Fathers? The answer is simple: The Hemingses have turned the accusation into a political and morality play, exonerating or condemning races and genders, and the nation by proxy. If you, the jury, allow your verdict to be some sort of a political irrigation on slavery that clouds the true facts, your verdict will be a grave injustice. You, the jury, are the arbitrator of what the facts are. And if you allow this to happen, you do so at the expense of a man's reputation and the corrosion of justice.

The standing of African Americans in our shared history should not depend upon one DNA test. Descendants of Sally have reasons to be proud of their heritage. They overcame slavery to produce in later generations a doctor, a legislator, and a musician, among other professions. And as much as they emotionally want to claim the honor and privilege to be descended from a president, they cannot. If this jury, and the jury of public opinion, is forced to accept an "official story" by means of a process more political than scientific, we do so at the expense of truth.[5]

The lesson is obvious: Since the inception of the Sally myth two hundred years ago, many Americans want passionately to believe that Thomas Jefferson fathered some or all of Sally's children, whether or not the evidence supports the venal charge or not. The legend that Jefferson took Sally as his lover refuses to die because it is not good enough for some to know that his brother, Randolph, or his nephews, the Carrs, kept Sally as their mistress— for neither Randolph nor Peter Carr can be made a symbol for America.

Indignant revisionism, however, is not a substitute for concrete facts and relevant evidence. Blatant speculation is not drawn with a sharp pencil, but a broad brush. Thomas Jefferson, both the man and his family, amounts to something more important than sordid gossip now obscuring his memory.

Jefferson was arguably the most accomplished man who ever occupied the White House—naturalist, lawyer, educator, musician, architect, geographer, inventor, scientist, farmer, philosopher, and more. James Parton, one of Jefferson's biographers, characterized his subject as a man who "could calculate an eclipse, survey an estate, tie an artery, plan an edifice, try a cause, break a horse, dance a minuet, and play the violin." And Parton was describing a *young* Jefferson who had not yet written the Declaration of Independence.[6]

The Hemings case against Jefferson rests, essentially, on three skeletal pieces of evidence, framed by a selective exclusion of all the exculpatory evidence pointing to Mr. Jefferson's innocence: (1) the hearsay testimony of Sally's son, Madison; (2) the unreliable documentation of Jefferson's physical presence at the time of conception of Sally's children; and (3) the misleading DNA, which would be excluded or discredited in whole or part.

Ladies and gentleman, the Hemingses have failed to show beyond and to the exclusion of every "reasonable doubt" that Jefferson had an affair with Sally Hemings. Their case is based on a pyramiding of inferences, wild speculation, conjecture, and witnesses whose credibility and memories have been severely impeached. In fact, their entire case is devoid of credible, corroborated evidence.

Let us talk about the most credible and plausible evidence that proclaims Mr. Jefferson's innocence:

1. Randolph Jefferson is Sally's most likely sexual partner. He would have the same Jefferson Y chromosome as his older brother that matched perfectly the DNA. Randolph had a reputation for socializing with Jefferson's slaves and he was expected at Monticello *approximately nine months* before the birth of Eston, the DNA match. This is not mere coincidence, since the oral history of Eston's family held that they descended from a Jefferson "uncle." Randolph was known at Monticello as "Uncle Randolph."

2. The only DNA matched Sally's male son, Eston Hemings. Randolph Jefferson had *six male children*. Thomas Jefferson, however, had all *female* children—except for a nonviable male infant—making it a virtual certainty that Randolph, both genetically and by common sense, fathered the male child, Eston. Thomas Jefferson, for whatever genealogical reason, was inclined to produce only female children. This is a monumental point in Jefferson's defense, missed by all of the paternity historians.

3. The confusing testimony of Madison Hemings has been discredited and amounts to nothing more than scripted hearsay, gossip, and speculation. Moreover, his capacity to observe events that occurred some thirty to forty years earlier lacks certainty, clarity, and veracity.

4. Madison was coached by a political activist editor, S. F. Wetmore, who had both a motive and political bias against Jefferson as a slaveholder. In fact, it is clear that Wetmore, a radical abolitionist, wrote some or all of Madison's interview.

5. The alcoholic, tabloid journalist James Callender has been destroyed as a credible witness. No reasonable person believes any of his malicious, political libel. And neither should you. As historian Winthrop Jordan stated, Callender's charge "has been dragged after Jefferson like a dead cat through the pages of formal and informal history."[7] He had a poisonous bias as Jefferson's political foe. The charges against Mr. Jefferson were suspect from the beginning because they issued from the vengeful pen of an unscrupulous man and were promulgated in the spirit of bitter, political partisanship. Yet, this jury is asked to believe that after Callender broadcast his lies to the world in 1802, President Jefferson was so brazen about public opinion that he fathered two more children with Sally. This defies good, common sense.

6. Three eyewitnesses who intimately knew both Sally and Jefferson (Martha, his daughter, and Ellen Coolidge and Jeff Randolph, his grandchildren), all found the accusations inconceivable and never witnessed any hint of a sexual liaison. In fact, there is not a scintilla of proof of "cohabitation" or any physical intimacy between Jefferson and Sally during the thirty-seven years she lived, on and off, at Monticello. Most importantly, at least four witnesses proved that Jefferson was not in physical proximity to Sally for fifteen months prior to the birth of her son who most resembled Jefferson: Martha J. Randolph, Thomas Jefferson Randolph, George Wythe Randolph, and biographer Henry Randall.

7. The most credible eyewitness is Edmund Bacon, Jefferson's overseer. He testified that he did not observe any evidence of a relationship and, in fact, saw another man leaving Sally's room many mornings, most probably one of the Carr brothers or Randolph Jefferson himself. Bacon made it clear it was not Thomas Jefferson.

8. The misleading DNA results would be excluded in a real trial under the case law of *Daubert*,[8] due to violations of acceptable

chain of custody and scientific methodology, as well as suspect independent controls. Assuming the DNA was admitted, the results are gross distortions at best, and utterly misleading at worse. They matched a male Jefferson, *not* Thomas Jefferson. The DNA does not rule out either one or both of the Carr brothers as the father of Sally's children, except Eston. In fact, at least eight other Jefferson males are candidates for Sally's paternity. In essence, the DNA shows only that one descendant of Sally had a Jefferson male-line haplotype.

9. The most notable, independent Jefferson scholars lent their expert opinions to this jury, and agreed that the accusation of an affair lacks not only credibility, but would be utterly outside the moral character of Jefferson. Revisionist slave historians have misread language and invoked chic psychological explanations to misinterpret Jefferson's motives. Many have clouded Jefferson's cultural views without regard to eighteenth-century norms. The Sally "story" reflects one of the most striking derelictions of scholarly integrity in American historiography. As one historian succinctly declared: "I'm afraid that Professor [Fawn] Brodie, despite her admirable qualities, is the worst thing to happen to Jefferson since James Callender."[9]

10. The sexual allegation is preposterously out of character for Jefferson, being unthinkable in a man of his standards and habitual conduct. His major weaknesses were not of this sort, and would have prevented any liaison. To charge Jefferson with this degree of remarkable imprudence requires extraordinary credulity.

11. Jefferson never denied the accusation publicly for to do so would have been to slander the reputations of his father-in-law (alleged father of Sally), his beloved wife's memory, and either his own brother or his two favorite nephews, the Carr brothers, as the true fathers of Sally's children. As a man of devotion and family honor, Jefferson chose to suffer in silence. It speaks volumes that in the Monticello graveyard, white tombstones clus-

ter around the stone monolith that marks the grave of Jefferson. Martha, his wife, lies at his feet.

12. Jefferson's health, especially in the last two decades of his life,
would physically prevent, and otherwise dissuade him, from
engaging in a vibrant sexual relationship with a fourteen-year-
old girl. His severe migraine headaches, diarrhea, rheumatoid
arthritis, and emotional distress over his finances and the death
of his wife and daughter contributed to a deteriorating physical
and mental health for a sixty-four-year-old man, at the time of
Eston's conception. It is simply beyond common sense to believe he was having an ongoing sexual affair at his age.

13. The Hemingses true believers, Annette Gordon-Reed and Peter Onuf, have turned the debate into an obsessive agenda on
the color of Sally's skin, and slave status. The previous friendship and influence between Gordon-Reed and Dianne Swann-
Wright, the Chairwoman of the Monticello Report, was not
known before today's trial. Their assessment that Madison's
interview must be taken on face value because "white" historians had previously ignored it, are not facts, but racial canards
and misinterpretations of the evidence itself. The slave historians have taken "diversity" and created a hostile environment in
the academic world in which scholars feel pressured to accept
the Hemings myth as historical truth.

Ladies and Gentlemen, justice is supposed to be color blind
and neither racism, nor gender, nor bias has any place in this
court of law. The only question before this jury is what is the
most credible and believable evidence. Not Jefferson's view on
slavery or race, but whether it is proved beyond and to the exclusion of every reasonable doubt that he had sexual relations
with a fourteen-year-old girl.

14. When it came to women, Jefferson's nature was sheepish, some
would say awkward and "geekish," but certainly not lustful, except for his youthful indiscretion in the Betsey Walker affair.
His marriage proposal to his first love, Rebecca Burwell, in

1763, illustrates this point. Jefferson became so nervous that he could barely utter his words. He later reflected on his disastrous experience in the famous Apollo room at the Raleigh tavern: Jefferson wrote that he was overwhelmed with "strange confusion" that deteriorated into "a few broken sentences." Later in life, he was cloistered in his tranquil home life with his wife, "Patty," and then deeply conflicted over his romantic feelings for the married Maria Cosway. The sexual allegation and conduct is contrary to Jefferson's refined and reticent nature toward women.

15. Some paternity believers are quick to believe Jefferson was a brutal, "rapist" slaveholder. Yet, when Jefferson arrived at Monticello from Paris, his slaves were so overjoyed to see him they unhitched his horses and pulled his carriage up the last ridge of the mountain, then carried "Master" in their arms into his house. "It seemed impossible to satisfy their anxiety to touch and kiss the very earth which bore him," Patsy Jefferson wrote.[10]

16. The Hemingses would have you believe that the absence of any letters to or from Sally in any Jefferson correspondence is evidence of a family "cover up." This is one of many examples of authorial presumption: to use the total lack of information as "proof" of their sordid allegation. It merely shows that some ardent Hemings believers will "fill in the blanks" to convert innocent information into incriminating evidence.[11]

Commenting on the John F. Kennedy assassination in 1967, Walter Cronkite said: "Only in fiction do we find all the loose ends neatly tied. Real life is not all that tidy."[12] And neither is the Jefferson-Hemings case.

Obviously a large number of people, for various reasons, passionately want to believe they have a place in American history and that Thomas Jefferson fathered Sally Hemings's children. But it is not the role of historians, or this jury, to make people feel good about their widespread family stories. As Professor David Mayer testified from the witness stand, the role of historians is simply to explain the past by following objective methodology and the evidence. However upsetting this conclusion may be, it is simply the case that no credible evidence proves that Jefferson fathered any of Sally's children.

Coming to terms with Jefferson is not easy for some in the twenty-first century. Jefferson was no saint, but none of his biographers claimed he was. His opinions about race and slavery cannot be glossed over. No one will deny that the facts about the paternity of Sally's children are repulsive evidence of one of the worst aspects of the slave system—the manner by which some enslaved women were sexually abused by their masters.

Nevertheless, that is not the question we have before us. Whether Jefferson, or others at Monticello, were racists is an entirely different scholarly issue than whether he had sex with a fourteen-year-old Sally Hemings. The issues are not linked in any way, shape, or form. You should not let the Hemingses tie these politically charged issues to the evidence proving Jefferson's innocence.

The Hemings myth has now come full circle. In 1840, Citizens of Albemarle County passed a resolution "vindicating the memory of Mr. Jefferson from posthumous slanders" with regard to his private character. These individuals were his neighbors, who "had an opportunity of personally knowing the true state of facts."[13]

When you visit Monticello, it is but a short walk from the pastoral west lawn, down a sloping hill to Jefferson's gravesite. As one enters the cemetery you feel closer to history, to the real Thomas Jefferson, who once wrote that "politics was a subject I never loved, and now hate."[14] Without a doubt, the Hemings controversy embodies Mr. Jefferson's sentiment. On his deathbed, Jefferson spoke of the slanders and libel against him, uttering: "[T]hey had never known him. They had created an imaginary being clothed with odious attributes, to whom they had given his name."[15]

Finally, only two people know the absolute truth: One was Sally Hemings, who wrapped herself in the mantle of silence her entire life on the accusation. Perhaps, she believed that it deserved nothing more. As expert historian John C. Miller testified: "[W]e know virtually nothing of Sally Hemings, or her motives [and] she is hardly more than a name."[16] The other witness was Thomas Jefferson, who denied the charge to friends and colleagues, declaring that "truth is . . . great and will prevail if left to herself . . . she is the proper and sufficient antagonist to error."[17]

Ladies and gentleman of the jury, "there are such things as moral impossibilities." And although the Sally rumor survives, no reasonable, sensible person hearing *all* the evidence has ever declared his belief in it.

And neither should this jury.

ACKNOWLEDGMENTS

This book could not have been written without the valuable assistance of three outstanding people: Herbert Barger, a true Jeffersonian and indefatigable patriot who had the political courage to seek the truth wherever it led; Dr. Ken Wallenborn, friend, mentor, and leading Jefferson authority; and author Cynthia Burton, whose meticulous research and valuable comments saved me from various errors and contributed immensely to improving my rough manuscript. I would encourage anyone interested in the Jefferson-Hemings controversy to read Cynthia's indispensable book, *Jefferson Vindicated*.

I am also grateful to several of my father's colleagues who lent their time in critically reading all or part of the manuscript. I have benefited from their comments: Strobe Talbot, Jim Hoge, Peter Grose, and the late Peter Rodman. I am also particularly grateful to Professor Forrest McDonald and John Works for their kind comments and scholarly insight. I also gave portions of the manuscript to several of my legal colleagues, whose opinions I respect. They generously contributed to improving the book, and I owe them a special debt of thanks: John Bothwell and Jack Evans, and my college roommates Dick Barron and Chip Welch. Dr. Jan Duvoisin also provided his medical expertise on Jefferson's health.

I would also like to thank the Thomas Jefferson Heritage Society, and especially Pam Buell, for her assistance with references, illustrations, e-mails, and arranging valuable interviews. My in-laws, Leo and Colleen Ruffini, also gave of their personal time and attention, and provided valued comments, as well as my mother, Lynn Hyland, who encouraged me to write this book "for father."

Similar gratitude is owed to the staff at the Alderman Library at the University of Virginia (Special Collections Department) who provided me with valuable research material.

No book is complete without the assistance of a passionate editor. I was fortunate to have one of the best, Rob Kirkpatrick, who took a controversial manuscript and shaped it into a readable book. I also am indebted to all the fine people at my publisher, Thomas Dunne Books, especially David Stanford Burr, Lorrie Grace McCann, and Jason Ramirez. I also wish to thank my literary agent, Jim Fitzgerald, who began it all and kept me on track.

Finally, I am indebted most of all to my loving family: my children, Tori and Will, provided me with encouragement and inspiration and, at times, a quiet place to work. Yet the person I owe the most to, in both my personal and professional life, is my selfless wife, Delia. She endured my writing "moods," constant travel for research and writing conferences, and has shown great patience so I could finally write "my book." Honey, you are "the best of wives and the best of women."

APPENDIX A[1]

JEFFERSON-HEMINGS TIMELINE

EVENT	YEAR
Birth of Thomas Jefferson	13 Apr 1743
Jefferson enters William & Mary	1760
Jefferson graduates, studies law with George Wythe	1762
Jefferson passes bar exam	1765
Construction begins on Monticello	1768
Shadwell burns down	1770
Jefferson marries Martha Wayles Skelton	1772
Martha Jefferson (Patsy) born	1772
Death of John Wayles	1773
Martha Jefferson inherits Hemings family	1773
Birth of Sally Hemings	1773
Jane Randolph Jefferson born	1774
Jane Randolph Jefferson dies	1775
Betty Hemings and children come to Monticello	1775
Jefferson writes Declaration of Independence	1776
Jefferson's infant son born/dies within two weeks	1777
Mary Jefferson (Polly) born	1778

Lucy Elizabeth Jefferson born	1778
Jefferson elected governor of Virginia (one-year term)	1779
Lucy Elizabeth Jefferson dies	1781
Lucy Elizabeth Jefferson (II) born	1782
Death of Jefferson's wife Martha Jefferson	6 Sep 1782
Jefferson goes to Paris with daughter Martha (Patsy), James Hemings accompanies him	July 1784
Lucy Elizabeth Jefferson (II) dies	Oct 1784
Daughter Mary joins Jefferson in Paris, Sally Hemings accompanies Mary to Paris	July 1787
Jefferson returns to Monticello, Sally and James return with Jefferson	1789
Martha (Patsy) marries Thomas Mann Randolph, Jr.	1790
Jefferson becomes secretary of state	1790
Birth of Tom Woodson to Sally	1790
Jefferson resigns as secretary of state	1793
Birth of Harriet I to Sally	Oct 1795
Jefferson elected vice-president	1796
Mary (Polly) marries John Wayles Eppes	Oct 1797
Death of Harriet I to Sally	Dec 1797
Birth of Beverly Hemings to Sally	1 Apr 1798
Birth/death of daughter to Sally	7 Dec 1799
Jefferson elected president	1800–1801
Birth of Harriet II to Sally	May 1801
James Callender articles in *Richmond Recorder*	Sep–Oct 1802
Death of Mary Jefferson	1804
Jefferson reelected president	1804
Birth of Madison Hemings to Sally	January 1805
Birth of Eston Hemings to Sally	21 May 1808
Jefferson retires to Monticello	March 1809
Founding of the University of Virginia	1817

Harriet and Beverly "run away"   1822

Death of Thomas Jefferson   4 July 1826

Madison and Eston freed by Jefferson will   1827

Sally Hemings leaves with Madison and Eston   1827

Death of Sally Hemings   1835

APPENDIX B[1]

MINORITY REPORT BY DR. WALLENBORN

DATE: March 23, 2000
TO: Readers of the Attached Reports
FROM: Daniel P. Jordan, President, TJF
SUBJECT: Dr. Wallenborn's Minority Report

White McKenzie (Ken) Wallenborn, M.D., was a conscientious member of the *ad hoc* staff committee that I appointed in late 1998 to review, comprehensively and critically, all the evidence, scientific and otherwise, relating to the relationship of Thomas Jefferson and Sally Hemings and to report its findings and recommendations to me in a timely manner. Twice in the spring of 1999, during and after the conclusion of the work of the committee, Ken expressed some reservations to me, and I encouraged him to write up his concerns. It was my understanding at the time that he wanted his report to be for my review and consideration, not general circulation, but Ken now feels that it should be distributed more broadly—and I agree. I subsequently learned that Ken gave a copy to the committee chairman.

For the record, Ken's concerns were reviewed and considered systematically and seriously. I believe the issues he raised are addressed in the research report of the committee, and I concur with the findings of the committee. **I would encourage anyone interested in the general subject to read both reports and draw their own conclusions.**

I recognize that honorable people can disagree on this subject, as indeed they have for over two hundred years. Further, we know that the historical record has gaps that perhaps can never be filled, and mysteries that may never be fully resolved. The Foundation stands ready to review any fresh evidence at any time and to reassess our understanding of the matter in light of more complete information. In the meantime, while respecting fully Ken's opinions, I stand by the research report as circulated.

Thomas Jefferson Foundation
DNA Study Committee
Minority Report
April 12, 1999

Preface:

When Daniel P. Jordan, President of the Thomas Jefferson Foundation, convened the DNA Study Committee on 12/21/98, he asked the committee to evaluate the DNA study (Eugene Foster et al) in context of all evidence, to assess the impact on historical interpretation at Monticello, and to formulate a course of action for the Thomas Jefferson Foundation. As a result, numerous meetings of the committee were held. Voluminous material was presented and studied, outside opinions were obtained, a discussion meeting was held with the African American Advisory Committee, and discussion and debate freely occurred between members of the committee. As the DNA Study Committee began to formulate its report to Mr. Jordan, certain areas of disagreement became apparent and this has prompted the preparation of a minority report. Because there were many areas of agreement among all of the committee members, these will not be included in the minority report.

Areas of Disagreement:

Historical Evidence

The DNA Study Committee majority appears to agree that the DNA study showed that Eston Hemings direct male line descendants had an identical DNA haplotype to that of Field Jefferson's direct male line descendants and that assuming that Thomas Jefferson's DNA haplotype was identical to his uncle's descendants DNA haplotype, this would prove that Thomas Jefferson was related to Eston Hemings (Sally Hemings' youngest son). The DNA Study Committee agrees that this finding alone does not prove that Thomas Jefferson was the father of Eston Hemings. However the majority of the committee feels that in view of multiple strands of documentary and statistical evidence combined with the DNA findings substantiates the paternity of all the children listed under Sally Hemings' name in Jefferson's Farm Book. The minority report agrees that there is significant historical evidence that would show that Thomas Jefferson could be the father of Eston Hemings but also strongly feels that there is significant historical evidence of equal stature that indicates that Thomas Jefferson was not the father of Eston Hemings (or any of Sally Hemings's children).

These events happened more or less two hundred years ago and only four or possibly five people (Thomas Jefferson, Sally Hemings, Randolph Jefferson, Peter Carr, and Samuel Carr) would have known the truth about the paternity question. Only one of them has left us direct evidence in their own words and handwriting. On July 1, 1805, Thomas Jefferson wrote a letter to Robert Smith, Secretary of the Navy, in which he said: "The inclosed copy of a letter to Mr. Levi Lincoln will so fully explain it's own object, that I need say nothing in that way. I communicate it to particular friends because I wish to stand with them on the ground of truth; neither better nor worse than that makes me. You will perceive that I plead guilty to one of their charges, that when young and single, I offered love to a handsome lady. I acknowledge its incorrectness. It is the only one founded on truth among all their allegations against me . . ." This has to be a very straight forward denial of all the Federalist charges which included the report of a sexual liaison with Sally Hemings (that he had fathered Sally Hemings' children). Some feel that this statement is ambiguous but how can it be? Mr. Jefferson and his cabinet members Robert Smith and Levi Lincoln certainly knew all of the Federalist charges against the president. Thomas Jefferson was not known to issue falsehoods to his intimate associates. The minority report maintains that this statement by Thomas Jefferson is a significantly powerful denial.

In a letter to Dr. George Logan (Penn.) in 1816, Thomas Jefferson said "As to Federal slanders, I never wished them to be answered, but by the tenor of my life, half a century of which has been on a theater at which the public have been spectators and competent judges of its merit. Their approbation has taught a lesson, useful to the world, that the man who fears no truths has nothing to fear from lies. I should have fancied myself half guilty had I condescended to put pen to paper in refutation of their falsehoods, or drawn to them respect by any notice of myself."

In the courtroom-like atmosphere of this committee study, the defendant has made two rather significant denials in his own words and handwriting of the Federalist charges against him. None of the others who would have had first hand knowledge of the facts have put down statements in their own handwriting and their own words.

Edmund Bacon (born March 28, 1785 near Monticello) had the title of overseer at Monticello from September 29, 1806 until about October 15, 1822 (sixteen years). Edmund Bacon was interviewed at length (several weeks) by the Rev. Hamilton Wilcox Pierson, president of Cumberland College, Princeton, WVA around 1861 or 1862 at Mr. Bacon's home. Mr. Bacon recalled that he went to live with Mr. Jefferson on Dec. 27, 1800 and was with him precisely twenty years but Mr. Jefferson recorded his employment as overseer for sixteen years. Possibly Mr. Bacon had started working as early as age sixteen but was not hired as overseer until age twenty and if so would have been working at Monticello when Harriet Hemings was conceived and born. Mr. Bacon's recollections and letters from Thomas Jefferson provided a remarkable record of the years that he was at Monticello. At times his memory was not absolutely accurate on minor matters. Mr. Bacon had many observations about Mr. Jefferson including: "his skin was very clear and pure—just like he was in principle." He also commented on William C. Rives, a youngster, who would stay and play at Monticello with the other boys (most likely the Randolphs, Carrs, and Maria's son, Francis) . . . Willie would stay with Mr. Bacon rather than at the house (Monticello) because the other boys were too intimate with the negro women to suit him. Bacon also said "he (TJ) could not bear to have a servant whipped, no odds how much he deserved it."

Edmund Bacon also shed some light on the Sally Hemings controversy. "He freed one girl some years before he died, and there was a great deal of talk about it. She was nearly as white as anybody and very beautiful. People said he freed her because she was his own daughter. She was not his daughter, she was ___'s daughter (Rev. Pierson apparently left the name blank to protect that individual). I know that. I have seen him come out of her mother's room many a morning when I was up to Monticello very early." Bacon had to be referring to Harriet Hemings. If Bacon had actually come to live at Monticello at age sixteen, on December 27, 1800 (before Th. Jefferson was inaugurated for his first term as president), he would have been working at Monticello during the time of conception and birth of Sally Hemings' last three children—Harriet, Madison, and Eston. Bacon's observations are certainly valid information and do strongly suggest that another male was having a sexual liaison with Sally Hemings.

Thomas Jefferson Randolph (1792–1875) was the oldest grandson of Thomas Jefferson and was Mr. Jefferson's farm manager and later executor of his estate. T.J. Randolph is a primary witness who was involved directly and who saw a past situation with his own eyes according to Douglass Adair.

Thomas Jefferson Randolph emphatically denied that Mr. Jefferson had commerce with Sally or any other of his female slaves. Since he "had spent a good share of his life closely about Mr. Jefferson at home and on journeys—in all sorts of circumstances," he could testify that his grandfather was in sexual matters "chaste and pure"—indeed as "immaculate a man as God ever created." Randall as quoted in Adair's treatise said that Col. Randolph said that he "Slept within sound of his (TJ's) breathing at night." He said that "he had never seen a motion, or a look, or a circumstance which led him to suspect for an instant that there was a particle of familiarity between Mr. Jefferson and Sally Hemings than between him and the most repulsive servant in the establishment—and that no person ever at Monticello dreamed of such a thing."

Thomas Jefferson Randolph also told Randall "Mr. Jefferson had two nephews, Peter Carr and Samuel Carr whom he brought up in his own house. They were the sons of Jefferson's sister and her husband Dabney Carr . . . who died in 1773 . . . Sally Hemings was the mistress of Peter and her sister Betsey (she was actually the daughter of Sally's half sister) the mistress of Samuel—and from these the progeny which resembled Mr. Jefferson. Both Hemings girls were light colored and decidedly good looking . . . Their connection with the Carrs was perfectly notorious at Monticello, and scarcely disguised by the latter—never disavowed by them. Samuel's proceedings were particularly open." Col. Randolph told Randall that his mother, Mrs. Gov. Randolph took the Dusky Sally stories much to heart, not long before her death she called two of them—the Colonel and George Wythe Randolph—to her. She asked the Colonel if he remembered when _____ Hemings (the slave who most resembled Mr. Jefferson) was born. The Col. turned to the book containing the list of slaves and found his birthdate. Martha Jefferson Randolph directed her son's attention to the fact that Mr. Jefferson and Sally Hemings could not have met and were far distant from each other—for fifteen months prior to such a birth. Col. Randolph later while examining an old account book of Jefferson's came on the birthdate again and was able from well known circumstances to prove the fifteen months separation. T.J. Randolph never recorded those circumstances.

Now if those circumstances confirming the fifteen months separation between Mr. Jefferson and Sally Hemings before the birth of _____ Hemings who most resembled Mr. Jefferson—and this by most accounts would be Eston Hemings—this would dramatically change the thinking in regards to the DNA studies . . . Thomas Jefferson would not be the father of Eston. Another Jefferson DNA Haplotype carrier would be the father of Eston and the stories about Peter Carr and Sally Hemings would probably indicate Peter as the father of Sally's other four children. Intensive research by outstanding historical investigators may be able to uncover this answer.

The Monte Carlo Simulation:

This is an interesting simulation to determine the probability that the timing of Th. Jefferson's known visits to Monticello were related to the conception dates of Sally Hemings' five children (the study used six children but the significant evidence indicates only five children) as opposed to the null hypothesis that they were unrelated. According to the results obtained, there is only a 1% chance that Sally Hemings's conceptions are coincidental to TJ's presence at Monticello. Based on the Monte Carlo Evaluation, the fact that all 6 conceptions occur during TJ's visits is 100 times more likely if TJ or someone with the same pattern of presence and absence at Monticello is the father.

Comments from the minority:

Statistics can be misleading. The basis for the numbers used in calculating statistical results has to be proven as true representations. In this simulation, two of the three proofs necessary are probably reliable . . . conception dates and timing of Mr. Jefferson's visits to Monticello. The third proof cannot be proven . . . Sally Hemings' presence at Monticello is not accurately recorded and her presence or absence cannot be proven as also coinciding with Mr. Jefferson's presence.

A good example would be that if Martha Jefferson's message to her sons that Mr. Jefferson was not in the presence of Sally Hemings for fifteen months prior to the birth of Eston (assuming that she was referring to Eston), the odds that were one hundred to one that TJ was the father would be meaningless.

Also because it is impossible to determine the timing of the presence or absence of other males with the Jefferson DNA haplotype at Monticello, you have no way to compare the probability of there being the father of Sally Hemings' children with the probability that Mr. Thomas Jefferson was the father. This evidence just is not there for vital comparison studies.

Wetmore's "Memoirs of Madison Hemings":

The minority feels that Madison was telling the truth as he remembered it in his interview by Mr. Wetmore. However it appears that Mr. Wetmore might have harmed his case because of the use of journalistic license. Mr. Madison Hemings admittedly had no formal education but in the memoirs, Mr. Wetmore has Madison using an amazing vocabulary and grammar, and having a remarkable knowledge of history. All of this was remembered some thirty five or forty years after he was at Monticello. Wetmore's use of direct quotes instead of paraphrasing would have helped make the memoirs more believable. As far as the minority can tell, Wetmore's handwritten notes covering his interview have not been found and as a result it is hard to tell when the words were Madison's or Wetmore's.

Summary:

The results of the DNA studies enhance the possibility that Thomas Jefferson was the father of one of Sally Hemings' children, Eston Hemings, but the findings do not prove that Thomas Jefferson was the father of Eston. This is a very important difference.

There is historical evidence of more or less equal stature on both sides of this issue that prevent a definitive answer as to Thomas Jefferson's paternity of Sally Hemings' son Eston Hemings or for that matter the other four of her children. In fairness to the descendants of Sally Hemings and the descendants of Thomas Jefferson and Martha Wayles Jefferson, the Thomas Jefferson Foundation should continue to encourage in depth historical research in hopes that accurate answers to very sensitive questions may be found.

In regards to the historical interpretation of Thomas Jefferson and his family, Monticello, and slavery at Monticello, the Thomas Jefferson Foundation should continue to present a properly weighted historical interpretation to visitors. As new historical evidence is found, it should continue to be incorporated into interpretive presentations. However, historical accuracy should never be overwhelmed by political correctness, for if it is, history becomes meaningless. Construction of historically inaccurate buildings on the mountaintop at Monticello would detract from the historically accurate picture that the Thomas Jefferson Foundation is trying to portray.

In summary, the Thomas Jefferson Foundation should continue to seek the truth. If the truth is not known, it should be so stated. The minority feels that it would be improper to accept that portion of the DNA Study Committee's report that says "the DNA study when combined with the multiple strands of documentary and statistical evidence, substantiates Thomas Jefferson's paternity of all the children listed under Sally Hemings' name in Jefferson's Farm Book." The historical evidence is not substantial enough to confirm nor for that matter to refute his paternity of any of the children of Sally Hemings. The DNA studies certainly enhance the possibility but to repeat, do not prove Thomas Jefferson's paternity. These events happened almost two hundred years ago and there were four (five) people who might have known the truth about this issue. Only one of them has answered in his own handwriting and words. Thomas Jefferson denied all the allegations except for the "Walker" affair which he admitted.

Respectfully Submitted,
White McKenzie Wallenborn, M.D.
Author of the Minority Report

APPENDIX C[1]

REPLY TO THOMAS JEFFERSON FOUNDATION RESPONSE TO THE MINORITY REPORT TO THE DNA STUDY COMMITTEE

Reply by White McKenzie Wallenborn, M.D.
Author of the Minority Report
Former Clinical Professor, University of Virginia School of Medicine
Former Historical Interpreter, Monticello
June 2000

This is the reply to the response to the Minority Report of the DNA Study Committee by the Thomas Jefferson Foundation through Lucia C. Stanton. With respect to the introductory comments by Mr. Daniel P. Jordan, President of the Thomas Jefferson Foundation, on March 23, 2000 presenting the "Minority Report": Mr. Jordan's invitation to the public to read both reports (DNA Study Committee and Minority Report) and draw their own conclusions has produced an immense positive response to the "Minority Report" from Jefferson scholars, historians, physicians, scientists, statisticians, active and retired college professors, attorneys, genealogists, and the general public. Many of those who have taken the time to read the TJMF report have been shocked to see the evidence that the committee used to reach their conclusions.

Several opening comments should be recorded before beginning the point by point discussion. The Foundation response by Ms. Stanton said that the committee as a whole did not feel the Minority Report was of sufficient weight to warrant a different conclusion. *This statement is anything but the truth because the committee as a whole did not see the Minority Report until well after the release of the final committee report on January 27, 2000. In other words, the chair of the committee did not share the dissenting report (which was submitted on April 12, 1999) with the complete committee.* As a matter of fact, the committee as a whole did not even see the final DNA Study Committee report until 72 hours prior to the release of this report to the public and there was no time to discuss the contents at that time (the committee had finished its deliberations in April 1999— nine months earlier). There will be more comment about the elastic conception of the truth in section 1.

1. Jefferson denied the relationship (and Ms. Stanton says: "and by implication, Jefferson would not lie").

In the fall of 1802, James Thomson Callender in a series of scandalous articles in a pro-Federalist weekly newspaper, the "Richmond Recorder" charged Thomas Jefferson with three basic misdeeds. These were as follows: 1) he had a son called Tom by his slave Sally; 2) that he had an affair with a married woman; and 3) that he had paid off a loan with devaluated currency. Although the Federalists continued to attack Mr. Jefferson most of his public life and throughout his retirement, primarily their charges echoed Callender's charges of 1802. The Federalists used them repeatedly against Jefferson.

Callender's allegations concerning the Walker affair with a reference to the "sable damsel", to whom Mr. Jefferson supposedly turned to after he was rejected by Mrs. Walker, were revived and printed again in 1805 in northern papers. This brought about a national political debate about Th. Jefferson's morality in the cases of Mrs. Walker and the concubinage of Sally Hemings.

Usually the Walker story and the Sally affair were lumped together in the same articles which confirm his distinct denial in the following letter. On July 1, 1805, Thomas Jefferson wrote a cover letter to Robert Smith, Secretary of the Navy, and enclosed a copy of a letter to Mr. Levi Lincoln, the Attorney General. In this letter Mr. Jefferson pled guilty to one of the Federalists' charges, that when young and single, he offered love to a handsome lady. He acknowledged the incorrectness of the act but said that it is the only one founded on truth among all their allegations against me. There is no element of ambiguity in Jefferson's denial. The other allegations were well known to all.

In his letter to Dr. George Logan in 1816 he uses the exact phrase and capitalization as James T. Callender used, e.g. "As to Federal slanders, I never wished them to be answered, . . . Their approbation has taught a lesson, useful to the world that the man who fears no truths, has nothing to fear from lies. I should have fancied myself half guilty had I condescended to put pen to paper in refutation of their falsehoods, or drawn to them respect by any notice of myself." So it would appear that in this denial he was again specifically referring to Callender's slanders as picked up by the Federalists.

Ms. Stanton quotes Joanne Freeman as saying Mr. Jefferson had an *elastic conception* of the truth, when he believed the stakes of the nation were high. We are not talking about the stakes of the nation here but the private communication between Th. Jefferson and two of his close personal and political friends. There is no proof, that I am aware of, that would show that Mr. Jefferson told anything but the truth to any of his adult family, friends, or close political associates.

Ms. Stanton also states: "We know Jefferson's rationalizing talents and can imagine ways he could find a fairly comfortable place for this relationship in his view of himself". This statement belies all of Mr. Jefferson's professions of morality, his assertions that a slave master must not abuse those under his control, and especially his strong and well known feelings about miscegenation. An even less scholarly comment was referenced by Ms. Stanton that Jefferson might have considered a sexual liaison with a slave necessary for his health as he had books on the subject of health and sexual activity. This is preposterous . . . in my library are books by Fawn Brodie and Annette Gordon-Reed but by no means do I agree with them nor should anyone make a supposition that I do just because they are in my collection. Th. Jefferson himself never wrote about or was quoted as saying anything that would give credence to these statements.

Robert McDonald writing in "Southern Cultures" said that Callender's allegations had "*scant credibility*" to readers, and even "*Jefferson's reticence which regularly characterized his responses to attacks*" did nothing to enhance their believability.

In summary, the 1805 letter to Robert Smith is both an incisive and direct denial by a primary subject and is certainly not fraught with ambiguity or falsehood. Daniel P. Jordan, President of the Thomas Jefferson Foundation, said in reference to Ms. Stanton's responses "*Her views reflect my own*" but in commenting on the possibility of Mr. Jefferson having a sexual relationship with a slave said in an interview for the Ken Burns documentary on PBS-TV: "*My own belief is that, as one of the contemporaries of Jefferson said, it would be morally impossible for that to have occurred.*"

2. Edmund Bacon denied the relationship (and Ms. Stanton says: "and by implication, Bacon too would not lie").

Edmund Bacon said in his interview with Rev. H. Pierson that he began working for Mr. Jefferson on Dec. 27, 1800 and had the title of overseer from Sept. 29, 1806 until Oct. 15, 1822. In Thomas Jefferson's *Farm Book* and *Garden Book* there are at least two references to Bacon having several jobs at Monticello before he became overseer in 1806. His father had apparently done some contract jobs for Mr. Jefferson and so Edmund Bacon was known to Mr. Jefferson well before 1806. In his interview with Rev. Pierson, Mr. Bacon produced letters of Mr. Jefferson's to him, bills from Monticello, etc. to back up some of his remarks. Thomas Jefferson provided a letter of recommendation for Mr. Bacon when he went West looking for land and employment. Whether or not he was at Monticello at Harriet's or Madison's conception is not nearly as important as his observation that Sally's male companion was not Thomas Jefferson. Remember that he was there by all accounts when Eston was conceived (if Eston was conceived at Monticello). There are no secrets on a farm and Monticello was no different, so Edmund Bacon would have been aware of who was having an affair with Sally Hemings even if the affair had been going on before Bacon's arrival. Edmund Bacon, being a primary witness, gives a significant observation that Mr. Thomas Jefferson was not involved with Sally Hemings at least for one of her conceptions.

Now again we see undocumented assumptions on the part of the TJMF responder with an attempt to read the mind of Edmund Bacon. Ms. Stanton says: "First we have to consider reasons Bacon might have had for absolving Jefferson of the Hemings connection (he was talking to a clergyman in 1860, when mores were decidedly different from those of 1800; he was deeply loyal to Jefferson and proud of his association with a great man, and so forth)". Of course the main reason Bacon had for absolving Mr. Jefferson was that he was telling the truth about the situation. As to the mores being different in 1860 from those of 1800, it is doubtful that telling a truism (or a falsehood) to a clergyman in 1860 would be different from telling one in 1800. And what would be wrong with being proud of your association with a great man as long as you are willing to tell the truth about him? There just is no good reason for Mr. Bacon to tell lies during his interview. Being forgetful on minor points is understandable after not being around Mr. Jefferson for thirty eight years. *As a primary witness, Edmund Bacon's revelations are of significant value in discrediting the purported Jefferson-Hemings affair.*

3. Thomas Jefferson Randolph denied the relationship (and Ms. Stanton says: "and by implication, Thomas Jefferson Randolph would not lie").

Actually the DNA evidence may have strengthened Thomas Jefferson Randolph's version of the events. The DNA applies only to Eston Hemings and not to Sally Hemings's other four children and in no way eliminates Peter or Samuel Carr from being the father of those four children. The DNA evidence indicates that Eston's father was someone carrying the Jefferson Y-Chromosome. Thomas Jefferson Randolph (and Henry S. Randall) reported that Thomas Jefferson and Sally Hemings could not have met—were far distant from each other—for fifteen months prior to the birth of the Hemings who looked most like Thomas Jefferson and this most likely would have been Eston . . . and here Ms. Stanton erroneously gives these dates as July 1806 to September 1807 when these dates of 15 months separation should be February 1807 to May 1808 (see section 4 of the response). Thus if Eston's father was a Jefferson and Mr. Jefferson was not around Sally for fifteen months prior to Eston's birth, then the most likely father would be Randolph Jefferson or one of his sons. Eston is said to be the son of Sally that most resembled Thomas Jefferson. He was six feet one inch tall and decidedly very light skinned. Madison Hemings was five feet seven inches and a darker mulatto. Beverly's appearance is only vaguely described. Eston was noted by one person in Cincinnati to look just like a Jefferson bust in Washington, thus it would appear that Eston was most likely the one referred to in TJR's comments to Henry S. Randall.

In response to Ms. Stanton's statement that "we know, however, from the Memorandum Books and other sources that Jefferson was at Monticello at the right time to father all of Sally Hemings' children". A study of the Memorandum Books, the Farm Book, the Garden Book, and the

Monticello Research Staff's Chronology Record of time and location of Mr. Jefferson do not support Ms. Stanton's statement. We do know the dates of Mr. Jefferson's departures from Philadelphia and Washington and the dates of his departures from Monticello to return to those cities. However it is difficult to pinpoint his presence at Monticello on or near the estimated dates of conception. Mr. Jefferson was a man on the move when he returned to Monticello and would make visits overnight or for longer periods to places such as Poplar Forest, Enniscorthy, Warren, Scottsville, Montpelier, Natural Bridge, etc. We do know that he was at Monticello on April 17, 1804 which is ten days before the estimated date of Madison Hemings's conception. He was there at the time of the death of his younger daughter, Maria Jefferson Eppes. She was the daughter that looked most like Th. Jefferson's wife and died from the same cause, late complications of childbirth. It is extremely unlikely that he would show his grief at that time with all of the family around by having a sexual liaison with Sally Hemings ten days after Maria's death. As to Sally's presence or absence from Monticello, there is only sketchy evidence of her whereabouts prior to 1801. From 1801 until 1810, there is almost no evidence bearing on this matter. While Mr. Jefferson was serving as President (1801–1809) and away from Monticello, the house was kept locked. During this time he leased some of his slaves out and it would not be unreasonable to think that Sally and some of the other house staff might have been loaned out to neighbors or nearby relatives at Edgehill, Snowden, Varina, Farmington, etc.

In summary, Thomas Jefferson Randolph's comments to Henry S. Randall were quite candid and were most likely closer to the truth on these matters. *And because he was a primary witness, they are very meaningful.*

4. There is insufficient information about Sally Hemings and other Jeffersons to make a valid statistical estimate of probability.

This was discussed in point three but to be more specific let me give here the estimated dates of conception (EDC), F. Neiman's dates that Th. Jefferson was supposed to be at Monticello (FND), and the dates that the Farm Book, Garden Book, Memorandum Books, and Monticello Research Department's Chronological Record can give Mr. Jefferson's exact location on specific date (SLD):

EDC	FND	SLD
Jan. 11, 1795 **Harriet 1**	Jan. 16, 1794–Feb. 20, 1797 No exclusions by Neiman	Jan. 1, 1795 Feb. 1, 1795 only
July 8, 1797 **Beverly**	July 11, 1797–Dec. 4, 1797 No exclusions by Neiman	July 1, 1797 (only date with reference to TJ's presence in this entire time).
Aug. 21, 1800 **Harriet**	May 29, 1800–Nov. 1800 No exclusions by Neiman	From Aug. 12 until Sept. 8, TJ's location unknown
Apr. 27, 1804 **Madison**	Apr. 5, 1(434) May 11, 1804 No exclusions by Neiman	Apr. 8, 12, and May 9 are the only dates listing TJ's location at Monticello.*
Aug. 28, 1807 **Eston**	Aug. 5, 1807–Oct. 1, 1807 No exclusions by Neiman	July 23, 1807 only. The next date recording TJ's location was Sept. 13, 1807 and he was actually at Warren and Enniscorthy this date.

*He was known to be at Monticello on April 17, 1804 because this is the date that his daughter Maria died at Monticello.

There are some striking coincidences which also add to the perplexity. For example, when Jefferson finally came home after his second term as President, for some reason Sally quit having children. Randolph Jefferson (TJ's brother and a possible father of Eston) was widowed probably as early as 1796 but as soon as he remarried in late 1808 or early 1809, Sally had no more children. Thomas Jefferson, Jr. (Randolph's son and a possible father of Eston) married on Oct. 3, 1808 and after this date, Sally had no more children. Obstetrical calculations are notoriously fallible and coupled with early or late deliveries being entirely possible, throw more doubt on the Monte Carlo Simulation studies based on these factors. At any rate, Neiman's statistics cry out for valid comparative studies of the other Jefferson males who might have fathered Eston and in the absence of these comparisons, the results are inconclusive. Because no accurate records were kept of these other Jefferson male visits to Monticello, no comparisons can be performed. And given the fact that there is no proof of Sally Hemings's presence at Monticello when Eston was conceived, the picture really becomes muddled.

(*A chronology of Jefferson's whereabouts throughout his life compiled by former Monticello Curator, James A. Bear, Jr., lists Jefferson at Monticello on many more dates than Dr. Wallenborn notes. The chronology is available at Monticello's* Jefferson Library *in Charlottesville, VA.*)

5. Madison Hemings's recollection lacks credibility because of language used (Ms. Stanton says: "amazing grammar and vocabulary") and his age 68.

Wetmore's article about Madison Hemings can not be called an "accurate reflection of Hemings's statements" as there are not direct quotations of Madison Hemings before and/or subsequent to the publication that reaffirm Wetmore's opinions. To make such a statement without access to Wetmore's interview notes just is not acceptable. Madison Hemings did not sign the original document or at least there is no record of a signature to affirm concurrence with Wetmore's statements. There can be no doubt that the language is Wetmore's and whether or not he changed the content to fit his (Wetmore's) strong political agenda is unknown but becomes suspect. *In other words, this document is very problematic and should not be considered as a primary source of evidence.*

In response to Ms. Stanton's statement that "Hemings would not have forgotten who his father was, no matter his age", it is almost impossible for anyone to say with absolute certainty who his father was. DNA can rule out paternity but does not prove it as we have seen in the case of Eston Hemings. Your parent(s) can tell you who your father is but even this is sometimes wrong, as is seen in the case of Thomas Woodson, who certainly did not know who his father was. If you read Wetmore's article carefully, at no time does Madison Hemings say that his mother told him that Thomas Jefferson was his father.

In final response to Ms. Stanton's comment that "the details of language and historical facts are irrelevant to the main issue: paternity", the entire questionable composition of Wetmore's publication, coupled with the fact that Madison never acknowledged the source of his information as to whom his father was, are very relevant to the main issue of paternity.

The author of the Minority Report of the DNA Study Committee would like to conclude with a statement: If the Thomas Jefferson Foundation and the DNA Study Committee majority had been seeking the truth and had used accurate legal and historical information rather than politically correct motivation, their statement should have been something like this: "*After almost two hundred years of study including recent DNA information, it is still impossible to prove with absolute certainty whether Thomas Jefferson did or did not father any of Sally Hemings's five children.*" This statement is accurate and honest and it would have helped discourage the campaign by leading universities (including Thomas Jefferson's own University of Virginia), magazines, university publications, national commercial and public TV networks, and newspapers to denigrate and destroy the legacy of one of the greatest of our founding fathers and one of the greatest of all of our citizens.

White McKenzie Wallenborn, M.D.
Second Revision: June 29, 2000

APPENDIX D

RANDOLPH JEFFERSON'S WILL

NOTE: Randolph Jefferson's will was made six days after Eston Hemings's birth. This is actually a typescript of Randolph Jefferson's "draft" will dated May 27, 1808. The final will was edited and dated May 28, 1808. This was copied from the Thomas Jefferson Papers on the microfilm from the University of Virginia, interlibrary loan. Roll 6.

Randolph Jefferson of Buckingham County in Virginia, being in sound health, do make the following testamentary disposition of my estate.

I give all the negroes which I shall own at the time of my death to be equally divided between my five sons, Thomas, Robert Lewis, Field, Randolph and Liburne, each of them to whom I have given slaves during my life time bring the value of those slaves into hotchpot with those being divided and drawstaking from those to be divided only so much as with those before given shall make his portion of slaves equal to that of each of his other brothers.

It is my will that all my lands and other property whatsoever, be sold after my death and the proceeds be equally divided among my said five sons, my son Thomas bring into hotch pot with those proceeds the some of one thousand pounds (at which I estimate the advantages I have given him during my life) and taking from the proceeds only so much as, being added do the said thousand pounds, shall make his portion under this bequest equal to that of his other brothers.

I give\ to my\ son Lewis \my\ violin,\ and to my son

Lastly I make my friends Harding Perkins and Robert Craig, and my son Robert Lewis, and my brother Thomas Jefferson executors of this my will, revoking all others heretofore made and writing in testimony here of I have written the whole with my own hand this 27th day of may 1808.

MR. JEFFERSON'S WILL

I, Thomas Jefferson of Monticello in Albemarle being of sound mind and my ordinary state of health make my last will and testament in manner and form as follows.

I give to my grand son Francis Eppes son of my dear deceased daughter Mary Eppes in fee simple all that part of my lands at Poplar Forest lying west of the following lines to-wit: Beginning at Radford's upper corner near the double branches of Bear Creek and the public road & running thence in a straight line to the fork of my private road near the barn thence along the private road (as it changed in 1817) to its crossing of the main branch of north Tomahawk creek and from then crossing in a direct line over the main ridge which devided the North and South Tomahawk to South Tomahawk and at the confluence of the two branches where the old road to the waterlick crossed it and from that confluence up the northern-most branch which separates McDaniel & Perrys field to its source & thence by the shortest line to my western boundary and having in a former correspondence with my deceased son in law John Eppes contemplated laying off for him with remainder to my grand son Francis a certain portion in the southern part of my lands in Bedford and Campbell which I afterwards found to be generally more indifferent than I had supposed I therefore determined to change its location for the better now to remove all doubt if any could arise on a purpose merely voluntary & unexecuted I hereby declare that where I have herein given to my sd grandson Francis is instead of and not additional to what I have formerly contemplated.

I subject all my other property to the payment of my debts in the first place considering the insolvent state of affairs friend and son in law Thomas Mann Randolph and that what will remain of my property will be the only resource against the want in which his family would otherwise be left, it must be his wish as it is my duty to guard that resource against all liability for his debts, engagements or purposes whatsoever, and to preclude the rights powers and authorities over it which might result to him by operation of law, and which might independantly of his will bring it in the power of his creditors, I do hereby devise and bequeath all the residue of my property real and personal, in possession or in action, whether held in my own right, or in that of my dear deceased wife, according to the powers vested in me by deed of settlement for that purpose to my grand son Thomas J. Randolph and my friends Nicholas P. Trist and Alex Garrett & their heirs during the life of my son in law Thomas M. Randolph, to be held & administered by them in trust, for the sole and separate use and behoof of my dear daughter Martha Randolph and heirs and aware of the nice and difficult distinctions of the law in these cases, I will further explain by saying that I understand and intend the effect of these limitation to be that legal estate and actual occupation shall be vested in my said trustees and held by them in base fee, determinable on the death of my said son in law, and the remainder during the said time be vested in my said daughter and her heirs, and of course disposable by her last will, and at the death of my sd son in law, the particular estate of sd trustees shall be determined and the remainder, in legal estate, possession and use become vested in my sd daughter and her heirs, in absolute property forever.

In consequence of the variety and indescribableness of the articles of property within the house at Monticello, and the difficulty of inventorying and appraising them separately and specifically, and its inutility, I dispense with having them inventoryed and appraised, and it is my will that my Executors be not held to give any security for their administration of my estate. I appoint my grand son Thomas Jefferson Randolph my sole executor during his life and after his death, I constitute executors my friends Nicholas P. Trist and Alexander Garrett joining to them my daughter Martha Randolph after the death of my sd son in law Thomas M. Randolph.

Lastly I revoke all former wills by me heretofore made in Witness that this is my will I have written the whole with my own hand on two pages, and have subscribed my name to each of them this 16th day of March one Thousand eight hundred and twenty six. Th: Jefferson

I, Thomas Jefferson of Monticello in Albemarle make and add the following codicil to my will controling the same so far as its provisions go.

I recommend to my daughter Martha Randolph the maintenance and care of my well beloved sister Anna Scott Marks, and trust confidently that from affection to her as well as for my sake, she will never let her want a comfort.

I have made no specific provision for the comfortable maintenance of my son in law Thomas M. Randolph, because of the difficulty and uncertainty of devising terms which shall vest any beneficial interest in him which the law will not transfer to the benefit of his creditors to the destitution of my daughter and her family and disablement of her to supply him: whereas property placed under the executive right of my daughter and her independance will, as if she were a femme sole, considering the relations in which she shared both to him and his children will be a certain resource against want for all.

I give to my friend James Madison of Montpellier my gold mounted walking staff of animal horn as a token of the cordial and affectionate friendship which for nearly now a half century, has united us in the same principles and pursuits of what we have deemed for the greatest good of our country.

I give to the University of Virginia my library except such particular books only and of the same edition as it may already possess, when this legacy shall take effect. The rest of my said library remaining after those given to the University, shall have been taken out, I give to my two grandsons in law Nicholas P. Trist and Joseph Coolidge.

To my grandson Thomas Jefferson Randolph I give my silver watch in preference of the golden one, because of its superior excellence. My papers of business going of course to him as my executors all others of a literary or other character I give to him as of his own property. Th: Jefferson

I give a gold watch to each of my grand children who shall not have already received one from me to be purchased and delivered by executors to my grandson at the age of 21 and grand daughters at that of sixteen.

I give to my good affectionate and faithful servant Burwell his freedom and the sum of Three Hundred Dollars to buy necessaries to commence his trade of painter and glasier or to use otherwise as he pleases. I give also to my good servant John Hemings and Joe Fossett their freedom at the end of one year after my death and to each of them respectively all the tools of their respective shops or callings: and it is my will that a comfortable log house be built for each of the three servants so emancipated on some part of my lands convenient to them with respect to their wives, and Charlottesville and the University, where they be mostly employed, and reasonably convenient to the interest of the proprietor of the lands; of which houses I give the use of one with a curtilage of an acre to each, during his life or personal occupation thereof.

I give also to John Hemings the services of his two apprentices, Madison and Eston Hemings, until their respective ages of twenty-one years, at which period respectively, I give them their freedom. I humbly and earnestly request of the legislature of Virginia a confirmation of the bequest of freedom of these servants, with permission to remain in this state where their families and connections are, as an additional instance of the favor, of which I have received so many other manifestations, in the course of my life, and for which I now give them my last, solemn, and dutiful thanks.

In testimony that this is a codicil to my will of yesterdays date and that it is to modify so far the provisions of that will, I have written it all with my own hand, in two pages, to each of which I subscribe my name this 17th day of March one thousand eight hundred and twenty six. Th: Jefferson

At a court held for Albemarle County the 7th of August 1826. This instrument of writing purporting to be the last will and testament of Thomas Jefferson was produced into Court and hand writing of the testator proved by the oath of Valentine W. Southall and ordered to be recorded. Teste: Alexander Garrett CC

APPENDIX F[1]

"THE FAMILY DENIAL"

Ellen (Eleanora) Wayles Randolph Coolidge to Joseph Coolidge, Jr.
Edgehill 24 October 1858

I am just from church, a church originally planned by Grandpapa, where I heard a good sermon from an Episcopalian Clergyman, a young man, the Revd. Mr. Butler.

I have been talking freely with my brother Jefferson on the subject of the 'yellow children' and will give you the substance of our conversation, with my subsequent reflections.

It is difficult to prove a negative. It is impossible to prove that Mr. Jefferson never had a coloured mistress or coloured children and that these children were never sold as slaves. The latter part of the charge however is disproved by it's atrocity, and it's utter disagreement with the general character and conduct of Mr. Jefferson, acknowledged to be a humane man and eminently a kind master. Would he who was always most considerate of the feelings and the well being of his slaves, treat them barbarously only when they happened to be his own children, and leave them to be sold in a distant market when he might have left them free as you know he did several of his slaves, directing his executor to petition the Legislature of Virginia for leave for them to remain in the State after they were free. Some of them are here to this day.

It was his principle (I know that of my own knowledge) to allow such of his slaves as were sufficiently white to pass for white men, to withdraw quietly from the plantation; it was called running away, but they were never reclaimed. I remember four instances of this, three young men and one girl, who walked away and staid away. Their whereabouts was perfectly known but they were left to themselves for they were white enough to pass for white. Some of the children currently reported to be Mr. Jefferson's were about the age of his own grandchildren. Of course he must have been carrying on his intrigues in the midst of his daughters family and insulting the sanctity of home by his profligacy. But he had a large family of grandchildren of all ages, older & younger. Young men and young girls. He lived, whenever he was at Monticello, and entirely for the last seventeen years of his life, in the midst of these young people, surrounded by them, his intercourse with them of the freest and most affectionate kind. How comes it that his immoralities were never suspected by his own family that his daughter and her children rejected with horror and contempt the charges brought against him? That my brother, then a young man certain to know all that was going on behind the scenes, positively declares his indignant disbelief in the imputations and solemnly affirms that he never saw or heard the smallest thing which could lead him to suspect that his grandfather's life was other than perfectly pure. His apartments had no private entrance not perfectly accessible and visible to all the household. No female domestic ever entered his chambers except at hours when he was known not to be there and none could have entered without being exposed to the public gaze. But again I would put it to any fair mind to decide if a man so admirable in his domestic character as Mr. Jefferson, so devoted to his daughters and their children, so fond of their society, so tender, considerate, refined in his intercourse with them, so watchful over them in all respects, would be likely to rear a race of half breeds under their eyes and carry on his low amours in the circle of his family.

Now many causes existed which might have given rise to suspicions, setting aside the inveterate rage and malice of Mr. Jefferson's traducers.

The house at Monticello was a long time in building and was principally built by Irish workmen. These men were known to have had children of whom the mothers were black women. But these women were much better pleased to have it supposed that such children were their master's. 'Le Czar m'a fait l'honneur de me faire cet enfant.' There were dissipated young men in the neighborhood who sought the society of the mulattresses and they in like manner were not anxious to establish any claim of paternity in the results of such associations.

One woman known to Mr. J.Q. Adams and others as 'dusky Sally' was pretty notoriously the mistress of a married man, a near relation of Mr. Jefferson's, and there can be small question that her children were his. They were all fair and all set free at my grandfather's death, or had been suffered to absent themselves permanently before he died. The mother, Sally Hemings, had accompanied Mr. Jefferson's younger daughter to Paris and was lady's maid to both sisters. Again I ask is it likely that so fond, so anxious a father, whose letters to his daughters are replete with tenderness and with good counsels for their conduct, should (when there were so many other objects upon whom to fix his illicit attentions) have selected the female attendant of his own pure children to become his paramour! The thing will not bear telling. There are such things, after all, as moral impossibilities.

The habit that the southern slaves have of adopting their master's names is another cause of misrepresentation and misapprehension. There is no doubt that such of Mr. Jefferson's slaves as were sold after his death would call themselves by his name. One very notorious villain who never had been the property of Mr. Jefferson, took his name and proclaimed himself his son. He was as black as a crow, and born either during Mr. Jefferson's absence abroad, or under some other circumstances which rendered the truth of his assertion simply impossible.

I have written thus far thinking you might chose to communicate my letter to Mr. Bulfinch. Now I will tell you in confidence what Jefferson told me under the like condition. Mr. Southall and himself being young men together, heard Mr. Peter Carr say with a laugh, that the old gentleman had to bear the blame of his and Sam's (Col. Carr) misdeeds.

There is a general impression that the few children of Sally Hemings were all the children of Col. Carr, the most notorious good-natured Turk that ever was master of a black seraglio kept at other men's expense. His deeds are as well known as his name. I have written in very great haste for I have very little time to write. We sat down sixteen at my brother's table to day, and are never less than twelve Children, grandchildren, visitors, friends I am in a perfect whirl. Yet this is the way in which I lived during all my girlish days, and then it seemed the easiest and most natural thing imaginable. Now I wonder how any head can bear it long. But Jefferson [her brother] and Jane [his wife] are the most affectionate parents and the kindest neighbors that I know.

[Signed]

The second part of the "Family Denial" is a letter from Henry S. Randall, reporting a conversation between himself and Thomas Jefferson Randolph in which Randolph stated that Peter Carr had fathered Sally Hemings's children. This letter was published in full in MILTON E. FLOWER, JAMES PARTON—THE FATHER OF MODERN BIOGRAPHY 236–39 (1951), and also printed in Fawn Brodie's biography of Jefferson: (In the original letter Hemings was spelled Henings.) And PBS's program, "Frontline: Jefferson's Blood" (5/2/2000), see http://www.pbs.org/wgbh/pages/frontline/shows/jefferson.

Dear Sir [to James Parton],
Courtland Village, N.Y. June 1, 1868

The "Dusky Sally Story"—the story that Mr. Jefferson kept one of his slaves, (Sally Henings) as his mistress and had children by her, was once extensively believed by respectable men, and I believe both John Quincy Adams and our own Bryant sounded their poetical lyres on this very poetical subject!

Walking about mouldering Monticello one day with Col. T. J. Randolph (Mr. Jefferson's oldest grandson) he showed me a smoke blackened and sooty room in one of the colonnades and informed me it was Sally Henings' room. He asked me if I knew how the story of Mr. Jefferson's connection with her originated. I told him I did not. "There was a better excuse for it, said he, than you might think: she had children which resembled Mr. Jefferson so closely that it was plain that they had his blood in their veins." He said in one case the resemblance was so close, that at some distance or in the dusk the slave, dressed in the same way, might have been mistaken for Mr. Jefferson. He said in one instance, a gentleman dining with Mr. Jefferson looked so startled as he raised his eyes from the latter to the servant behind him, that his discovery of the resemblance was so perfectly obvious to all. Sally Henings was a house servant and her children were brought up house servants that the likeness between master and slave was blazoned to all the multitudes who visited this political mecca.

Mr. Jefferson had two nephews, Peter Carr and Samuel Carr whom he brought up in his house. They were the sons of Jefferson's sister and her husband Dabney Carr, that young and brilliant orator described by Wirt, who shone so conspicuously in the dawn of the Revolution, but who died in 17–. Peter was peculiarly gifted and amiable. Of Samuel I know less. But he became a man of repute and sat in the State Senate of Virginia. Col. Randolph informed me that Sally Henings was the mistress of Peter, and her sister Betsey the mistress of Samuel and from these connections sprang the progeny which resembled Mr. Jefferson. Both the Hening girls were light colored and decidedly good looking. The Colonel said their connection with the Carrs was perfectly notorious at Monticello, and scarcely disguised by the latter never disavowed by them. Samuel's proceedings were particularly open. Col. Randolph informed me that there was not the shadow of suspicion that Mr. Jefferson in this or any other instance had commerce with female slaves. At the periods when these Carr children were born, he, Col. Randolph, had charge of Monticello. He gave all the general directions, gave out their clothes to the slaves, etc., etc. He said Sally Henings was treated, dressed, etc., exactly like the rest. He said Mr. Jefferson never locked the door of his room by day: and that he (Col. Randolph) slept within sound of his breathing at night. He said he had never seen a motion, or a look, or a circumstance which led him to suspect for an instant that there was a particle more of familiarity between Mr. Jefferson and Sally Henings than between him and the most repulsive servant in the establishment and that no person ever living at Monticello dreamed of such a thing. With Betsy Henings, whose children also resembled him, his habitual meeting, was less frequent and the chance of suspicion still less, and his connection with her was never indeed alleged by any of our northern politicians, or poets.

Col. Randolph said that he had spent a good share of his life closely about Mr. Jefferson at home and on journeys in all sorts of circumstances and he fully believed him chaste and pure as "immaculate a man as God ever created." Mr. Jefferson's oldest daughter Mrs. Gov. Randolph, took the Dusky Sally stories much to heart. But she never spoke to her sons but once on the subject. Not long before her death she called two of them the Colonel and George Wythe Randolph—to her. She asked the Colonel if he remembered "_____ Henings (the slave who most resembled Mr. Jefferson) was born." He said he could answer by referring to the book containing the list of slaves. He turned to the book and found that the slave was born at the time supposed by Mrs. Randolph. She then directed her son's attention to the fact that Mr. Jefferson and Sally Henings could not have met—were far distant from each other for fifteen months prior to such birth. She bade her sons remember this fact, and always to defend the character of their grandfather. It so happened when I was afterwards examining an old account book of Jefferson's I came pop on the original entry of this slaves birth: and I was then able from well known circumstances to prove the fifteen months separation—but those circumstances have faded from my memory. I have no doubt I could recover them however did Mr. Jefferson's vindication in the least depend upon them.

Colonel Randolph said that a visitor at Monticello dropped a newspaper from his pocket or accidentally left it. After he was gone, he (Colonel Randolph) noticed the paper and found some very insulting remarks about Mr. Jefferson's mulatto children. The Colonel said he felt provoked. Peter and Sam Carr were lying not far off under a shade tree. He took the paper and put it in Peters hands, pointing out the article. Peter read it, tears coursing down his checks, and then handed it to Samuel. Samuel also shed tears. Peter exclaimed "Ar'nt you and I a couple of pretty fellows to bring this disgrace on poor old uncle who has always fed us! We ought to be _____ by _____!"

I could give fifty more facts were there time and were there any need of it, to show Mr. Jefferson's innocence of this and all similar offenses against propriety.

I asked Col. R. why on earth Mr. Jefferson did not put these slaves who looked like him out of the public sight by sending them to his Befond [Bedford] estate or elsewhere. He said Mr. Jefferson never betrayed the least consciousness of the resemblance and although he (Col. Randolph) and he had no doubt his mother, would have been very glad to have them removed, that both and all venerated Mr. Jefferson too deeply to broach such a topic to him. What suited him, satisfied them. Mr. Jefferson was deeply attached to the Carrs especially to Peter. He was extremely indulgent to them and the idea of watching them for faults or vices probably never occurred to him.

Do you ask why I did not state, or at least hint the above facts in my Life of Jefferson? I wanted to do so, but Colonel Randolph, in this solitary case alone, prohibited me from using at my discretion the information he furnished me with. When I rather pressed him, on the point, he said, pointing to the family graveyard, "You are not bound to prove a negation. If I should allow you to take Peter Carr's corpse into Court and plead guilty over it to shelter Mr. Jefferson, I should not dare again to walk by his grave: he would rise and spurn me." I am exceedingly glad Col. Randolph did overrule me in this particular. I should have made a shameful mistake. If I had unnecessarily defended him (and it was purely unnecessary to offer any defense) at the expense of a dear nephew and a noble man hating a single folly.—

I write this currente calamo, and you will not understand that in telling what Col. Randolph and others said, I claim to give their precise language. I give it as I now recall it. I believe I hit at least the essential purport and spirit of it in every case.

Do you wonder that the above explanations were not made by Mr. Jefferson's friends when the old Federal Party were hurling their villanes at him for keeping a Congo Harem. Nobody could have furnished a hint of explanation outside the family. The secrets of an old Virginia Manor house were like the secrets of an Old Norman Castle. Dr. Dungleson, and Professor Tucker had lived years near Mr. Jefferson in the University and were often at Monticello. They saw what others saw. But Dr. D. told me that neither he nor Prof. T. ever heard the subject named in Virginia. An awe and veneration was felt for Mr. Jefferson among his neighbors which in their view, rendered it shameful to even talk about his name in such a connexion. Dr. D. told me that he never heard of Col. Randolph talking with anyone on the subject but me. But he said in his own secret mind he had always believed the matter stood just as Col. Randolph explained it to me.

You ask if I will not write a cheap Life of Jefferson of 600 pages, to go into families who will not purchase a larger work. I some years ago commenced such a condensed biography. I suspended the work when the storm of Civil War burst over the land. I have not again resumed it. I may yet do so hereafter—I have been strongly urged to the work by a prominent publishing house, and if I find time I may again mount my old hobby.

I must again express my regret that I cannot send you a fine autograph letter of Mr. Jefferson on some interesting topic but I am stripped down to those his family expected me to keep. But I send you some characteristic leaves—one from his draft of his Parliamentary Law.

Very truly yours,
Henry S. Randall

James Parton, Esq.

APPENDIX G[1]

APPENDIX B: OPINIONS OF SCIENTISTS CONSULTED

DR. KENNETH K. KIDD, PROFESSOR OF GENETICS, YALE UNIVERSITY, JANUARY 1999

I have read and thought about the article quite a bit. First, there is nothing wrong with the science. The markers on the Y are well documented and most have been studied in several hundred men. The male to male transmission is about as basic in mammalian biology as you can get. All of the authors that I know personally (less than half of them) are very reputable and I trust them. So, the only 'controversy' that exists is over the interpretation.

I think Eric Lander and Joseph Ellis in their News and Views commentary over-interpreted the results as proving that Jefferson was the father of Eston [emphasis added]; I think the actual authors are more correct when they consider other explanations 'unlikely.' What the data do prove, beyond any reasonable doubt, is that Thomas Jefferson and H21, a descendant of Eston Hemings, had Y chromosomes that were identical by descent. The Y chromosome data do not prove that Thomas Jefferson himself was the ancestor of H21, but that is certainly one of the likely specific scenarios within the 'identical by descent' family of explanations.

The term 'identical by descent' is standard population genetics terminology and means that the instances being considered, in this case the two Y chromosomes, Thomas Jefferson's and H21's, can be traced to a single common ancestral Y chromosome. That could be Thomas Jefferson's OR it could be an ancestor of Thomas Jefferson who was also an ancestor of H21. Obviously, the evidence favors Eston being the Great-Great Grandfather of H21 since there is no reason to question that lineage. Thus, the question becomes one of who Eston's father was. For example, J5, J12, J6, J13, and J14 look likely to have been alive and old enough to have fathered Eston and they have Y chromosomes identical by descent with Thomas Jefferson's. How many other male-line relatives of Thomas Jefferson were alive at that time? Did Thomas Jefferson II (Peter's and Field's father) have any brothers and/or any paternal uncles? One can go back this way to other male-line ancestors and then forward again among their male-line descendants to the relevant time. In sum, a male-line relative quite remotely related to President Thomas Jefferson would likely have the same Y chromosome as Jefferson. (For example, J41 and J49 are fifth cousins once removed and have the same Y chromosome.)

The data do prove that Thomas Woodson was not the son of Thomas Jefferson or any close male-line relative of Jefferson. The Carr brothers are also excluded from being fathers of Eston or Thomas Woodson. Thus, as with modern day paternity testing, we can prove a man is/was not the father, but we cannot absolutely prove a man is/was the father.

So, the proof ultimately rests on demonstrating that Thomas Jefferson was present at the time Eston was conceived and that no other male relative with the same Y chromosome was hiding in the bushes. This is something I have no knowledge of, but some of the people there at Monticello probably do know a lot in this area of history. Obviously, this can all get very sensitive if people get emotionally or personally involved. I personally think the simplest answer is that Jefferson was the father of Eston. He may have been the father of all of Sally Hemings's children except Thomas Woodson, and she may have thought that Jefferson was the father of Thomas Woodson as well.

'A comment about the statistics. There is fair uncertainty in the exact numbers that should be used because it is very difficult to estimate accurately a small number. But, it is clear that the specific Y chromosome pattern is rare—it was not seen elsewhere in a sample of over 600 European men. Thus, the authors are right when they say these results for H21 are at least 100 times more likely if Thomas Jefferson is Eston's father than if someone unrelated [to Jefferson] was the father. As noted above, however, that statement says 'unrelated' and J5, J6, etc. are all related. It is also correct to say 'these results for H21 are at least 100 times more likely if

Thomas Jefferson's cousin J5 [or J6 or J12 or . . .] is Eston's father than if someone unrelated [to the Jeffersons] was the father.'

One final comment. I notice that the pattern for the Woodson descendants is very similar to the pattern for the Carrs. It would not take many mutations to convert one into the other. That makes it possible that John Carr and Thomas Woodson had fathers who were male-line relatives within a few generations. That could just mean that their fathers came from the same town or county back in Europe since I do not know how common these particular allelic combinations are in Europe (England?).

APPENDIX H

REBUTTAL OF THE JOHN HARTWELL COCKE LETTERS
TJMF REPORT, SEPTEMBER 11, 2000

ASSESSED BY JEFFERSON FAMILY HISTORIAN, HERBERT
BARGER, DR. E. A. FOSTER'S DNA STUDY ASSISTANT

Much emphasis has been placed upon the two John Hartwell Cocke letters on pages 13 and 14 of the Thomas Jefferson Memorial Foundation Report. Proponents of the Thomas Jefferson–Sally Hemings liaison are always quick to point out that even Mr. Jefferson's great friend and one of the founding officials of the University of Virginia, Mr. Cocke, also accused Mr. Jefferson of fathering children by Sally Hemings. It must be remembered that Mr. Cocke never charged Mr. Jefferson with Callender's rumors and Campaign Lies while Jefferson was alive but he wished to make sure Mr. Jefferson was not around.

In the case of these two letters, one written 27 years after Mr. Jefferson's death and the other 33 years after his death, are general statements originally discussing the overall "institution" of fathering illegitimate slave children and cited some instances.

1853: The January 26, 1853 letter (pg. 13), tells of Rev. Lemuel Hatch informing him of two wealthy friends of Virginia sending away from their premises a slave woman who had a number of illegitimate children of the "INSTITUTION," defined in the dictionary as "an established practice." We might ask, is this not in reference to the "institution of slavery," not a reference and indictment of any one individual. He further states, "A "SAMPLE" of the moral and social blessing of the "INSTITUTION" (institution of slavery). NOTE: As a preacher he is against this "institution" and may possibly be anti-Jefferson as were many of the clergy of that era, because of his insistence on the separation of state and religion. He next says, "I can enumerate a score of such cases in our beloved Ant. Dominion (Virginia) that have come in my way thro' life, they would be found by hundreds—nor is it to be wondered at . . . when Mr. Jefferson's notorious 'EXAMPLE' is considered." Please note: Yes, the mulattos can be found everywhere, but does he (the Rev. Hatch), actually know who fathered them or was it just a result of the "institution" and generally accepted, expected and yes sometimes rumored in the press and especially of someone in the limelight and politically connected? He goes on to say it was sustained by other such dignitaries of the Republic. While the monstrous doctrine, finds men in other respects respectable, who assert that slavery is a moral, social, and political blessing.

As we can see, a preacher is giving John Hartwell Cocke, who wrote it in his journal, his opinion of slavery and cites instances of what are the results of "this institution of slavery." In no way did the Reverend Hatch state that Thomas Jefferson (himself) fathered a Hemings child, he was merely speaking of "the institution of slavery." Many in the year 1853 remembered the charges spread by James T. Callender's article of September 1802 naming Thomas Jefferson the father of Sally's child, Tom "Hemings" Woodson . . . DNA testing eliminated (on two separate tests) any connection of the Woodson and Jefferson descendants' DNA.

1859: The April 23, 1859 letter (pg. 14), tells of a rich planter, Mr. Nixon, a bachelor, building a splendid mansion and lived with a mulatto girl. The defenders of "THE INSTITUTION" (meaning slave-owners, one of which was Jefferson as we all know), omit to look at the future,—that all bachelors—or a large majority—at least—keep as a substitute for a wife—some individual of their own slaves. NOTE: This is not news and we know it went on, but how can Mr. Cocke say first, all then change it to or a large majority (sounds like the headlines of today to grab attention). Now he proceeds to involve Mr. Jefferson by stating, "In Virginia, this damnable practice prevails as much as anywhere—and probably more— as Mr. Jefferson's example can be () for its defense." What is he saying? He is merely saying that the practice of slavery is probably more prevalent in Virginia and that "all or a large majority of bachelors engage in this practice." Yes, we all know about the numerous mulattos at Monticello of which he is referring to. However, he has not accused Thomas Jefferson of personally fathering a Sally Hemings child. Remember that accusation goes back to James T. Callender's . . . article of 1802, which has been proven by DNA to be a lie. Please read all the revealing Callender articles compiled by Dr. & Mrs. James McMurry. Callender was most unkind in his references to Sally Hemings and had never seen or met her, she was just being slandered because he wished to "get" Thomas Jefferson. These Callender accusations, complete with the same misspelling of the name, "Wales," which should be "Wayles," and other thoughts, are just repeated in the article of Pike County, Ohio by Madison Hemings, son of Sally Hemings, who NEVER stated that his mother TOLD HIM these accusations. They were just stated in the reporter's words in the article.

1840: Something even more revealing about General John Hartwell Cocke comes to us from a book/manuscript by Lucius Manlius Sargent, "Reminiscences of Lucius Manlius Sargent," a leather-bound type written, privately printed book. He wrote it sometime before his death in 1867. Mr. Sargent describes his father, a staunch Federalist and his grief at the death of George Washington. After describing the scene (which took place in Boston), Mr. Sargent notes, "In the spring of 1840 (Barger notes: well before the 1853 and 1859 letters mentioned above), when I related this anecdote to my friend, Gen. Cocke, in Richmond, Va. he observed, that the people of the North cherished the memory of Washington, much more gracefully, than those of the South; and added, that no persons had done more to injure his reputation, than two Virginians, Jefferson & Randolph." SO we can see that Gen. John Hartwell Cocke, now political enemy and FORMER friend of Jefferson, had a reason as early as 1840 to paint Mr. Jefferson in a bad light and proceeded to do so in those two letters cited by TJMF as "proof of some kind of truth." It was no more than a further assignation of Mr. Jefferson's character, NOT first hand statements of fact that Jefferson fathered any Hemings child.

Historian Andrew Burstein writing in his 2005 book, "Jefferson's Secrets," (five years after my above rebuttal of 2000), states that he (Cocke), felt antagonistic toward Jefferson's undemanding Unitarianism, a feeling that had built over decades. Even the week of Jefferson's death, brought a suggestion from a friend, that they might want to lobby for a replacement for Jefferson on the university's Board of Visitors who better satisfied the "friends of Religion." And here comes the clincher, Burstein states, "So we cannot, without pause, consider Cocke an unimpeachable observer on the subject of Thomas Jefferson's private conduct." Yes, in the earlier founding days of the University of Virginia they were friends but "reli-gion" changed all that we can see. So now it was time for Cocke to throw in some old rumors that James Callender had written as part of his Cam-paign Lies against Jefferson in 1802 . . . Callender's lies were forever put to rest when DNA indicated there was NO DNA match between Jefferson DNA and Woodson DNA. This was where Mr. John Hartwell Cocke had gotten his rumors of a Thomas-Sally liaison. Mr. Burstein then remarks, "Certainly he knew the content of the Callender articles, as a young adult, out of college and newly married when they were published." Mr. Burstein further states that Cocke does not indicate how he knows firsthand of Jef-ferson's complicity in race mixing . . . whether he even [saw] Sally or the Hemings children.

Herbert Barger
Jefferson Family Historian
Assisted Dr. Foster on the DNA Study

ENDNOTES

PREFACE

1. Eyler Robert Coates, Sr., ed., "Research Report on the Jefferson-Hemings Controversy," *The Jefferson-Hemings Myth: An American Travesty*, 76.

2. The Hemings, as other slaves at Monticello, were referred to as "servants"—none were ever called "slaves." Elizabeth Langhorne, *Monticello: A Family Story*, 17.

3. Dr. Wallenborn is an M.D. in Charlottesville, Virginia. Dr. Wallenborn graduated from the University of Virginia School of Medicine in 1955 and served as flight surgeon and Aircraft Accident Investigator with both the Air Force and FAA. He served on the Otolaryngology—Head and Neck Surgery faculty for thirty-four years before retiring as clinical professor in 1994. Dr. Wallenborn was employed as a Guide at Monticello for five years and served on the DNA Study committee at Monticello. He wrote the dissenting report. Wallenborn is also a member of the Thomas Jefferson Chapter of the Sons of the American Revolution. See Report of the Research Committee on Thomas Jefferson and Sally Hemings, Thomas Jefferson Memorial Foundation, January 2000, 10. The report is available at www.monticello.org.

4. Herbert Barger is a Jefferson Family Historian, whose wife is a lineal descendant of Thomas Jefferson's uncle, Field Jefferson. It was Barger's authoring of *The Jefferson Family of Virginia* that led to his assisting Dr. E. A. Foster with the Jefferson-Hemings DNA Study. Barger has researched and compiled four family genealogical books including, *The Jefferson Family of Virginia* on file at Monticello. Barger served for over twenty-seven years as a

career member of the military services, his last six years being in the position as Audio-Visual Superintendent at Headquarters, U.S. Air Force, at the Pentagon. During WWII Mr. Barger served in the infantry in Italy.

5. Professor D'Entremont, History Department, Randolph Macon woman's college, Forum, 1998, C-SPAN Radio.

6. In a modern *civil* trial, the burden of proof is by a "preponderance of the evidence," that is "the greater weight of the evidence. Greater weight of the evidence means the more persuasive and convincing force and effect of the entire evidence in the case." In a *criminal* trial, the burden of proof is much higher: One must prove an accused guilty by and to the exclusion of "every reasonable doubt." Reasonable doubt "is not a mere possible doubt, a speculative, imaginary or forced doubt. Such a doubt must not influence you to return a verdict of not guilty if you have an abiding conviction of guilt. On the other hand, if, after carefully considering, comparing and weighing all the evidence, there is not an abiding conviction of guilt, or, if, having a conviction, it is one which is not stable but one which wavers and vacillates, then the charge is not proved beyond every reasonable doubt and you must find the defendant not guilty because the doubt is reasonable. It is to the evidence introduced in this trial, and to it alone, that you are to look for that proof. A reasonable doubt as to the guilt of the defendant may arise from the evidence, conflict in the evidence or the lack of evidence. If you have a reasonable doubt, you should find the defendant not guilty. If you have no reasonable doubt, you should find the defendant guilty." Florida Criminal Jury Instructions. WestLaw Online, July 30, 2008. I will attempt to meet, and exceed, *both* burdens of proof in Jefferson's defense.

7. John C. Miller, "Slavery," in Merrill Peterson, ed., *Thomas Jefferson: A Reference Biography*, 428.

8. Winthrop Jordan, "Hemings and Jefferson Redux," in Jan Lewis and Peter S. Onuf, eds., *Sally Hemings and Thomas Jefferson: History, Memory, and Civic Culture*, 44–45 (letter from Jefferson to William Short, quoted in *White Over Black: American Attitudes Toward the Negro, 1550–1812* by Winthrop Jordan, 467).

9. Gore Vidal, *Inventing a Nation*, 36.

10. Gloria R. Polites, "Thomas Jefferson: Family Man," *Cobblestone*, September 1989, 39–40 (a letter from Jefferson to his grandson, Francis Eppes).

11. David McCullough, "History in Danger," *Parade Magazine*, June 22, 2008, 11.

12. George Will, "The Last Word," *Newsweek*, August 11, 2008, 64.

INTRODUCTION

1. Eyler Robert Coates, Sr., ed., "Introduction," *The Jefferson-Hemings Myth: An American Travesty*.

2. James Madison is now the target of a recent DNA allegation; see "Trying to Prove Link to a Noted Forefather Woman Has Been Working to Show Kinship to Madison," Jonathan Mummolo, *Washington Post* Staff Writer Sunday, August 24, 2008, C01—"It's been four years since Bettye Kearse set out to prove a story that has been handed down through generations of her family: that she, an African American, is a direct descendant of founding father James Madison. But after a prolonged attempt to arrange DNA testing with Madison family descendants in the United States, the two sides have been unable to agree on how to do it. . . . According to stories told by Kearse's family, Madison fathered a child named Jim with her great-great-great-great-grandmother, a slave cook named Coreen. Kearse, sixty-five, has no documentation to bolster the claim, so in 2004, she enlisted the help of geneticist Bruce Jackson to investigate."

3. David N. Mayer, "The Thomas Jefferson–Sally Hemings Myth and the Politicization of American History, Individual Views of David N. Mayer, Concurring with the Majority Report of the Scholars Commission on the Jefferson-Hemings Matter," April 9, 2001, http://www.ashbrook.org/articles/mayer-hemings.html; Report of the Research Committee on Thomas Jefferson and Sally Hemings, Thomas Jefferson Memorial Foundation, January 2000, 10. The report is available at www.monticello.org; see Thomas Jefferson Heritage Society, Report of the Scholars Commission on the Jefferson-Hemings Matter, April 12, 2001, 6, 2. This report is available at www.tjheritage.org. The members of the Scholars Commission were Lance Banning of the University of Kentucky (political history and history of ideas); James Ceaser of the University of Virginia (political science); Robert H. Ferrell of Indiana University (diplomatic history); Charles R. Kesler of Claremont McKenna College (political science, history of ideas); Alf J. Mapp, Jr., of Old Dominion University (Jefferson biographer and Virginia historian); Harvey C. Mansfield, Jr., of Harvard University (political science, political theory, government, and history of ideas); David N. Mayer of Capital University (constitutional history, history of ideas); Forrest McDonald of the University of Alabama (constitutional history, political history, history of ideas); Paul Rahe of the University of Tulsa (history of ideas and classical history); Thomas Traut of the University of North Carolina (biology and medicine); Robert F. Turner of the University of Virginia Law

School (law, diplomacy, government); Walter E. Williams (economics and journalism); and Jean Yarborough of Bowdoin College (history of ideas, political history, political science, government).

4. Virginius Dabney, *The Jefferson Scandals: A Rebuttal*, 15.

5. Hamilton W. Pierson, "Jefferson at Monticello: The Private Life of Thomas Jefferson," in James A. Bear, Jr., ed., *Jefferson at Monticello*, 25, 99.

6. A male son of Thomas Jefferson's died as a two-week old infant in 1777.

7. Merrill Peterson, ed., *Thomas Jefferson: A Reference Biography*, 429.

8. John H. Works, Jr., "Foreword," in Eyler Robert Coates, Sr., ed., *The Jefferson-Hemings Myth: An American Travesty*, 9–10. As a side note, Jefferson's descendants are entitled to burial in the Monticello cemetery. An organization of descendants called the Monticello Association (which is not affiliated with the Thomas Jefferson Foundation) controls the half-acre burial site and has resisted calls that the Hemingses and their descendants be allowed into the Monticello graveyard. In April 2002 the Association issued its own report into the matter suggesting that a separate cemetery be created at Monticello, out of the land owned by the TJF, for the descendants of all of Monticello's slaves and artisans. The Association met in Charlottesville in early May 2002 to vote on the proposal. The TJHS's John H. Works, a former president of the Monticello Association, criticized the proposal because he feared that the lines between the two cemeteries "would blur" over time and lead to "a graveyard of Jefferson's descendants, real and imagined." On May 5, 2002, the Monticello Association voted by a margin of 74–6 to deny the descendants of Sally Hemings the right to join the Association and to be buried at the Monticello graveyard. They also voted against creating a separate burial site for Monticello's slaves. "Jefferson's Heirs Plan Cemetery for Slave's Kin at Monticello," *New York Times*, April 21, 2002; Leef Smith, "Monticello's Theories of Relativity," *Washington Post*, May 4, 2002, B1; Leef Smith, "Jefferson Group Bars Kin of Slave," *Washington Post*, May 6, 2002, B1. John H. Works had been concerned about the implications of the misleading DNA testing for the membership of the Monticello Association. On December 23, 1999, he wrote a lengthy letter to the membership of the Association to oppose the admission of the Hemings descendants to the Monticello Association. He argued that there was no legal, scientific, or historical basis for their admission to the group. "John H. Works to the Monticello Association, December 23, 1999," www.monticello-assoc.orgljhw-Letter.htm.

9. Dr. Foster passed away on July 21, 2008.

10. Joseph Ellis, *William and Mary Quarterly*, January 2000, 130.

11. Joseph Ellis, "Money and that Man from Monticello," *Reviews in American History*, 23, 588.

12. David Murray, "Anatomy of a Media Run Away," in Eyler Robert Coates, Sr., ed., *The Jefferson-Hemings Myth: An American Travesty*, 38–39; *William and Mary Quarterly*, January 2000, 129.

13. Jefferson-Hemings Scholar report, Conclusion.

14. Cynthia Burton, "Exploration of the Record Pinpoints Enormous Gaps," *Richmond Times-Dispatch*, January 14, 2007, E1.

15. *Ibid.*

16. David N. Mayer gives a tangible name to this heated Jefferson-Hemings debate: "Presentism." The term wrongly presumes that the historical past can be judged by the contemporary standards of the present.

17. David Dubuisson, "Revisiting the Thomas Jefferson–Sally Hemings Story," *Greensboro News & Record*, July 29, 2001, H3.

18. Virginius Dabney, *The Jefferson Scandals: A Rebuttal*, 6.

19. Scot A. French and Edward L. Ayers, "The Strange Career of Thomas Jefferson: Race and Slavery in American Memory," in Peter S. Onuf, ed., *Jeffersonian Legacies*, 418–56, 431.

1. JAMES CALLENDER:
"HUMAN NATURE IN A HIDEOUS FORM"

1. Douglass Adair, "The Jefferson Scandals," in Trevor Colbourn, ed., *Fame and the Founding Fathers: Essays by Douglass Adair*, 227–73, 240.

2. Dumas Malone, *Jefferson the President*, 212.

3. Andrew Burstein, *Jefferson's Secrets*, 160.

4. "Mudslinging isn't what it used to be," *St. Petersburg Times*, October 24, 2008, 15A, reprinted from the *Washington Post* (no author cited).

5. Andrew Burstein, *Jefferson's Secrets*, 227.

6. Rebecca L. McMurry and James F. McMurry, Jr., "The Origins of the 'Sally' Story," in Eyler Robert Coates, Sr., ed., *The Jefferson-Hemings Myth: An American Travesty*, 16.

7. Rebecca L. McMurry and James F. McMurry, *Jefferson, Callender and the Sally Story*, 7; Robert M. S. MacDonald, "Race Sex and Reputation: Thomas Jefferson and the Sally Hemings Story," *Southern Cultures* 4, Summer 1998, 48.3; James Callender, *Richmond Recorder*, September 1, 1802 quoted in Michael Durey, *With the Hammer of Truth*, 157–60; *Richmond Recorder*, September 1, 1802, October 20, 1802. The relevant extracts have been reprinted in Jan Ellen Lewis and Peter S. Onuf, eds., *Sally Hemings and Thomas Jefferson: History, Memory, and Civic Culture*, 259–61.

8. Michael Knox Beran, *Jefferson's Demons*, 158.

9. Andrew Burstein, *The Inner Jefferson: Portrait of a Grieving Optimist*, 227.

10. Letter from Thomas Jefferson to James Monroe, May 26, 1800, in Barbara B. Oberg, ed., *The Papers of Thomas Jefferson, 1800–1801*, 590.

11. Letter from James Callender to James Madison, April 27, 1801, in William T. Hutchinson and William M. E. Rachal, eds., *The Papers of James Madison: Secretary of State Series, 1800–1801*, 117.

12. See Michael Durey, *With the Hammer of Truth*, 146–47 (quoting Meriwether Jones).

13. Nathan Schachner, *Thomas Jefferson: A Biography*, 678.

14. Letter from James Monroe to James Madison, June 6, 1801, in William T. Hutchinson and William M. E. Rachal, eds., *The Papers of James Madison: Secretary of State Series, 1800–1801*, 244–45; William G. Hyland Jr. and William G. Hyland, "A Civil Action: Hemings v. Jefferson," *American Journal of Trial Advocacy*, 2007, vol. 31:1.

15. Andrew Burstein, *The Inner Jefferson: Portrait of a Grieving Optimist*, 227.

16. Rebecca L. McMurry and James F. McMurry, *Anatomy of a Scandal*, 69, 75–76; Henry Adams, *History of the United States of America During the Administration of Thomas Jefferson*, 221.

17. Rebecca L. McMurry and James F. McMurry, *Anatomy of a Scandal*, 70.

18. Christopher Hitchens, *Thomas Jefferson*, 65; Henry Adams, *History of the United States of America During the Administration of Thomas Jefferson*, 220–21.

19. Henry Adams, *History of the United States of America During the Administration of Thomas Jefferson*, 220.

20. Fawn M. Brodie, *Thomas Jefferson: An Intimate History*, 350.

21. Winthrop Jordan, *White Over Black: American Attitudes Toward the Negro, 1550–1812*, 461–69.

22. David McCullough, *John Adams*, 580; Joseph J. Ellis, *American Sphinx: The Character of Thomas Jefferson*, 261, 365, 260. Another major study of Jefferson's character that appeared in the mid-1990s, Andrew Burstein's *The Inner Jefferson: Portrait of a Grieving Optimist*, also cast doubt on the Hemings-Jefferson relationship.

23. David McCullough, *John Adams*, 584.

24. *Ibid.*, 577.

25. Merrill Peterson, *Thomas Jefferson and the New Nation*, 711; John C. Miller, "Slavery," in Merrill Peterson, ed., *Thomas Jefferson: A Reference Biography*, 429.

26. Andrew Burstein, *The Inner Jefferson: Portrait of a Grieving Optimist*, 229; Douglass Adair, "The Jefferson Scandals," in Trevor Colbourn, ed., *Fame and the Founding Fathers: Essays by Douglass Adair*, 227–73, 233.

27. Letter from Jefferson to William A. Burwell, 1808, available at http://etext.lib.virginia.edu/etcbin/foleyx-browse?id=Lies.

28. Letter from Jefferson to Dr. George Logan, June 20, 1816, in Paul Leicester Ford, ed., *The Works of Thomas Jefferson,* "Federal Edition"; Douglass Adair, "The Jefferson Scandals," in Trevor Colbourn, ed., *Fame and the Founding Fathers: Essays by Douglass Adair*, 227–73, 234.

29. B. L. Rayner, *Life of Thomas Jefferson*, 299.

30. E-text of Jefferson letters, Alderman Library, http://etext.virginia .edu/etcbin/ot2www-singleauthor?specfile=/web/data/jefferson/texts/jefall .o2w&act=text&offset=5423832&textreg=2&query=abigail+adams, letters Jefferson, Thomas, 1743–1826, Merrill D. Peterson, ed.

31. B. L. Rayner, *Life of Thomas Jefferson*, 298.

32. Frank J. Klingberg, et al. eds., *The Correspondence between Henry Stephens Randall and Hugh Blair Grigsby 1856–1861*, 39 (Grigbsy to Randall, February 19, 1856); Cynthia Burton, *Jefferson Vindicated: Fallacies, Omissions, and Contradictions in the Genealogical Search*, 35.

33. Henry Adams, *History of the United States of America During the Administration of Thomas Jefferson*, 220–21; letter from Jefferson to R. R. Livingston, October 10, 1802, in Paul Leicester Ford, ed., *The Works of Thomas Jefferson*, iv, 448.

34. John C. Miller, "Slavery," in Merrill Peterson, ed., *Thomas Jefferson: A Reference Biography*, 429.

35. Willard Sterne Randall's interview on John McLaughlin's *One on One*, PBS television broadcast, November 6, 1998.

36. Andrew Burstein, *Jefferson's Secrets: Death and Desire at Monticello*, 117.

37. Eyler Robert Coates, Sr., ed., *The Jefferson-Hemings Myth*, 19; Michael Durey, *With the Hammer of Truth,* 171; Dumas Malone, *Jefferson the President: 1805–1809*, 212.

2. MISLEADING DNA

1. Dr. Eugene Foster in remarks on February 1, 1999 at Randolph Macon woman's college, Forum on the DNA Study, C-SPAN Radio.

2. Lucian K. Truscott IV, "Children of Monticello," *American Heritage Magazine*, February/March 2001, vol. 52, issue 1, http://www.american heritage.com/articles/magazine/ah/2001/1/2001_1_50.shtml.

3. Margalit Fox, *New York Times*, October 15, 2006, http://www.nytimes .com/2006/10/15/us/15bennett.html?pagewanted=print. Mrs. Bennett died of kidney failure on Oct. 7, 2006, at her home in Arlington, Virginia. She was seventy-one.

4. John H. Works, Jr., "A Primer on Jefferson DNA," in Eyler Robert Coates, Sr., ed., *The Jefferson-Hemings Myth: An American Travesty*, 35–36.

5. Byron Woodson, *A President in the Family*, Foreword.

6. Chain of custody is used to establish that the object is in substantially the same condition as it was at the time at issue. Some objects that are vulnerable to intentional alteration, or items that are susceptible to undetected contamination or deterioration, such as blood samples, require that a chain of custody be established to prove that there has been no alteration during custody. *Rabovsky v. Com.*, 973 S.W.2d 6, 77 A.L.R.5th 711 (Ky. 1998). Blood tests inadmissible due to lack of chain of custody where samples transferred and stored within hospital and at two different outside laboratories.

7. "Frontline: Jefferson's Blood," PBS television broadcast, May 2, 2000, (transcript on file at http://www.pbs.org/wgbh/pages/frontline/shows/ jefferson/etc/script.html).

8. John H. Works, Jr., "A Primer on Jefferson DNA," in Eyler Robert Coates, Sr., ed., *The Jefferson-Hemings Myth: An American Travesty*, 35–36, 30.

9. Herbert Barger, Jefferson family historian, personal interview with Author, April 2007 and June 10, 2008; taped interview with Mrs. Bennett at her home in Arlington, Virginia, 1999.

10. *Ibid.*; Correspondence from Barger to Author, July 2008.

11. William Branigin, *Washington Post*, January 4, 2000; reprinted in the *Boston Globe*, January 4, 2000, A09.

12. Eyler Robert Coates, Sr., "Research Report on the Jefferson-Hemings Controversy: A Critical Analysis," in Eyler Robert Coates, Sr., ed., *The Jefferson-Hemings Myth: An American Travesty*, 90.

13. Eugene A. Foster, "In Jefferson-Hemings Tie, a Family's Pride; Tenable Conclusions," *New York Times*, November 9, 1998, A24.

14. Correspondence from Dr. Eugene Foster to Herbert Barger. "From: EAFOSTER@aol.com To: <herbar@erols.com>, Sent: Wednesday, November 11, 1998 10:00 PM, Subject: reply to today's"; From: <EAFOSTER@. . . . , To: <herbar@. . . . Sent: Wednesday, November 11, 1998 10:00 PM, Subject: reply to today's . . .

15. Willard Sterne Randall's interview on John McLaughlin's *One on One*, PBS television broadcast, November 6, 1998.

16. See Steven T. Corneliussen, "Sally Hemings, Thomas Jefferson, and the Authority of Science," www.tjscience.org/HemingsTJscience.htm.

17. Dr. Edwin M. Knights, Jr., "Genealogy and GENETICS: Marital Bliss or Shotgun Wedding," *Family Chronicle,* March/April 2003, 20.

18. Dr. Eugene Foster, "Which Jefferson was the Father?," *Science,* www .sciencemag.org.

19. 509 U.S. 579 (1993). Although it is true that the Virginia Supreme Court has not adopted all the features of *Daubert* as the controlling test in Virginia, the court has noted that "[p]rior to *Daubert* . . . [it] discussed the trial court's role in making a threshold finding of scientific reliability when unfamiliar scientific evidence is offered." *John v. Im*, 559 S.E.2d 694, 698 n.3 (Va. 2002) (citations omitted).

20. William G. Hyland Jr. and William G. Hyland, "A Civil Action: Hemings v. Jefferson," *American Journal of Trial Advocacy*, vol. 31:1, 2007, 33.

3. SALLY HEMINGS AND RANDOLPH JEFFERSON: "THE UNKNOWN BROTHER"

1. Taped interview by Herbert Barger, March 29, 2000, conducted at The Colonnades Retirement Home, Charlottesville, Virginia.

2. Virginius Dabney, *The Jefferson Scandals: A Rebuttal*, 120; see Annette Gordon-Reed, *The Hemingses of Monticello*; see Annette Gordon-Reed, *Thomas Jefferson and Sally Hemings: An American Controversy*.

3. Isaac Jefferson, "Memoirs of a Monticello Slave," in James A. Bear, Jr. ed., *Jefferson at Monticello*, 3, 4 [hereinafter: *Jefferson at Monticello*]; Cynthia Burton, *Jefferson Vindicated: Fallacies, Omissions, and Contradictions in the Hemings Genealogical Search*, 134–36.

4. Rebecca McMurry and James McMurry, *Anatomy of a Scandal,* 101.

5. Official Monticello Web site, http://www.monticello.org/plantation/ hemingscontro/hemings-jefferson_contro.html.

6. This evidence is debatable, and discussed more thoroughly. Some historians dispute that Wayles was Sally's father, pointing out that Wayles was sick the last two years of his life. Moreover, Sally was born at Guines Plantation, a hard three days trip from Wayles's home, "The Forest." Wayles died several months before Sally's actual birth, See Rebecca McMurry, *Anatomy of a Scandal*, 24–25.

7. Douglass Adair, "The Jefferson Scandals," in Trevor Colbourn, ed., *Fame and the Founding Fathers: Essays by Douglass Adair*, 247.

8. *Jefferson at Monticello*, 4; Jon Kukla, *Mr. Jefferson's Women*, 120.

9. Lucia Cinder Stanton, *Free Some Day*, 106; Elizabeth Langhorne, *Monticello: A Family Story*, 182; John Hemings, Betty's son had been apprenticed to Jefferson's principal builder, James Dinsmore, and became a master builder and cabinet maker. Joe Fossett, son of Mary Hemings, was Monticello's blacksmith, who had learned his trade from William Stewart, see Langhorne, 182.

10. Donald Jackson, *A Year at Monticello: 1795*, 91–92.

11. Annette Gordon-Reed, *Thomas Jefferson and Sally Hemings: An American Controversy*, 209 (noting that Sally Hemings was listed as white); Thomas Jefferson Memorial Foundation, Statement on the TJMF Committee Report on Thomas Jefferson and Sally Hemings, January 2000, 30; Report of the Research Committee on Thomas Jefferson and Sally Hemings, Thomas Jefferson Memorial Foundation, January 2000, 10. The report is available at www.monticello.org. http://www.monticello.org/plantation/hemingscontro/jefferson-hemings_report.pdf [hereinafter: Report] noting that Sally Hemings was listed as a "free person of color."

12. Jon Kukla, *Mr. Jefferson's Women*, 121.

13. Annette Gordon-Reed, *Thomas Jefferson and Sally Hemings: An American Controversy*, 209, 240.

14. Andrew Burstein, *The Inner Jefferson: Portrait of a Grieving Optimist*, 3; Edwin M. Betts and James A. Bear, Jr., eds., *The Family Letters of Thomas Jefferson*, Preface.

15. "Maria's maid produced a daughter about a fortnight ago, and is doing well"; Jefferson to John Wayles Eppes, December 21, 1799, UVA, quoted in Lucia Cinder Stanton, *Free Some Day*, 113.

16. Cynthia Burton, *Jefferson Vindicated: Fallacies, Omissions, and Contradictions in the Hemings Genealogical Search*, 21.

17. Lucia Cinder Stanton, *Free Some Day*, 103–104.

18. Cynthia Burton, *Jefferson Vindicated: Fallacies, Omissions, and Contradictions in the Hemings Genealogical Search*, 21.

19. Douglass Adair, "The Jefferson Scandals," in Trevor Colbourn, ed., *Fame and the Founding Fathers: Essays by Douglass Adair*, 227–73, 265.

20. Christopher Hitchens, *Thomas Jefferson*, 2.

21. Henry S. Randall, *The Life of Thomas Jefferson*, 544–55.

22. Sarah N. Randolph, *The Domestic Life of Thomas Jefferson*, 429.

23. Andrew Burstein, *The Inner Jefferson: Portrait of a Grieving Optimist* 265.

24. *Ibid.*, 271.

25. Cynthia Burton, *Jefferson Vindicated: Fallacies, Omissions, and Contradictions in the Hemings Genealogical Search*, 54; Thomas Jefferson Deposition, Buckingham Co. Court, September 15, 1815, Jefferson Papers at UVA, microfilm.

26. *Ibid.*, 54.

27. *Ibid.*, 57.

28. Katt Henry, *Cavalier Daily*, April 25, 2007, interview with Cynthia Burton. Charlottesville genealogist at http://www.cavalierdaily.com/CVArticle_print.asp?ID=29556&pid1557.

29. *Jefferson at Monticello*, 22 (referring to himself in the first person).

30. Forrest McDonald, *The Presidency of Thomas Jefferson*, 31.

31. Merrill Peterson, *Thomas Jefferson: A Reference Biography*, xii.

32. Andrew Burstein, *The Inner Jefferson: Portrait of a Grieving Optimist*, 21–22.

33. Cynthia Burton, *Jefferson Vindicated: Fallacies, Omissions, and Contradictions in the Hemings Genealogical Search*, 52–53. Burton's book is the most thoroughly detailed book I have researched concerning Jefferson's younger brother, Randolph.

34. Ellen Randolph to Jefferson, April 21, 1808, and Martha Jefferson Randolph to Jefferson, January 30, 1808, in Edwin M. Betts and James A. Bear, Jr., eds., *The Family Letters of Thomas Jefferson*; Cynthia Burton, *Jefferson Vindicated: Fallacies, Omissions, and Contradictions in the Hemings Genealogical Search*, 53.

35. Bernard Mayo and James Bear, Jr., eds., *Thomas Jefferson and His Unknown Brother*, 21.

36. *Ibid.*

37. Eyler Robert Coates, Sr. ed., *The Jefferson-Hemings Myth: An American Travesty*, 91.

38. Mr. Coates was the Head Librarian, Shenandoah College, Winchester, Virginia (1969–74) and Section Head (Supervisor), DBPH, Library of

Congress (1974–78). He designed the Web site, Thomas Jefferson on Politics & Government, adopted by the University of Virginia.

39. Media release by Herbert Barger, Jefferson Family Historian, on February 6, 2006 in e-mail from Barger to Author, June 2008.

40. Cynthia Burton, *Jefferson Vindicated: Fallacies, Omissions, and Contradictions in the Hemings Genealogical Search*, 60.

41. TJMF Report at http://www.monticello.org/plantation/hemingscontro/appendixd.html; Report of the Research Committee on Thomas Jefferson and Sally Hemings, Thomas Jefferson Memorial Foundation, January 2000, 10. The report is available at www.monticello.org.

42. Cynthia Burton, *Jefferson Vindicated: Fallacies, Omissions, and Contradictions in the Hemings Genealogical Search*, 52–70.

43. J. H. Battle, *The History of Todd Co., Ky.*, 296.

44. Herbert Barger personal interview with Author, Charlottesville, June 10, 2008; correspondence May 28, 2008.

45. Eyler Robert Coates, Sr., ed., *The Jefferson-Hemings Myth: An American Travesty*, 96.

46. Monticello Committee Report, Appendix J; Report of the Research Committee on Thomas Jefferson and Sally Hemings, Thomas Jefferson Memorial Foundation, January 2000, 10. The report is available at www.monticello.org.

47. Herbert Barger, "The Jefferson-Hemings DNA Study," in Eyler Robert Coates, Sr., ed., *The Jefferson-Hemings Myth: An American Travesty*, 34.

48. Rebecca L. McMurry and James F. McMurry, *Jefferson, Callender and the Sally Story*, iii; Eyler Robert Coates, Sr., ed., *The Jefferson-Hemings Myth: An American Travesty*, 94.

49. Mia Bay, "In Search of Sally Hemings in the Post-DNA Era," *Reviews in American History*, December 2006, fn 19.

50. Lucia Cinder Stanton, *Free Some Day*, 115; Jack McLaughlin, *Jefferson and Monticello: Biography of a Builder*, 122—according to Isaac, John Hemings's father was "an Englishman named Nelson" who was a carpenter who worked on the original Monticello house and was identified by Isaac as "an inside worker, a finisher"; also see, Elizabeth Langhorne, *Monticello: A Family Story*, 76: "Martin, Betty Hemings's son by a black father before her connection with John Wayles, was also a trained coachman."

51. Herbert Barger, "The Jefferson-Hemings DNA Study," in Eyler Robert Coates, Sr., ed., *The Jefferson-Hemings Myth: An American Travesty*, 35.

52. http://www.unc.edu/depts/uncspeak/pdfs/Traut_Karyn.pdf.

53. http://gazette.unc.edu/archives/02may22/morestories.html; Online Gazette, The Faculty/Staff Online Newspaper of the University of North Carolina at Chapel Hill, May 22, 2002.

4. "AN AMERICAN IN PARIS"

1. Jon Kukla, *Mr. Jefferson's Women*, 64.

2. Jack McLaughlin, *Jefferson and Monticello: Biography of a Builder*, 198; Jon Kukla, *Mr. Jefferson's Women*, 82.

3. Andrew Burstein, *Jefferson's Secrets*, 12; see also Burstein, *The Inner Jefferson*.

4. *Ibid.*; Walter Kirn with reporting by Andrea Dorfman, "Life, Liberty and the Pursuit of Thomas Jefferson," *Time*, July 5, 2004; taped interview Frank Berkeley, March 29, 2000, with Herbert Barger.

5. David McCullough, *John Adams*, 313.

6. Merrill Peterson, ed., *Thomas Jefferson: Writings*, 46; Jan Kukla, *Mr. Jefferson's Women*, 63, 67.

7. E. M. Halliday, *Understanding Thomas Jefferson*, 29.

8. Winthrop Jordan, "Hemings and Jefferson Redux," in Jan Lewis and Peter S. Onuf, eds., *Sally Hemings and Thomas Jefferson: History, Memory, and Civic Culture*, 43.

9. Sarah N. Randolph, *The Domestic Life of Thomas Jefferson*, 44; Claude G. Bowers, *The Young Jefferson*, 47.

10. Merrill Peterson, *Thomas Jefferson and the New Nation*, 27.

11. Jon Kukla, *Mr. Jefferson's Women*, 67.

12. Elizabeth Langhorne, *Monticello: A Family Story*, 24.

13. Letter from Jefferson to Francis Eppes, August 30, 1785, in Julian P. Boyd et. al, *The Papers of Thomas Jefferson*, vol. XV, 621–22, vol. VIII, 451; Edwin M. Betts and James A. Bear, Jr., eds., *The Family Letters of Thomas Jefferson*, 5.

14. Edwin M. Betts and James A. Bear, Jr., eds., *The Family Letters of Thomas Jefferson*, 5–7; Lucia Cinder Stanton, *Free Some Day*, 108; Sarah N. Randolph, "Mrs. Thomas Mann Randolph," in Mrs. O. J. Wister and Miss Agness Irwin, eds., *Worthy Women of Our First Century*, 16, 17, 23.

15. Letter from Abigail Adams to Thomas Jefferson, June 27, 1787, in Lester J. Cappon, ed., *The Adams-Jefferson Letters*, 179.

16. Letter from Abigail Adams to Thomas Jefferson, July 6, 1787, in Lester J. Cappon, ed., *The Adams-Jefferson Letters*, 183.

17. William Howard Adams, *The Paris Years of Thomas Jefferson*, 222.

18. David McCullough, *John Adams*, 322.

19. Mia Bay, "In Search of Sally Hemings in the Post-DNA Era," *Reviews in American History*, December 2006, fn 32.

20. Lucia Cinder Stanton, *Free Some Day*, 109.

21. James A. Bear, Jr., and Lucia Stanton eds., *Jefferson's Memorandum Books: Accounts, with Legal Record and Miscellany, 1767–1826*, 749–71 [hereinafter: *Memorandum Books*].

22. Report at 53; Report of the Research Committee on Thomas Jefferson and Sally Hemings, Thomas Jefferson Memorial Foundation, January 2000, 10. The report is available at www.monticello.org.

23. Report at app. K.; Report of the Research Committee on Thomas Jefferson and Sally Hemings, Thomas Jefferson Memorial Foundation, January 2000, 10. The report is available at www.monticello.org.

24. Lucia Cinder Stanton, *Free Some Day*, 110.

25. *Ibid.*

26. Edwin Morris Betts, ed., *Thomas Jefferson's Farm Book*, 7.

27. Dumas Malone, *Jefferson the President*, 185; Jack McLaughlin, *Jefferson and Monticello: Biography of a Builder*, 142.

28. Fawn M. Brodie, *Thomas Jefferson: An Intimate History*, 233.

29. *Memorandum Books*, 729–34; Jon Kukla, *Mr. Jefferson's Women*, 121.

30. Lucia Cinder Stanton, *Free Some Day*, 112.

31. Fawn M. Brodie, *Thomas Jefferson: An Intimate History*, 292, 435; Edwin Morris Betts, ed., *Thomas Jefferson's Farm Book*, 130.

32. Fawn M. Brodie, *Thomas Jefferson: An Intimate History*, 475; "Last Will of Thomas Jefferson," in Eyler Robert Coates, Sr., ed., *The Jefferson-Hemings Myth: An American Travesty*, 192.

33. Richard E. Dixon, "The Case Against Thomas Jefferson: A Trial Analysis of the Evidence on Paternity," in Eyler Robert Coates, Sr., ed., *The Jefferson-Hemings Myth: An American Travesty*, 151.

34. Douglass Adair, "The Jefferson Scandals," in Trevor Colbourn, ed., *Fame and the Founding Fathers: Essays by Douglass Adair*, 227–73.

35. *Ibid.*

36. Claude G. Bowers, *The Young Jefferson*, 25.

37. Jon Kukla, *Mr. Jefferson's Women*, 121.

5. TIMING AND CONCEPTION

1. Gore Vidal, *Inventing a Nation*, 82.

2. Virginius Dabney, *The Jefferson Scandals: A Rebuttal*, 27–28. According to Dr. Wallenborn, Jefferson's records and Madison Hemings's account only show five children born to Sally. Lucia Cinder Stanton, Monticello historian, tried to make a case for a sixth child. She references a casual comment by Jefferson in a letter to a friend that said Maria's maid had a child (1797) a fortnight ago. In 1797, Betsy Hemings (not Sally) was Maria's maid.

3. Winthrop Jordan, *William and Mary Quarterly*, 3rd series, vol. 55, no. 2, April 1998, 318, 316–318.

4. Winthrop Jordan, "Hemings and Jefferson Redux," in Jan Lewis and Peter S. Onuf, eds., *Sally Hemings and Thomas Jefferson: History, Memory, and Civic Culture*, 41.

5. See Edwin Morris Betts, ed., *Thomas Jefferson's Farm Book*.

6. There were no eyewitness accounts that Sally was in a pregnant state when she returned to the United States from Paris.

7. Report at app. H.; Report of the Research Committee on Thomas Jefferson and Sally Hemings, Thomas Jefferson Memorial Foundation, January 2000, 10. The report is available at www.monticello.org.

8. *Ibid.*

9. *Ibid.*

10. Eppington was the home of Elizabeth Wayles Eppes (half sister to Jefferson's wife), located on the Appomattox River in southern Chesterfield County.

11. Edwin M. Betts and James A. Bear, Jr., eds., *The Family Letters of Thomas Jefferson*, 232.

12. Elizabeth Langhorne, *Monticello: A Family Story*, 259.

13. *Ibid.*, 258–59. Some historians have disputed that this "Sally" was Sally Hemings, since Jefferson owned three slaves with the name Sally.

14. Cynthia Burton, *Jefferson Vindicated: Fallacies, Omissions, and Contradictions in the Hemings Genealogical Search*, 23.

15. Report at 24 (citing Edwin Morris Betts, ed., *Thomas Jefferson's Farm Book*, 130); Report of the Research Committee on Thomas Jefferson and Sally Hemings, Thomas Jefferson Memorial Foundation, January 2000, 10. The report is available at www.monticello.org.

16. *Jefferson at Monticello*, 4.

17. Report at app. H.; Report of the Research Committee on Thomas Jef-

ferson and Sally Hemings, Thomas Jefferson Memorial Foundation, January 2000, 10. The report is available at www.monticello.org.

18. Joyce Appleby, *Thomas Jefferson*, 72–73.

19. Edwin M. Betts and James A. Bear, Jr., eds., *The Family Letters of Thomas Jefferson*; William G. Hyland Jr. and William G. Hyland, "A Civil Action: Hemings v. Jefferson," *American Journal of Trial Advocacy*, vol. 31:1, 2007, 22.

20. *Ibid.*

21. Media release by Herbert Barger, Jefferson Family Historian, in e-mail from Barger to Author, February 6, 2006.

22. Fraser D. Neiman, "Coincidence or Causal Connection? The Relationship between Thomas Jefferson's Visits to Monticello and Sally Hemings's Conceptions," *William and Mary Quarterly*, vol. 57, 2000, 198–211.

23. Correspondence to Author, July 21, 2008.

24. David Murray, "Present at the Conception," in Eyler Robert Coates, Sr., ed., *The Jefferson-Hemings Myth: An American Travesty*, 119; Fraser D. Neiman, "Coincidence or Causal Connection? The Relationship between Thomas Jefferson's Visits to Monticello and Sally Hemings's Conceptions," *William and Mary Quarterly*, vol. 57, 2000, 198–211.

25. Dr. White McKenzie Wallenborn, Thomas Jefferson Foundation, DNA Study Committee, Minority Report, April 12, 1999. Dr. Wallenborn's minority report was added to the Monticello Web site in March 2000, three months after the majority report was released to the public. Although the tone of his minority report is balanced, Dr. Wallenborn is much more outspoken in his criticism of the research committee and its methods in White McKenzie Wallenborn, M.D., "A Committee Insider's Viewpoint," Eyler Robert Coates, Sr., ed., *The Jefferson-Hemings Myth: An American Travesty*, 55–68. Dr. Daniel P. Jordan, the president of the Thomas Jefferson Foundation, asked Lucia C. Stanton, the Shannon Research Historian at Monticello, to prepare a response to Wallenborn's criticisms. Her Response to the Minority Report was submitted in April 2000.

26. Cynthia Burton, "Exploration of the Record Pinpoints Enormous Gaps," *Richmond Times-Dispatch*, January 14, 2007, E1.

27. David N. Mayer, "The Thomas Jefferson–Sally Hemings Myth and the Politicization of American History," John M. Ashbrook Center for Public Affairs, Ashland University, www.ashbrook.org. This paper is available through a link at the TJHS Web site, www.tjheritage.org. Mayer, V. PART B—"The TJMF Monticello Report"; Dr. White McKenzie Wallenborn, "A

Committee Insider's Viewpoint," in Eyler Robert Coates, Sr., ed., *The Jefferson-Hemings Myth: An American Travesty*, 53.

28. Lucia Cinder Stanton, *Free Some Day,* 107.

29. David N. Mayer, "The Thomas Jefferson–Sally Hemings Myth and the Politicization of American History," John M. Ashbrook Center for Public Affairs, Ashland University, www.ashbrook.org. This paper is available through a link at the TJHS Web site, www.tjheritage.org. Mayer, V. PART B—"The TJMF Monticello Report"; Letter from Henry S. Randall to James Parton, June 1, 1868, in Milton E. Flower, *James Parton: The Father of Modern Biography*, 237–38.

30. Steven T. Corneliussen, *Richmond Times-Dispatch*, on February 25, 2007, 2:07; Fraser D. Neiman, "Coincidence or Causal Connection? The Relationship between Thomas Jefferson's Visits to Monticello and Sally Hemings's Conceptions," *William and Mary Quarterly*, vol. 57, 2000, 198–211.

31. Steven T. Corneliussen, "Sally Hemings, Thomas Jefferson, and the Authority of Science Whether or not Hemings and Jefferson had children together, misreported DNA and misused statistics have skewed the paternity debate, discrediting science itself," http://www.tjscience.org/HemingsTJscience.htm.

32. *Ibid.*

33. *Ibid.*

34. *Ibid.*

35. *Ibid.*

36. *Ibid.*

37. *Ibid.*

6. CARR BROTHERS AND OTHER MALE JEFFERSONS

1. Merrill Peterson, ed., *Thomas Jefferson: A Reference Biography*, 429.

2. Thomas J. Randolph. Draft Letters, c. 1874, UVA, Alderman Library, 8937; Cynthia Burton, *Jefferson Vindicated: Fallacies, Omissions, and Contradictions in the Hemings Genealogical Search*, 86.

3. Donald Jackson, *A Year at Monticello: 1795*, 95–96.

4. Letter from Ellen Coolidge to Joseph Coolidge, October 24, 1958, in Eyler Robert Coates, Sr., ed., *The Jefferson-Hemings Myth: An American Travesty*, 196.

5. Annette Gordon-Reed, *Thomas Jefferson and Sally Hemings: An American Controversy*, 254–55.

6. Fawn M. Brodie, *Thomas Jefferson: An Intimate History*, 496. As an aside, in a modern-day trial, the defendants would undoubtedly file a "third

party" complaint against the Carr brothers and possibly Jefferson's own brother, Randolph.

7. David N. Mayer, "The Thomas Jefferson–Sally Hemings Myth and the Politicization of American History, Individual Views of David N. Mayer, Concurring with the Majority Report of the Scholars Commission on the Jefferson-Hemings Matter," April 9, 2001, http://www.ashbrook.org/articles/mayer-hemings.html; Thomas Jefferson Randolph letter, c. 1874, UVA, 238.

8. In a civil trial, this is the burden of proof, by the "greater weight of the evidence."

9. Taped interview with Frank Berkeley by Herbert Barger conducted March 29, 2000 at The Colonnades Retirement Home, Charlottesville, Virginia; Francis Lewis Berkeley, Jr., was the University of Virginia's archivist and professor emeritus. Berkeley, who retired in 1974, was cited numerous times for his outstanding service to the library, in particular his efforts to develop and enrich its manuscript resources. An Albemarle County native, Berkeley received his bachelor's and master's degrees from UVA. He joined the faculty in 1938 as the University's first curator of manuscripts. Berkeley also helped to create the principal documentary publications of the new press, The Papers of James Madison and The Papers of George Washington. As curator, Berkeley devised a cataloguing system based on the British Museum's Catalogue of Additional Manuscripts, and he began the creation of a central archives for the University. Berkeley received the Raven Society Award in 1973 for distinguished service to the University. He served for twenty-nine years on the board of Monticello.

10. Bernard Mayo and James Bear, Jr., eds., *Thomas Jefferson and His Unknown Brother*, 8–9.

11. Ellen Wayles Coolidge to Joseph Coolidge, October 25, 1858, Acc 9090, ViU; Cynthia Burton, *Jefferson Vindicated: Fallacies, Omissions, and Contradictions in the Hemings Genealogical Search*, 63.

12. Interview with Herbert Barger, (stating "the official Thomas Jefferson Foundation Monticello Report lists Randolph Jefferson's sons and specifically Thomas Jefferson, Jr., as being schooled at Monticello in 1799, 1800 and possibly in 1801 (all three dates coincide with Sally's three children conceptions). However . . . the study group's assessment was that these Jefferson boys, at ages 16, 17 and 20 were too young."); Report of the Research Committee on Thomas Jefferson and Sally Hemings, Thomas Jefferson Memorial Foundation, January 2000, 10. The report is available at www.monticello.org.

13. Cynthia Burton, *Jefferson Vindicated: Fallacies, Omissions, and Contradictions in the Hemings Genealogical Search*, 61–63.

14. *Ibid.*, 63–65.

15. Monticello Household Accounts, DLC; Cynthia Burton, *Jefferson Vindicated: Fallacies, Omissions, and Contradictions in the Hemings Genealogical Search*, 64.

7. JEFFERSON'S DECLINING HEALTH

1. David McCullough, *John Adams*, 451.

2. John T. Morse, Jr., *Thomas Jefferson*, 5; the most thorough discussion of Jefferson's health can be found in Cynthia Burton's book, *Jefferson Vindicated*.

3. Author Cynthia Burton, in her book, *Jefferson Vindicated*, has superbly detailed Jefferson's health in explicit detail through correspondence and Jefferson's own health records, pp. 40–46.

4. See Edwin M. Betts and James A. Bear, Jr., eds., *The Family Letters of Thomas Jefferson*; Cynthia Burton, *Jefferson Vindicated: Fallacies, Omissions, and Contradictions in the Hemings Genealogical Search*, 40.

5. Katt Henry, *Cavalier Daily*, April 25, 2007, interview with Cynthia Burton. Charlottesville genealogist at http://www.cavalierdaily.com/CVArticle_print.asp?ID=29556&pid1557.

6. Sarah N. Randolph, *The Domestic Life of Thomas Jefferson*, 232–33; transcript of Jefferson to James Madison, April 27, 1795; Letter from Jefferson to Thomas Mann Randolph, January 31, 1796; DLC.

7. Alan Pell Crawford, *Twilight at Monticello*, 76.

8. Gore Vidal, *Inventing a Nation*, 81.

9. Alan Pell Crawford, *Twilight at Monticello*, 124.

10. Alan Pell Crawford, "Thomas Jefferson survives 'Equality, unalienable rights—and a duality,' FINAL YEARS WERE ONES OF HOPE, DISAPPOINTMENT," *Free Lance-Star*, February 3, 2008.

11. *Ibid.*

12. *Ibid.*

13. David McCullough, *John Adams*, 322.

14. Jon Kukla, *Mr. Jefferson's Women*, 127–28; Letter from Jefferson to Madison, June 9, 1793, *Jefferson Papers*, 26:240.

15. Sam Hodges, "Paternity dispute: Professors lock horns over Jefferson," *Mobile Register*, March 11, 2001, B01.

16. John T. Morse, *Thomas Jefferson*, 6.

17. David McCullough, *John Adams*, 145.

18. Jon Kukla, *Mr. Jefferson's Women*, 17.

19. Gary L. Cohen, M.D., and Loren A. Rolak, M.D., "Thomas Jefferson's Headaches: Were They Migraines?" *Headache: The Journal of Head and Face Pain*, vol. 46, issue 3, March 2006, 492–97.

20. Jon Kukla, *Mr. Jefferson's Women*, 35.

21. Gary L. Cohen, M.D., and Loren A. Rolak, M.D., "Thomas Jefferson's Headaches: Were They Migraines?" *Headache: The Journal of Head and Face Pain*, vol. 46, issue 3, March 2006, 492–497.

22. Merrill D. Peterson, *Thomas Jefferson and the New Nation*, 348.

23. Fawn M. Brodie, *Thomas Jefferson: An Intimate History*, 243.

24. B. John Melloni, *Melloni's Illustrated Medical Dictionary*, 3rd ed., 50; WEB MD at http://www.webmd.com/migraines-headaches/guide/migraines -headaches-basics.

25. Gary L. Cohen, M.D., and Loren A. Rolak, M.D., "Thomas Jefferson's Headaches: Were They Migraines?" *Headache*, March 2006, 492–97.

26. Gore Vidal, *Inventing a Nation*, 10.

27. Cynthia Burton, *Jefferson Vindicated*, 40–41.

28. Letter from Jefferson to Monroe, March 18, 1785, DLC (Papers, VIII, 43); Letter from Jefferson to William Dunbar, January 12, 1801, DLC; Cynthia Burton, *Jefferson Vindicated*, 41.

29. Letter from Jefferson to William Thornton, February 14, 1801, William Thornton Papers, vol. 3, no. 395, DLC.

30. Letter from Dr. Robert Patterson to Jefferson, rec'd July 14, 1807, Massachusetts Historical Society, Boston; Letter from Jefferson to Ellen Wayles Randolph, October 25, 1808, MHi; Letter from Martha Jefferson Randolph, October 27, 1808, ViU.

31. WEB MD at http://www.webmd.com/rheumatoid-arthritis/guide/ rheumatoid-arthritis-basics.

32. Cynthia Burton, *Jefferson Vindicated*, 42.

33. Donald Jackson, *A Year at Monticello: 1795*, 90; Letter from Washington to Jefferson, October 4, 1795, in John C. Fitzpatrick, ed., *The Writings of George Washington, from the Original Manuscript Sources, 1745–1799*, 34:325.

34. Cynthia Burton, *Jefferson Vindicated*, 42–43.

35. Dr. Jan Duvoisin, M.D., Anesthesiologist, in correspondence to Author, June 30, 2008.

36. *Ibid.*

37. Andrew Burstein, *The Inner Jefferson: Portrait of a Grieving Optimist*, 264.

38. Cynthia Burton, *Jefferson Vindicated*, 44.

39. Dumas Malone, *Jefferson the President*, 186–88.

40. Cynthia Burton, *Jefferson Vindicated*, 43–44.

41. Dumas Malone, *Jefferson the President*, 188; Letter from Henry Dearborne to Thomas Jefferson, August 15, 1802, DLC.

42. David McCullough, *John Adams*, 319.

43. Cynthia Burton, *Jefferson Vindicated*, 42.

44. *Ibid.*, 45

45. *Ibid.*, 46.

46. *Ibid.*, 40.

47. *Ibid.*, 46.

48. Joseph J. Ellis, *American Sphinx: The Character of Thomas Jefferson*, 273–74, 365, 260. Another major study of Jefferson's character that appeared in mid-1990, Andrew Burstein's *The Inner Jefferson: Portrait of a Grieving Optimist*, also cast doubt on the Hemings-Jefferson relationship.

49. Joseph J. Ellis, *American Sphinx: The Character of Thomas Jefferson*, 233, 365, 260.

50. Dumas Malone, *The Sage of Monticello*, xxi–xxii.

51. Frank Beardsley, "The Making of a Nation—Thomas Jefferson, Part 9 (The Last Days)," broadcast January 8, 2004, http://www.manythings .org/voa/04/040108mn_t.htm.

52. Dumas Malone, *The Sage of Monticello*, 458–59; Letter from Alexander Garrett to J. H. Cocke, June 18, 1825, Cooke-Shields Papers, UVA.

53. Dumas Malone, *The Sage of Monticello*, 458–59.

54. *Ibid.*, 496.

55. *Ibid.*

56. *Ibid.*, 497.

57. Cynthia Burton, *Jefferson Vindicated*, 42, n. 40, and pp. 40–42; see also Andrew A. Lipscomb and Albert E. Bergh, eds., *The Writings of Thomas Jefferson*, 296.

58. Cynthia Burton, *Jefferson Vindicated*, n. 40, and pp. 40–42; see also Massachusetts Historical Society, Microfilm; Letter from Jefferson to Edmund Randolph, September 7, 1794, DLC.

59. Cynthia Burton, *Jefferson Vindicated*, 42, n. 40, and pp. 40–42; Herbert Barger, "Why did Sally become pregnant only when Thomas Jefferson was at Monticello?" unpublished manuscript; see also Andrew A. Lipscomb and Albert E. Bergh, eds., *The Writings of Thomas Jefferson*; MHi-Massachusetts Historical Society, Boston, Massachusetts.

60. Andrew Burstein, *Jefferson's Secrets*, 19; Letter from Jefferson to Dr. Benjamin Waterhouse, January 8, 1825, in Paul L. Ford, ed., *The Works of Thomas Jefferson*.

8. THE SCHOLARS COMMISSION AND THE CHARACTER ISSUE

1. Interview, PBS *NewsHour*, November 2, 1998.

2. The members of the Scholars Commission were: Lance Banning, Professor of History, University of Kentucky; James Ceaser, Professor of Government and Foreign Affairs, University of Virginia.; Charles R. Kesler, Professor of Government, Claremont McKenna College Professor; Alf J. Mapp, Jr., Eminent Scholar, Emeritus and Louis I. Jaffe Professor of History, Emeritus, Old Dominion University Professor; Harvey C. Mansfield, William R. Kenan, Jr., Professor of Government, Harvard University; David N. Mayer, Professor of Law and History, Capital University; Professor Forrest McDonald, Distinguished Research Professor of History, Emeritus, University of Alabama; Thomas Traut, Professor of Biochemistry and Biophysics, School of Medicine, University of North Carolina; Robert F. Turner, (Chairman) University of Virginia Professor; Walter E. Williams, Professor of Economics, George Mason University; and Jean Yarbrough, Professor of Political Science Bowdoin College.

3. Winthrop Jordan, "Hemings and Jefferson Redux," in Jan Lewis and Peter S. Onuf, eds., *Sally Hemings and Thomas Jefferson: History, Memory, and Civic Culture*, 44–51; see Scholars Commission Report.

4. Sam Hodges, "Paternity disputed Scholars: No proof Jefferson fathered slave's children," *Mobile Register*, April 13, 2001.

5. *Ibid.*

6. *Ibid.*

7. *Ibid.*

8. Professor Joshua D. Rothman received his Ph.D. at the University of Virginia in 2000 and studied under the tutelage of History Professor Peter Onuf, an ardent and high-profile paternity believer.

9. Sam Hodges, "Paternity disputed Scholars: No proof Jefferson fathered slave's children," *Mobile Register*, April 13, 2001; personal interview with Author, Tuscaloosa, Alabama, July 19, 2008.

10. Sam Hodges, "Paternity disputed Scholars: No proof Jefferson fathered slave's children," *Mobile Register*, April 13, 2001.

11. David Dubuisson, "Revisiting the Thomas Jefferson–Sally Hemings Story," *Greensboro News & Record*, July 29, 2001.

12. *Ibid.*

13. Professor Willard Sterne Randall resigned from the commission before the report was issued.

14. Lisa Jones, "Author tracks history mystery," *Burlington Free Press*, October 9, 2000, infoweb@newsbank.com.

15. *Ibid.*

16. William Branigin, "Pruning Thomas Jefferson's Family Tree Historians' Report Attacks Theory That 3rd President Fathered Slave's Children," *Washington Post*, April 13, 2001, B3.

17. Final Report of The Jefferson-Hemings Scholars Commission, April 12, 2001 [in part], FOR THE MAJORITY: LANCE BANNING, Professor of History, University of Kentucky. Professor Banning formerly held the John Adams Chair in American History at the University of Groningen in the Netherlands. Two of his award winning books (*The Jeffersonian Persuasion* and *Jefferson and Madison*) were nominated for the Pulitzer Prize in History. JAMES CEASER, Professor of Government and Foreign Affairs, University of Virginia. Professor Ceaser is the author of *Reconstructing America* and has taught at Harvard, the University of Montesquieu, the University of Basel, and Marquette. He is the author or editor of more than forty books; and was described as "the dean of American presidential historians" by the *Chicago Sun-Times*. CHARLES R. KESLER, Professor of Government, Claremont McKenna College Professor. Kesler is Director of the Henry Salvatori Center at Claremont McKenna College and former chairman of its Department of Government. He has written extensively on the American founding and American political thought, and is coeditor of a widely used edition of *The Federalist Papers*. ALF J. MAPP, JR., Eminent Scholar, Emeritus, and Louis I. Jaffe Professor of History, Emeritus, Old Dominion University. Professor Mapp is the author of *Thomas Jefferson: A Strange Case of Mistaken Identity*. A reference source for *Encyclopedia Britannica* and *World Book*, his numerous awards include Commonwealth of Virginia Cultural Laureate and a medal from the Republic of France's Comité Français du Bicentenaire de l'Indépendence des États Unis. HARVEY C. MANSFIELD, William R. Kenan, Jr., Professor of Government, Harvard University. A former Guggenheim Fellow and National Endowment for the Humanities Fellow, he served as President of the New England Political Science Association and on the Council of the American Political Science Association. DAVID N. MAYER, Professor of Law and History, Capital University. Professor Mayer holds both a law degree and a Ph.D. in history, and is the author of *The Constitutional Thought of Thomas Jefferson*. FORREST MCDONALD, Distinguished Research Professor of History, Emeritus, University of Alabama. Professor McDonald has also taught at Brown and was the James Pinckney Harrison Professor of History at the College of William & Mary. His many awards and prizes include Thomas Jefferson Lecturer with the National Endowment for the Humanities. THOMAS TRAUT, Professor of Biochemistry and Biophysics, School of

Medicine, University of North Carolina. Professor Traut is Director of Graduate Studies and a former Ford Foundation and National Institute of Health Fellow. He is the author or coauthor of more than seventy publications. ROBERT F. TURNER, (Chairman) University of Virginia Professor. Turner holds both professional and academic doctorates from the University of Virginia School of Law, and is a former Charles H. Stockton Professor of International Law at the U.S. Naval War College and a Distinguished Lecturer at West Point. A former president of the congressionally established U.S. Institute of Peace, he has had a strong professional interest in Jefferson for three decades. WALTER E. WILLIAMS, Professor of Economics, George Mason University. Professor Williams is Chairman of the Department of Economics at George Mason University and the author of half a dozen books. He is a nationally syndicated columnist. JEAN YARBROUGH, Professor of Political Science, Bowdoin College. Professor Yarbrough is former Chair of the Department of Government and Legal Studies at Bowdoin and a National Endowment for the Humanities Bicentennial Fellow. She has lectured at the International Center for Jefferson Studies, is a consultant to the Jefferson Papers project, and serves on the editorial board of both the *Review of Politics* and *Polity*.

18. *Ibid.*

19. Henry Kissinger, *Diplomacy*, 32; For the origins of the character defense see Sarah N. Randolph, *The Domestic Life of Thomas Jefferson*, and Edwin Morris Betts and James Adam Bear, eds., *The Family Letters of Thomas Jefferson*.

20. Dumas Malone, *Jefferson and His Time, Volume Four: Jefferson the President, First Term, 1801–1805*, 214; Cynthia Burton, *Jefferson Vindicated*, 168.

21. John T. Morse, *Thomas Jefferson*, 145.

22. Douglass Adair, "The Jefferson Scandals," in Trevor Colbourn, ed., *Fame and the Founding Fathers: Essays by Douglass Adair*, 227–73.

23. Taped interview with Frank Berkeley by Herbert Barger, March 29, 2000.

24. Merrill Peterson, *Thomas Jefferson and the New Nation*, 709–11.

25. Letter from Thomas Jefferson to William Burwell, November 22, 1808, in Paul L. Ford ed., *The Works of Thomas Jefferson*, 78.

26. Cynthia Burton, *Jefferson Vindicated*, 138.

27. Walter Kirn, with reporting by Andrea Dorfman, "From Life, Liberty and the Pursuit of Thomas Jefferson," *Time*, July 5, 2004.

28. Letter from Ellen Randolph Coolidge to Joseph Coolidge, October 24, 1858, Coolidge Collection, UVA Library; For the origins of the character defense among Jefferson's descendants see Sarah N. Randolph, *The Domestic*

Life of Thomas Jefferson, and Edwin Morris Betts and James Adam Bear, eds., *The Family Letters of Thomas Jefferson*.

29. Letter from Jefferson to William Short, October 31, 1819, in Merrill D. Peterson, ed., *Jefferson's Writings*, 1432–33.

30. Taped interview with Frank Berkeley by Herbert Barger, March 29, 2000.

31. James Parton, *The Life of Thomas Jefferson*, 569.

32. *Ibid.*

33. John T. Morse, *Thomas Jefferson*, 157–58.

34. *Ibid.*, 157.

35. *Ibid.*, 157–58.

36. *Ibid.*, 223.

37. Henry S. Randall, *The Life of Thomas Jefferson*, 20–21.

38. See Dumas Malone, *Jefferson and His Time* (six-volume work chronicling the early life of Thomas Jefferson through his first years as president).

39. Merrill Peterson, *The Jefferson Image in the American Mind*, 186.

40. Dumas Malone, *Jefferson the President, First Term, 1801–1805*, 494.

41. *Ibid.*, 526.

42. Henry S. Randall, *The Life of Thomas Jefferson*, 477.

43. Douglass Adair, "The Jefferson Scandals," in Trevor Colbourn, ed., *Fame and the Founding Fathers: Essays by Douglass Adair*, 176, 227–73.

44. *Ibid.*, 181, 227–73.

45. *Ibid.*, 227–73.

46. *Ibid.*

47. Andrew Burstein, *The Inner Jefferson: Portrait of a Grieving Optimist*, xii.; Winthrop Jordan, "Hemings and Jefferson Redux," in Jan Lewis and Peter S. Onuf, eds., *Sally Hemings and Thomas Jefferson: History, Memory, and Civic Culture*, 46.

9. MADISON HEMINGS: GOSSIP AND HEARSAY

1. Judith Justus, *Down from the Mountain*, 79.

2. Madison was the second son, but only if we exclude Thomas Woodson from the mix.

3. Dumas Malone, *Jefferson the Virginian*, 496.

4. "Life among the Lowly, No. 1," *Pike County* (Ohio) *Republican*, March 13, 1873, reprinted in Annette Gordon-Reed, *Thomas Jefferson and Sally Hemings: An American Controversy*, 245–48; Herbert Barger, Jefferson Family Historian, states "that the use of an identical title was owned by Harriet Beecher, and possible copyright infringement. If so, then she and Wetmore must have been partners in this smear. We know they were both great abolitionists." Interview with Herbert Barger, Jefferson Family Historian, in Charlottesville, Virginia, and Washington, D.C., April and June 2007.

5. *Ibid.*

6. *Ibid.*

7. Cynthia Burton, *Jefferson Vindicated*, 145–46.

8. *Ibid.*

9. *Ibid.* According to Herbert Barger, Jefferson Family Historian:

The most glaring Madison/Wetmore lie is that Madison claims that he was named for James Madison by Dolley Madison on the date of his birth, January 19, 1805 while she was visiting Monticello. The Madison Papers indicate that the Madisons never left Washington for Virginia during the winter. Just imagine this scenario: Dolley announces to her Secretary of State husband, Mr. Madison, and to Mr. Jefferson, for whom she acts as Hostess that she has heard that a "male" slave is to be born (never mind that this was well before the sex of a child could be determined), to one of Mr. Jefferson's slaves and she must be present to name him after her husband. Never mind the hazardous winter route without support of these two important people left back in Washington. For extra measure Madison says she reneges on a promised present to his mother, thus fanning the flames of further resentment between the races. NOTE: This Pike County article was used by Annette Gordon-Reed and the Monticello in-house Jefferson-Hemings DNA Study to cite "truthful and believable" information from a son of Sally Hemings. We cannot believe anything gained from this article. The article was "torn apart" by the competing newspaper, The Waverly Watchman just five days later. Among other things stated in the article was, "The fact that Hemings claims to be the natural son of Jefferson does not convince the world of its truthfulness."

Interview with Herbert Barger, Jefferson Family Historian (quoting John A. Jones, Editorial, *Waverly Watchman*, March 18, 1873).

10. Virginius Dabney and Jon Kukla, "The Monticello Scandals: History and Fiction," *Virginia Cavalcade*, 29, Autumn 1979, 52–61.

11. Willard Sterne Randall's interview on John McLaughlin's *One on One*, PBS television broadcast, November 6, 1998.

12. William G. Hyland Jr., *Law Review, Hemings v. Jefferson.*

13. Edwin Morris Betts, ed., *Thomas Jefferson's Garden Book.*

14. Edwin Morris Betts, ed., *Thomas Jefferson's Farm Book*, xx, xvi.

15. "Monticello: A 40-year fixer-upper," *Times-Courier,* September 16, 2000.

16. David McCullough, *John Adams*, 314.

17. Ludwell H. Johnson, *Fort Sumter and Confederate Diplomacy*, 26 J. S. Hist. 441, 444.

18. Shannon Lanier and Jane Feldman, *Jefferson's Children: The Story of One American Family*, 56; see also Lucia Stanton and Dianne Swann-Wright, "Bonds of Memory: Identity and the Hemings Family," in Jan Lewis and Peter S. Onuf, eds., *Sally Hemings and Thomas Jefferson*, 161.

19. Interview with Jefferson family historian Herbert Barger, June 10, 2008, Charlottesville, Virginia.

20. David N. Mayer, "The Thomas Jefferson–Sally Hemings Myth and the Politicization of American History, Individual Views of David N. Mayer, Concurring with the Majority Report of the Scholars Commission on the Jefferson-Hemings Matter," April 9, 2001, http://www.ashbrook.org/articles/mayer-hemings.html.

21. Fawn M. Brodie, *Thomas Jefferson: An Intimate History*, 477.

22. *Ibid.,* 481–82.

23. Virginius Dabney, *The Jefferson Scandals: A Rebuttal*, 52; see also Fawn M. Brodie, *Thomas Jefferson: An Intimate History*, 438.

24. *Ibid.,* 53; *ibid.,* 481.

25. Virginius Dabney and Jon Kukla, "The Monticello Scandals: History and Fiction," *Virginia Cavalcade*, 29, Autumn 1979, 52–61.

26. William G. Hyland Jr., *Law Review, Hemings v. Jefferson.*

27. Letter from Thomas Jefferson Randolph, Thomas Jefferson's grandson, to the editor of the *Pike County* (Ohio) *Republican* on file at UVA Library, special collections, available at http://www.pbs.org/wgbh/pages/frontline/shows/jefferson/cron/1873randolph.html.

28. William G. Hyland Jr., *Law Review, Hemings v. Jefferson.*

10. JEFFERSON ON TRIAL

1. Gore Vidal, *Inventing a Nation*, 93.

2. Annette Gordon-Reed, *Thomas Jefferson and Sally Hemings: An American Controversy*, 63.

3. Dumas Malone, *Jefferson the President, First Term, 1801–1805*, 447–48, 450, n. 8.

4. Cynthia Burton, *Jefferson Vindicated*, 93–94.

5. *Ibid*; see Appendix H: Rebuttal to Cocke Letter.

6. Letter from Wallenborn to Author, July 21, 2008.

7. Dumas Malone, *Jefferson the President, First Term, 1801–1805*, 448–50, n. 8.

8. Merrill Peterson, *Thomas Jefferson and the New Nation*, 27.

9. Jon Kukla, *Mr. Jefferson's Women*, 94; see also Dumas Malone, *Jefferson and the Rights of Man*, 70.

10. Jon Kukla, *Mr. Jefferson's Women*, 100.

11. *Ibid.*, 86, 98.

12. *Ibid.*, 102, 103.

13. Joseph J. Ellis, *American Sphinx: The Character of Thomas Jefferson*, 115, 365, 260. Another major study of Jefferson's character that appeared in the mid-1990s, Andrew Burstein's *The Inner Jefferson: Portrait of a Grieving Optimist*, also cast doubt on the Hemings-Jefferson relationship.

14. Donald Jackson, *A Year at Monticello: 1795*, 84–85.

15. *Ibid.*, 85.

16. Jon Kukla, *Mr. Jefferson's Women*, 113.

17. Sarah N. Randolph, *The Domestic Life of Thomas Jefferson*, 213.

18. David N. Mayer, "The Thomas Jefferson–Sally Hemings Myth and the Politicization of American History: Individual Views of David N. Mayer, Concurring with the Majority Report of the Scholars Commission on the Jefferson-Hemings Matter," April 9, 2001, http://www.ashbrook.org/articles/mayer-hemings.html.; see also letters from Jefferson to Henry Lee, May 15, 1826, and Jefferson to William Duane, March 22, 1806.

19. David N. Mayer, "The Thomas Jefferson–Sally Hemings Myth and the Politicization of American History: Individual Views of David N. Mayer, Concurring with the Majority Report of the Scholars Commission on the Jefferson-Hemings Matter," April 9, 2001, http:www.ashbrook.org/articles/mayer-hemings.html.

20. Willard Sterne Randall's interview on John McLaughlin's, *One on One*, PBS television broadcast, November 6, 1998.

21. Dumas Malone, *Jefferson the President*, 497.

22. David N. Mayer, "The Thomas Jefferson–Sally Hemings Myth and the Politicization of American History," John M. Ashbrook Center for Pub-

lic Affairs, Ashland University, www.ashbrook.org. This paper is available through a link at the TJHS Web site, www.tjheritage.org.; David N. Mayer, "The Thomas Jefferson–Sally Hemings Myth and the Politicization of American History: Individual Views of David N. Mayer, Concurring with the Majority Report of the Scholars Commission on the Jefferson-Hemings Matter," April 9, 2001, http:www.ashbrook.org/articles/mayer-hemings.html.; Letter from Henry S. Randall to James Parton in Milton E. Flower, *James Parton: The Father of Modern Biography*, 239.

23. Sarah N. Randolph, *The Domestic Life of Thomas Jefferson*, 310.

24. *Jefferson at Monticello,* 110.

25. Correspondence from Cynthia Burton, Cyndihburton@aol.com, Sent: Thursday, April 12, 2007 8:04 PM To: Hyland, Jr., William G., Subject: Re: FW: Edmund Bacon Interview.

26. James Parton, "The Presidential Election of 1800," July 1873, http://www.theatlantic.com/politics/policamp/parton.htm.

27. *Jefferson at Monticello,* 88.

28. E-mail to Author from Herbert Barger, FW: Edmund Bacon Interview, Sent: Friday, April 13, 2007 6:12 PM.

29. *Jefferson at Monticello,* 110.

30. E-mail to Author from Herbert Barger, From:, Subject: FW: FW: Edmund Bacon Interview.

31. Douglass Adair, "The Jefferson Scandals," in Trevor Colbourn, ed., *Fame and the Founding Fathers: Essays by Douglass Adair*, 227–73.

32. Bernard A. Weisberger, *America Afire*, 1.

33. David McCullough, *John Adams*, 312–13.

34. Letter from Abigail Adams to Thomas Jefferson, July 6, 1787, in Lester J. Cappon, ed., *The Adams-Jefferson Letters*, 183.

35. Letter from Abigail Adams to Jefferson, in Julian Boyd, ed., *Papers of Thomas Jefferson*, vol. XI, 503; see Rebecca L. McMurry and James F. McMurry, *Anatomy of a Scandal*; Virginius Dabney, *The Jefferson Scandals*, 23.

36. David McCullough, *John Adams*, 372.

37. Rebecca L. McMurry and James F. McMurry, *Anatomy of a Scandal*, 85–97, 87, 142; Cynthia Burton, *Jefferson Vindicated*, 32–34.

38. Rebecca L. McMurry and James F. McMurry, *Anatomy of a Scandal*, 90.

39. *Ibid.,* 91.

40. Alan Pell Crawford, *Unwise Passions*, 180.

41. *Ibid.,* 276.

42. *Ibid.*

43. Letter from Henry S. Randall to James Parton, June 1, 1858, in James Parton Collection, Houghton Library, Harvard University; Cynthia Burton, *Jefferson Vindicated*, 80–81.

44. Andrew Burstein, *The Inner Jefferson*, 269.

45. Elizabeth Langhorne, *Monticello: A Family Story*, 95.

46. Letter from Ellen Coolidge to Joseph Coolidge, October 24, 1858, in Eyler Robert Coates, Sr., ed., *The Jefferson-Hemings Myth: An American Travesty*, 193–96.

47. Eyler Robert Coates, Sr., ed., *The Jefferson-Hemings Myth: An American Travesty*, 194.

48. *Ibid.*, 194–95.

49. Annette Gordon-Reed, *Thomas Jefferson and Sally Hemings: An American Controversy*, 258–60.

50. Letter from Ellen Coolidge to Joseph Coolidge, October 24, 1958, in Eyler Robert Coates, Sr., ed., *The Jefferson-Hemings Myth: An American Travesty*, 194.

51. *Ibid.*, 195.

52. *Ibid.*, 196.

53. Alan Pell Crawford, *Twilight at Monticello*, xxvi.

54. Douglass Adair, "The Jefferson Scandals," in Trevor Colbourn, ed., *Fame and the Founding Fathers: Essays by Douglass Adair*, 227–73; Letter from Henry Randall to James Parton, June 1, 1868, in Milton E. Flower, *James Parton: The Father of Modern Biography*, 236–39; see also Fawn M. Brodie, *Thomas Jefferson: An Intimate Portrait*, 494–97.

55. *Ibid.*

56. Rayford W. Logan, "Memoirs of a Monticello Slave: As Dictated to Charles Campbell in the 1840's by Isaac, One of Thomas Jefferson's Slaves," *The American Historical Review*, October 1952, 131–33.

57. Berkeley interview with Herbert Barger conducted March 29, 2000 at The Colonnades Retirement Home, Charlottesville, Virginia.

11. SECRET ROOMS AND OTHER HOLLYWOOD FANTASIES

1. Scot A. French and Edward L. Ayers, "The Strange Career of Thomas Jefferson," in Peter Onuf, ed., *Jefferson Legacies*, 437; see Barbara Chase-Riboud, *Sally Hemings*. Chase-Riboud wrote a sequel to *Sally Hemings* called *The President's Daughter*. Another popular fictional account that accepted the Jefferson-Hemings relationship was Gore Vidal's *Burr* (1974).

2. Elizabeth Langhorne, *Monticello: A Family Story*, 82; Thomas Jefferson quote, 1787.

3. Letter from Jefferson to Martha Jefferson Randolph, June 8, 1797, in Edwin M. Betts and James A. Bear, Jr., eds., *The Family Letters of Thomas Jefferson*, 3, 11.

4. Megan Barnett, "His home was his heart," *U.S. News & World Report*, July 4/July 11, 2005; infoweb@newsbank.com, Sent: Wednesday, April 30, 2008 5:02 PM, To: Hyland Jr., William G., Subject: Requested NewsBank Article(s).

5. Alan Pell Crawford, *Twilight at Monticello*, 145.

6. Cynthia Burton, *Jefferson Vindicated*, 102–104; second interview with Dr. Ken Wallenborn and the Author, June 10, 2008.

7. Jack McLaughlin, *Jefferson and Monticello*, 323.

8. Jon Kukla, *Mr. Jefferson's Women*, 125; Jack McLaughlin, *Jefferson and Monticello*, 323–26, 256.

9. Jack McLaughlin, *Jefferson and Monticello*, 326.

10. Richard Dixon, ed., *Jefferson Notes*, Spring 2008, no. 4, 5.

11. Cynthia Burton, *Jefferson Vindicated*, 102.

12. Jack McLaughlin, *Jefferson and Monticello*, 322.

13. Elizabeth Langhorne, *Monticello: A Family Story*, 86.

14. TJMF report, Appendix H, available at http://www.monticello.org/plantation/hemingscontro/jefferson-hemings_report.pdf.; Jefferson referred to "the closet over my bed" in a letter to his daughter Martha, November 4, 1815, in Edwin M. Betts and James A. Bear, Jr., eds., *The Family Letters of Thomas Jefferson*, 411.

15. David McCullough, *John Adams*, 451.

16. Letter from Jefferson to Thomas M. Randolph, May 19, 1793; see Cynthia Burton, *Jefferson Vindicated*.

17. See Henry S. Randall, *The Life of Thomas Jefferson*; Lucia Cinder Stanton, *Free Some Day*, 112–13.

18. Cynthia Burton, *Jefferson Vindicated*, 104.

19. *Saturday Night Live*, December 7, 2002, http://snltranscripts.jt.org/02/02g.phtml.

20. Original screenplay by Ruth Prawer Jhabvala, *Jefferson in Paris*, Merchant Ivory Productions (1995), 79, 94, 106.

21. Cynthia Burton, *Jefferson Vindicated*, 169.

22. William G. Hyland Jr., "Creative Malpractice: The Cinematic Lawyer," *Texas Review of Entertainment and Sports Law*, vol. 9, Spring 2008, no. 2, 272–73.

23. George Comstock, *Television in America*, 120–23; S. Robert Lichter, Linda S. Lichter, and Stanley Rothman, *Prime Time: How TV Portrays American Culture*, 430, 433; William G. Hyland Jr., "Creative Malpractice: The Cinematic Lawyer," *Texas Review of Entertainment and Sports Law*, vol. 9, Spring 2008, no. 2, 272–73.

24. Letter from Jefferson to William Wirt, August 14, 1814, Papers, DLC; Letter from Jefferson to Monsieur N. G. Dufief, April 19, 1814, Papers, DLC; Cynthia Burton, *Jefferson Vindicated*, 169.

12. THE MONTICELLO REPORT: A "RUSH TO JUDGMENT"

1. Taped interview with Frank Berkeley by Herbert Barger, March 29, 2000.

2. The Thomas Jefferson Memorial Foundation (TJMF) officially owns and runs Monticello. It is now called the "Thomas Jefferson Foundation," excising the word "memorial" from Mr. Jefferson.

3. Dr. White McKenzie Wallenborn, Thomas Jefferson Foundation, DNA Study Committee, Minority Report, April 12, 1999. Dr. Wallenborn's minority report was added to the Monticello Web site in March 2000, three months after the majority report was released to the public. Although the tone of his minority report is fairly balanced, Dr. Wallenborn is much more outspoken in his criticism of the research committee and its methods in White McKenzie Wallenborn, M.D., "A Committee Insider's Viewpoint," in Eyler Robert Coates, Sr., ed., *The Jefferson-Hemings Myth: An American Travesty*, 55–68.

4. One of the glaring errors, among many in this soap television movie is a scene where Sally is depicted as teaching a young male to read. There is no evidence that Sally herself was even literate. In another scene, Thomas Jefferson is depicted as fighting with Sally, in a jealous rage, over the advances by his nephew Peter Carr. It should be noted that the screenwriter, Tina Andrews, watched the premier of the movie with four hundred "crying" relatives of the Hemings's family at Ohio State University. See Byron Woodson, *A President in the Family*, 244.

5. David N. Mayer, "The Thomas Jefferson–Sally Hemings Myth and the Politicization of American History," John M. Ashbrook Center for Public Affairs, Ashland University, www.ashbrook.org. This paper is available through a link at the TJHS Web site, www.tjheritage.org. Mayer, V. PART B—"The TJMF Monticello Report"; Dan Jordan, interviewed in Shannon Lanier and Jane Feldman, *Jefferson's Children: The Story of One American Family*, pp. 112–14.

6. White McKenzie Wallenborn, M.D., "A Committee Insider's Viewpoint," in Eyler Robert Coates, Sr., ed., *The Jefferson-Hemings Myth: An American Travesty*, 55–68.

7. *Jefferson at Monticello*, 110.

8. Eyler Robert Coates, Sr., ed., *The Jefferson-Hemings Myth: An American Travesty*, 84.

9. Report at app. J.; Report of the Research Committee on Thomas Jefferson and Sally Hemings, Thomas Jefferson Memorial Foundation, January 2000, 10. The report is available at www.monticello.org.

10. Virginius Dabney, *The Jefferson Scandals: A Rebuttal*, 79–81.

11. Monticello official Web site is http://www.monticello.org/.

12. Joseph Ellis, *William and Mary Quarterly*, 134, fn 12, 134.

13. White McKenzie Wallenborn, M.D., "A Committee Insider's Viewpoint," in Eyler Robert Coates, Sr., ed., *The Jefferson Hemings Myth: An American Travesty*, 55–68.

14. Report at Minority Report; see also White McKenzie Wallenborn, M.D., "A Committee Insider's Viewpoint," in Eyler Robert Coates, Sr., ed., *The Jefferson Hemings-Myth: An American Travesty*, 55–68.

15. White McKenzie Wallenborn, M.D., "A Committee Insider's Viewpoint," in Eyler Robert Coates, Sr., ed., *The Jefferson-Hemings Myth: An American Travesty*, 55–68.

16. For twenty-five years Frank Berkeley was curator of manuscripts at the University of Virginia. He also sat on the Board of Trustees at Monticello. Along with current UVA president John Casteen they compiled an abstract of each Jefferson document with a separate "Sally Hemings file"; from taped interview with Herbert Barger, March 29, 2000.

17. Taped interview of Frank Berkeley with Herbert Barger, March 29, 2000.

18. David N. Mayer, "The Thomas Jefferson–Sally Hemings Myth and the Politicization of American History," John M. Ashbrook Center for Public Affairs, Ashland University, www.ashbrook.org. This paper is available through a link at the TJHS Web site, www.tjheritage.org. Mayer, V. PART B—"The TJMF Monticello Report"; White McKenzie Wallenborn, M.D., "A Committee Insider's Viewpoint," in Eyler Robert Coates, Sr., ed., *The Jefferson Hemings Myth: An American Travesty*, 55–68.

19. David N. Mayer, "The Thomas Jefferson–Sally Hemings Myth and the Politicization of American History," John M. Ashbrook Center for Public Affairs, Ashland University, www.ashbrook.org. This paper is available

through a link at the TJHS Web site, www.tjheritage.org. Mayer V. PART B—"The TJMF Monticello Report"; see *Jefferson at Monticello.*

20. David N. Mayer, "The Thomas Jefferson–Sally Hemings Myth and the Politicization of American History," John M. Ashbrook Center for Public Affairs, Ashland University, www.ashbrook.org. This paper is available through a link at the TJHS Web site, www.tjheritage.org. Mayer, V. PART B—"The TJMF Monticello Report."

21. Media release by Herbert Barger, Jefferson Family Historian, on February 6, 2006 in e-mail from Herbert Barger to Author, June 2008.

22. *Ibid.*

23. *Ibid.*

24. *Ibid.*

25. *Ibid.*

26. Tax returns and board of directors and trustees for official Monticello, years 2001 and 1997—taxpayer ID # 54-0505959, a 501 (C) (3) public charity available at www.guidestar.org., July 23, 2008.

27. E-mail from Herbert Barger to Author on May 7, 2008.

28. *Ibid.*

13. THE CHARLOTTESVILLE CONNECTION: TRUE BELIEVERS

1. Richard Dixon, "Courses on Jefferson-Hemings Slanted," *Jefferson Notes,* Spring 2007, no. 2, 2.

2. Monticello Newsletter, vol. 11, no. 2, Winter 2003.

3. Robert C. Lautman, Monticello Restoration vol. 12, no. 1; Spring 2001, Monticello Newsletter vol. 12, no. 1, 1.

4. Susan R. Stein, *Jefferson's Monticello,* Official Guidebook, Monticello, 13, 105.

5. Lea Marshall, "Excavating Real Life Discover the Quiet Revolution at Monticello," Richmond.com, Wednesday, July 2, 2003.

6. White McKenzie Wallenborn, M.D., "A Committee Insider's Viewpoint," in Eyler Robert Coates, Sr., ed., *The Jefferson-Hemings Myth: An American Travesty,* 55–68.

7. Lea Marshall, "Excavating Real Life Discover the Quiet Revolution at Monticello," Richmond.com, Wednesday, July 2, 2003.

8. *Ibid.*

9. Remarks by Dianne Swann-Wright on February 1, 1999 at Randolph Macon woman's college, C-SPAN Radio.

10. Kendra Hamilton, " 'Wrighting' " history's wrongs—African American Dianne Swann-Wright, special programs director at the Thomas Jefferson Memorial Foundation," *Black Issues in Higher Education*, August 5, 1999.

11. *Ibid.*

12. *Ibid.*

13. *Ibid.*

14. *Ibid.*

15. Taped interview with Frank Berkeley by Herbert Barger, March 29, 2000.

16. White McKenzie Wallenborn, M. D., e-mail to Author, June 29, 2008.

17. White McKenzie Wallenborn, M.D., "A Committee Insider's Viewpoint," in Eyler Robert Coates, Sr., ed., *The Jefferson-Hemings Myth: An American Travesty*, 55–68.

18. Martin A. Larson, Thomas Jefferson's Place in History, Institute for Historical Review, *Journal of Historical Review*, www.ihr.org/jhr/jhrindex.html.

19. "University of Virginia History Professor Peter Onuf's 'Age of Jefferson' Class Explores the Life and Works of the School's Founder," April 3, 2008, http://www.virginia.edu/uvatoday/newsRelease.php?print=1&id=4783.

20. Winthrop Jordan, *William and Mary Quarterly*, 3rd series, vol. 55, no. 2, 318, 316–18.

21. Annette Gordon-Reed, *Thomas Jefferson and Sally Hemings: An American Controversy*, 103.

22. William G. Hyland Jr. and William G. Hyland, "A Civil Action: Hemings v. Jefferson," *American Journal of Trial Advocacy*, vol. 31:1, 49; Annette Gordon-Reed, *Thomas Jefferson and Sally Hemings: An American Controversy*, 234–35.

23. Annette Gordon-Reed, *Thomas Jefferson and Sally Hemings: An American Controversy*, 103.

24. *Ibid.*

25. William G. Hyland Jr. and William G. Hyland, "A Civil Action: Hemings v. Jefferson," *American Journal of Trial Advocacy*, vol. 31:1, 49.

26. Annette Gordon-Reed, *Thomas Jefferson and Sally Hemings: An American Controversy*, 200.

27. Comments on February 1, 1999 at Randolph Macon woman's college forum on DNA, C-SPAN Radio.

28. White McKenzie Wallenborn, M.D., "A Committee Insider's Viewpoint," in Eyler Robert Coates, Sr., ed., *The Jefferson-Hemings Myth: An American Travesty*, 55–68.

29. Annette Gordon-Reed, "Engaging Jefferson: Blacks and the Founding Father," *William and Mary Quarterly*, January 2000, 174.

30. *Ibid.*

31. *Ibid.*, 175–76.

32. *Ibid.*, 181.

33. David N. Mayer, "The Thomas Jefferson–Sally Hemings Myth and the Politicization of American History," John M. Ashbrook Center for Public Affairs, Ashland University, www.ashbrook.org. This paper is available through a link at the TJHS Web site, www.tjheritage.org; Mayer, Part V. A— Annette Gordon-Reed's book *Thomas Jefferson and Sally Hemings: An American Controversy*, xiv, 234–35.

34. *Ibid.*

35. Annette Gordon-Reed, *Thomas Jefferson and Sally Hemings: An American Controversy*, 18.

36. David N. Mayer, "The Thomas Jefferson–Sally Hemings Myth and the Politicization of American History," John M. Ashbrook Center for Public Affairs, Ashland University, www.ashbrook.org. This paper is available through a link at the TJHS Web site, www.tjheritage.org. Mayer, Part V. A— Annette Gordon-Reed's book *Thomas Jefferson and Sally Hemings: An American Controversy*, 210.

37. Scot A. French and Edward L. Ayers, "The Strange Career of Thomas Jefferson: Race and Slavery in American Memory," in Peter S. Onuf, ed., *Jeffersonian Legacies*, 418–56, 430.

38. David N. Mayer, "The Thomas Jefferson–Sally Hemings Myth and the Politicization of American History," John M. Ashbrook Center for Public Affairs, Ashland University, www.ashbrook.org. This paper is available through a link at the TJHS Web site, www.tjheritage.org. Mayer, Part V. A—Annette Gordon-Reed's book *Thomas Jefferson and Sally Hemings: An American Controversy*, 258–60.

39. *Ibid.*

40. Annette Gordon-Reed, *Thomas Jefferson and Sally Hemings: An American Controversy*, 259.

41. David N. Mayer, "The Thomas Jefferson–Sally Hemings Myth and the Politicization of American History," John M. Ashbrook Center for Public Affairs, Ashland University, www.ashbrook.org. This paper is available through a link at the TJHS Web site, www.tjheritage.org. Mayer, Part V. A—Annette Gordon-Reed's book *Thomas Jefferson and Sally Hemings: An American Controversy*, 258–60.

42. Douglas R. Egerton, *The Journal of Southern History*, vol. 64, no. 2, 349, 348–50.

43. Annette Gordon-Reed, *Thomas Jefferson and Sally Hemings: An -American Controversy*, xix.

44. *Ibid.*, xx.

45. Annette Gordon-Reed, *The Hemingses of Monticello*, 24.

46. *Ibid.*, 25.

47. *Ibid.*, 667.

48. *Ibid.*, 31.

49. *Ibid.*, 315.

50. *Ibid.*, 361.

51. *Ibid.*, 361.

52. Winthrop Jordan, "Hemings and Jefferson Redux," in Jan Lewis and Peter S. Onuf, eds., *Sally Hemings and Thomas Jefferson: History, Memory, and Civic Culture*, 51.

53. Virginius Dabney, *The Jefferson Scandals*, 107.

54. *Ibid.*

55. Annette Gordon-Reed, *The Hemingses of Monticello*, 361.

56. *Ibid.*, 195.

57. Viginius Dabney, *The Jefferson Scandals*, 26.

58. Annette Gordon-Reed, *The Hemingses of Monticello*, 23.

59. *Ibid.*, 25.

60. See John Chester Miller, *The Wolf by the Ears: Thomas Jefferson and Slavery*.

61. Annette Gordon-Reed, *The Hemingses of Monticello*, 341.

62. *Ibid.*, 264.

63. *Ibid.*, 266.

64. *Ibid.*, 278.

65. Douglas R. Egerton, review of Annette Gordon-Reed's *Thomas Jefferson and Sally Hemings*, in *The Journal of Southern History*, vol. 64, no. 2, May 1998, 348–50.

66. Annette Gordon-Reed, *The Hemingses of Monticello*, 283.

67. *Ibid.*, 286.

68. Edmund S. Morgan and Marie Morgan, *Jefferson's Concubine*, October 9, 2008, *New York Review of Books*, A1.

69. Annette Gordon-Reed, *The Hemingses of Monticello*, 664.

14. THE "SALLY" BOOKS

1. Kendra Hamilton, " 'Wrighting' " history's wrongs—African American Dianne Swann-Wright, special programs director at the Thomas Jefferson Memorial Foundation," *Black Issues in Higher Education*, August 5, 1999.

2. Fawn M. Brodie, *Thomas Jefferson: An Intimate History*, 294–300, 229.

3. David N. Mayer, "The Thomas Jefferson–Sally Hemings Myth and the Politicization of American History, Individual Views of David N. Mayer, Concurring with the Majority Report of the Scholars Commission on the Jefferson-Hemings Matter," April 9, 2001, http://www.ashbrook.org/articles/mayer-hemings.html; Willard Sterne Randall, *Thomas Jefferson: A Life*, 476.

4. See Alf J. Mapp, *Thomas Jefferson: Passionate Pilgrim*.

5. See Noble E. Cunningham, Jr., *In Pursuit of Reason: The Life of Thomas Jefferson*.

6. See Willard Sterne Randall, *Thomas Jefferson: A Life*.

7. Noble E. Cunningham, Jr., *In Pursuit of Reason: The Life of Thomas Jefferson*, 116.

8. Willard Sterne Randall, *Thomas Jefferson: A Life*, 477.

9. Andrew Burstein, *Jefferson's Secrets*, 230–31.

10. Douglas Wilson, "Thomas Jefferson and the Character Issue," *Atlantic Monthly*, November 1992, 57–74.

11. *Ibid.*

12. Forrest McDonald, *The Presidency of Thomas Jefferson*, 179.

13. Scot A. French and Edward L. Ayers, "The Strange Career of Thomas Jefferson: Race and Slavery in American Memory," in Peter S. Onuf, ed., *Jeffersonian Legacies*, 418–56, 433.

14. Joseph J. Ellis, *American Sphinx: The Character of Thomas Jefferson*, 365, 260. Another major study of Jefferson's character that appeared in the mid-1990s, Andrew Burstein's *The Inner Jefferson: Portrait of a Grieving Optimist*, also cast doubt on the Hemings-Jefferson relationship.

15. Herbert Barger, "Jefferson-Hemings authority has active imagination," *The Washington Times*, June 21, 2001, A18.

16. E-mail from Herbert Barger to Author, May 7, 2008.

17. *Ibid.*

18. Walter Robinson and Patrick Healy, "Professor Apologizes for Fabrications," *Boston Globe*, June 19, 2001, A1; in a real trial, a person's reputation for truth and veracity in his community is also allowed into evidence as possible impeachment: Joseph Ellis, a Mount Holyoke College professor, never went overseas while in the army, according to the *Boston Globe* and the Associated

Press. Apparently, he also embellished his involvement in the antiwar and civil rights movements, among other things. In his Vietnam War lectures at Mount Holyoke College, Ellis included detailed recollections of his own duty as an airborne soldier in Vietnam—even though, the *Boston Globe* revealed he never served there. His army duty consisted of three years as a West Point teacher. Through cross-examination it can be shown that Mr. Ellis is prone to flights of fancy, most notoriously about himself. Following the report in the *Boston Globe*, Ellis admitted to even fabricating a stellar student football career. "I deeply regret having let stand and later confirming the assumption that I went to Vietnam," Ellis said in a statement. "For this and any other distortions about my personal life, I want to apologize to my family, friends, colleagues, and students." As for why the distortions occurred, he did not say; see Herbert Barger editorial "Jefferson and Hemings redux," *Washington Times*, July 11, 2001, A16.

19. Statement on Standards of Professional Conduct, American Historical Association, Paragraph 8. Reputation and Trust (2004).

20. Joseph Ellis, "Lies my teacher told me," *U.S. News & World Report*, vol. 131, July 2, 2001, 10.

21. David Murray, "Present at the Conception," in Eyler Robert Coates, Sr., ed., *The Jefferson-Hemings Myth: An American Travesty*, 42.

22. David N. Mayer, "The Thomas Jefferson–Sally Hemings Myth and the Politicization of American History, Individual Views of David N. Mayer, Concurring with the Majority Report of the Scholars Commission on the Jefferson-Hemings Matter," April 9, 2001, http://www.ashbrook.org/articles/mayer-hemings.html.

23. Annette Gordon-Reed, *The Hemingses of Monticello: An American Family*, http://www.amazon.com/Hemingses-Monticello-American-Family/dp/0393064778.

24. Andrew Burstein, *The Inner Jefferson*, 230, 231.

25. *Ibid.*

26. Andrew Burstein, *Jefferson's Secrets*, 182.

27. *Ibid.*, 154–58.

28. *Ibid.*, 156–58.

29. *Ibid.*, 116.

30. *Ibid.*, 187.

31. *Ibid.*, 130; Andrew Burstein, *Inner Optimist*, xiv.

32. Virginius Dabney and Jon Kukla, "The Monticello Scandals: History and Fiction," *Virginia Cavalcade*, Autumn 1979, 52–61, 61.

33. *Ibid.*

34. Jon Kukla, *Mr. Jefferson's Women*, 115.

35. E-text of Jefferson letters, Alderman Library, http://etext.virginia .edu/etcbin/ot2www-singleauthor?specfile=/web/data/jefferson/texts/jefall .o2w&act=text&offset=5423832&textreg=2&query=abigail+adams.

36. Jon Kukla, *Mr. Jefferson's Women*, 134.

37. *Ibid.*, 248, 270–71.

38. E-mail from Herbert Barger to Author on May 2, 2008, original e-mail from Judith Justus to Herbert Barger on May 1, 2008.

39. Virginius Dabney and Jon Kukla, "The Monticello Scandals: History and Fiction," *Virginia Cavalcade*, Autumn 1979, 52–61, 60–61.

15. JEFFERSON UNDER SIEGE: "PRESENTISM"

1. E-mail from Herbert Barger to Author on April 18, 2008.

2. Willard Sterne Randall's interview on John McLaughlin's *One on One*, PBS television broadcast, November 6, 1998.

3. David N. Mayer, "The Thomas Jefferson–Sally Hemings Myth and the Politicization of American History, Individual Views of David N. Mayer, Concurring with the Majority Report of the Scholars Commission on the Jefferson-Hemings Matter," April 9, 2001, http://www.ashbrook.org/ articles/mayer-hemings.html.

4. Christopher Shea, "Ivory Tower, Historical Revisionism," *Slate*, http://www.salon.com/it/feature/1998/11/cov_18featurea.html.

5. Richard Dixon, "Courses on Jefferson-Hemings Slanted," *Jefferson Notes*, Spring 2007, no. 2, 2.

6. *Ibid.*

7. *Ibid.*

8. Timothy Sandefur, "Anti-Jefferson, Left and Right," *Liberty*, October 1999, 52.

9. David N. Mayer, "The Thomas Jefferson–Sally Hemings Myth and the Politicization of American History, Individual Views of David N. Mayer, Concurring with the Majority Report of the Scholars Commission on the Jefferson-Hemings Matter," April 9, 2001, http://www.ashbrook.org/ articles/mayer-hemings.html.

10. Andrew Ferguson "Don't Know Much About History," *New York Times Book Review*, May 4, 2008, BR14.

11. Gary Emerling, "Exploring legacy of Columbus—At annual celebration, advocates lament a new world of revisionism," *Washington Times*, October 11, 2005, B1.

12. Robert Stacy McCain, "Washington's name seen as sullied—Founding Fathers are victims of historical revisionism," *Washington Times*, February 23, 2004, A04.

13. Robert Stacy McCain, "Pilgrims' progress?—Historical revisionism taking toll on holiday of settlers," *Washington Times*, November 25, 2003, A02.

14. Correspondence from Herbert Barger to Author, April 23, 2008; original e-mail to Barger: ——Original Message—From: _____, Sent: Friday, December 11, 1998 11:27 PM, To: herbar@erols.com.

15. Douglas L. Wilson, "Thomas Jefferson and the Character Issue," *Atlantic Monthly*, November 1992, 62–64; Joseph J. Ellis, *American Sphinx: The Character of Thomas Jefferson*, 18, 365, 260. Another major study of Jefferson's character that appeared in the mid-1990s, Andrew Burstein's *The Inner Jefferson: Portrait of a Grieving Optimist* also cast doubt on the Hemings-Jefferson relationship.

16. Douglas L. Wilson, "Thomas Jefferson and the Character Issue," *Atlantic Monthly*, November 1992, 62–64.

17. *Ibid.*

18. David N. Mayer, "The Thomas Jefferson–Sally Hemings Myth and the Politicization of American History, Individual Views of David N. Mayer, Concurring with the Majority Report of the Scholars Commission on the Jefferson-Hemings Matter," April 9, 2001, http://www.ashbrook.org/articles/mayer-hemings.html.

19. Daniel A. Farber and Suzanna Sherry, *Beyond All Reason: The Radical Assault on Truth in American Law*, 12, 15, 108–10.

20. David N. Mayer, "The Thomas Jefferson–Sally Hemings Myth and the Politicization of American History, Individual Views of David N. Mayer, Concurring with the Majority Report of the Scholars Commission on the Jefferson-Hemings Matter," April 9, 2001, http://www.ashbrook.org/articles/mayer-hemings.html; see for example, William R. Keylor, "Clio on the Campus: The Historical Society at Boston University," in *Bostonia*, Summer 1999, 20–23.

21. David N. Mayer, "The Thomas Jefferson–Sally Hemings Myth and the Politicization of American History, Individual Views of David N. Mayer, Concurring with the Majority Report of the Scholars Commission on the Jefferson-Hemings Matter," April 9, 2001, http://www.ashbrook.org/articles/mayer-hemings.html.

22. Scot A. French and Edward L. Ayers, "The Strange Career of Thomas Jefferson: Race and Slavery in American Memory," in Peter S. Onuf, ed., *Jeffersonian Legacies*, 418–56, 433.

16. FINAL ARGUMENT: AN INNOCENT MAN

1. Hal Alan, *Quotations for Successful Living*, 25.

2. See Florida Standard Jury instructions at http://www.floridabar.org.

3. Merrill Peterson, *Thomas Jefferson: A Reference Biography*, xi.

4. Virginius Dabney and Jon Kukla, "The Monticello Scandals: History and Fiction," *Virginia Cavalcade*, Autumn 1979, 52–61, 29.

5. David Murray, "Present at the Conception," in Eyler Robert Coates, Sr., ed., *The Jefferson-Hemings Myth*, 124.

6. Douglas L. Wilson, "Thomas Jefferson and the Character Issue," *Atlantic Monthly*, November 1992, 62–64.

7. Winthrop Jordan, "Hemings and Jefferson Redux," in Jan Lewis and Peter S. Onuf, eds., *Sally Hemings and Thomas Jefferson: History, Memory, and Civic Culture*, 35–51, 40.

8. See *Daubert v. Merrell Dow Pharm., Inc.*, 509 U.S. 579 (1993).

9. Virginius Dabney, *The Jefferson Scandals: A Rebuttal*, 128 (citing Margot Hornblower, "Mr. Jefferson, With Passion: A Founding Father Revisited," *Washington Post*, August 28, 1975, B1).

10. David McCullough, *John Adams*, 419.

11. See Thomas Jefferson Heritage Society, Report of the Scholars' Commission on the Jefferson-Hemings Matter, April 12, 2001, 6, 2. This report is available at www.tjheritage.org.

12. Vincent Bugliosi, *The Kennedy Assassination*, xliii.

13. Cynthia Burton, *Jefferson Vindicated*, back cover.

14. David McCullough, *John Adams*, 451.

15. Henry Randall, *The Life of Thomas Jefferson*, vol. 3, 544; Cynthia Burton, *Jefferson Vindicated*, 170.

16. Virginius Dabney, *The Jefferson Scandals: A Rebuttal*, 120.

17. Thomas Jefferson: Bills for Establishing Religious Freedom, 1779; John H. Works, Jr., "Foreword," in Eyler Robert Coates, Sr. ed., *The Jefferson-Hemings Myth: An American Travesty*, 13.

APPENDIX A: JEFFERSON-HEMINGS TIMELINE

1. Eyler Robert Coates, Sr., ed., *The Jefferson-Hemings Myth: An American Travesty*, 197–99.

APPENDIX B: MINORITY REPORT BY DR. WALLENBORN

1. TJMF report, March 23, 2000, http://www.monticello.org/plantation/hemingscontro/minority_report.html.

APPENDIX C: REPLY TO THOMAS JEFFERSON FOUNDATION
RESPONSE TO THE MINORITY REPORT
TO THE DNA STUDY COMMITTEE

1. TJMF report, June 2000, http://www.monticello.org/plantation/hemingscontro/wallenborn_response.html.

APPENDIX E: MR. JEFFERSON'S WILL

1. Bryon Woodson, *A President in the Family*, Appendix 1, 253–255; Monticello.org at http://wiki.monticello.org/mediawiki/index.php/Jefferson's_Will.

APPENDIX F: "THE FAMILY DENIAL"

1. Fawn M. Brodie, *Thomas Jefferson: An Intimate Portrait*, Appendix III, 493–501.

APPENDIX G: APPENDIX B: OPINIONS OF SCIENTISTS CONSULTED

1. TJMF report at http://www.monticello.org/plantation/hemingscontro/appendixb.html.

BIBLIOGRAPHY

NOTES ON SELECTED PRIMARY SOURCES

A voluminous amount of information, misinformation, and speculation exists dealing with every phase of Thomas Jefferson's private life. What follows is a selected list tailored to the issue at hand, the Jefferson-Hemings controversy and chronology:

Jefferson's Memorandum Books, 2 vols: 1767–1826, eds. James A. Bear, Jr., and Lucia Cinder Stanton. (Princeton, NJ: Princeton University Press, 1997).

Thomas Jefferson's Farm Book, ed. Edwin M. Betts (Princeton, NJ: American Philosophical Society/Princeton University Press, 1953).

The Family Letters of Thomas Jefferson, eds. Edwin M. Betts and James A. Bear, Jr. (Columbia: University of Missouri Press, 1966).

The Domestic Life of Thomas Jefferson, ed. Sarah N. Randolph (Charlottesville: University Press of Virginia, 1978).

Thomas Jefferson's Garden Book, annotated by Edwin M. Betts (Philadelphia, PA: The American Philosophical Society, 1944).

Important documentary sources

Madison Hemings's interview in the *Pike County* (Ohio) *Republican*, March 13, 1873, reprinted in several books; the text in Fawn Brodie's *Thomas Jefferson: An Intimate History* seems the most reliable.

Israel Jefferson's interview also in *Pike County* (Ohio) *Republican*, December 25, 1873, also reprinted in Fawn Brodie's book.

Jefferson at Monticello, ed. James A. Bear, Jr., includes "The Monticello slave, Isaac Jefferson's, recollections" (1847); (Charlottesville: University Press

of Virginia, 1967); and "The recollections of Edmund Bacon" (overseer
     at Monticello).
Ellen Randolph Coolidge letter to Joseph Coolidge, October 24, 1858,
     printed in Eyler Robert Coates, Sr., ed., *The Jefferson-Hemings Myth*
     (Charlottesville: Thomas Jefferson Heritage Society, 2001).
Henry S. Randall letter to James Parton, June 1, 1868; also available in Fawn
     Brodie's book.

In addition to the foregoing, I relied on these important secondary sources:

Dumas Malone, *Jefferson and His Time*, 6 vols. Malone deals with the accu-
     sations of James Callender in vol. 4, *Jefferson the President: First Term
     1801–1805* (Boston: Little Brown, 1970), Appendix II, pp. 494–98.
Merrill D. Peterson, *Thomas Jefferson and The New Nation* (New York: Oxford
     University Press, 1970); also by Professor Peterson is his *The Jefferson Im-
     age in the American Mind* (New York: Oxford University Press, 1960); a
     second edition addresses Fawn Brodie's claims against Jefferson (1998).

Three full length books (pro-Hemings) deserve mention:

Fawn M. Brodie, *Thomas Jefferson: An Intimate History* (New York: Norton,
     1974).
Annette Gordon-Reed, *Thomas Jefferson and Sally Hemings: An American
     Controversy* (Charlottesville: University Press of Virginia, 1997).
Annette Gordon-Reed, *The Hemingses of Monticello* (New York: Norton, 2008).

A useful chronicle of the controversies sparked by both Fawn M. Brodie and
     the novelist Barbara Chase-Riboud is summarized in "The Strange Ca-
     reer of Thomas Jefferson, Race and Slavery in American Memory, 1943–
     1993," by Scot A. French and Edward L. Ayers, in *Jeffersonian Legacies*,
     ed. Peter S. Onuf (Charlottesville: University Press of Virginia, 1993).

The case for Jefferson

A collection of essays: *The Jefferson-Hemings Myth: An American Travesty*,
     ed. Eyler Robert Coates, Sr. (Charlottesville: Thomas Jefferson Heritage
     Society, 2001).
Anatomy of a Scandal, Rebecca L. McMurry and James F. McMurry, Jr.
     (Shippensburg, PA: White Mane Books, 2002).

Of the large body of recent biographies five are notable:

Joseph J. Ellis, *American Sphinx: The Character of Thomas Jefferson* (New York: Knopf, 1997).

Andrew Burstein, *Jefferson's Secrets: Death and Desire at Monticello* (New York: Basic Books, 2005).

Andrew Burstein, *The Inner Jefferson: Portrait of a Grieving Optimist* (Charlottesville: University Press of Virginia, 1995).

Jon Kukla, *Mr. Jefferson's Women* (New York: Knopf, 2007).

Alan Pell Crawford, *Twilight at Monticello* (New York: Random House, 2008).

Sally's Story

There is no biography of Sally Hemings as such, although Annette Gordon-Reed's *The Hemingses of Monticello* seems comprehensive. This is not surprising, since so little is known about Sally. There are valuable bits and pieces in a number of books and essays. The Thomas Jefferson Foundation has collected the known facts, available at their Web site, under the heading of Sally Hemings, at www.monticello.org. This site also includes a great deal of relevant information.

Fawn M. Brodie, *Thomas Jefferson: An Intimate History* (New York: Norton, 1974).

Barbara Chase-Riboud, *Sally Hemings* (New York: Viking, 1979).

The most scholarly recent collection is: *Sally Hemings and Thomas Jefferson: History, Memory, and Civic Culture*, eds. Jan Ellen Lewis and Peter S. Onuf (Charlottesville: University Press of Virginia, 1999).

Annette Gordon-Reed, *Thomas Jefferson and Sally Hemings* (Charlottesville: University Press of Virginia, 1997) also, her newest book, *The Hemingses of Monticello* (New York: Norton, 2008).

Slavery

Edmund S. Morgan, *American Slavery-American Freedom* (New York: Norton, 1975); Jefferson's various listing of slaves he owned can be found in *Thomas Jefferson's Farm Book* ed. by Edwin M. Betts (Charlottesville: Thomas Jefferson Memorial Foundation, 1999).

Lucia Cinder Stanton has published two books on slavery at Monticello: *Free Some Day: The African American Families of Monticello* (Charlottesville:

University Press of Virginia, 2000) and *Slavery at Monticello* (Charlottesville: University Press of Virginia, 1996).

John Chester Miller, *The Wolf by the Ears: Thomas Jefferson and Slavery* (1977; reissued, Charlottesville: University of Virginia Press, 1991).

A great deal has been written about Jefferson's years as minister in Paris. Most pertinent to the Sally story is Conor Cruise O'Brien, *The Long Affair: Thomas Jefferson and the French Revolution, 1785–1800* (Chicago: University of Chicago Press, 1996).

William Howard Adams, *The Paris Years of Thomas Jefferson* (New Haven, CT: Yale University Press, 1997).

Madison Hemings

Madison Hemings was interviewed by, or gave a statement to, the editor of the *Pike County* (Ohio) *Republican*, printed in March 1873. The text is reprinted, as a typescript, in various books: Fawn M. Brodie's seems to be the most reliable full text.

Dumas Malone and Steven Hochman, "A Note on Evidence: The Personal History of Madison Hemings," *Journal of Southern History*, XLI, November 1975, 523–38.

Conception and Births

Many authors refer to the match between the date of Sally's probable conception of her children and the presence at Monticello of Thomas Jefferson. Two essays that discuss this topic are: Winthrop D. Jordan, "Hemings and Jefferson Redux," in *Sally Hemings and Thomas Jefferson*, and Fraser D. Neiman, "Coincidence or Causal Connection?" in *William and Mary Quarterly*, January 2000.

The mystery of the paternity of Thomas Woodson is reflected in books by his descendants: Minnie Shumate Woodson, *The Sable Curtain* (Washington, DC: Stafford Lowery Press, 1987), and Byron W. Woodson, *A President in the Family* (Westport, CT: Praeger, 2001).

An interesting book is *Jefferson's Children: The Story of One American Family* by Shannon Lanier; he is a descendant of Madison Hemings. In the book he has assembled pictures and stories of the descendants of Madison and Eston Hemings and an artist's depiction of Sally Hemings (New York: Random House, 2000).

Steven T. Corneliussen, "Sally Hemings, Thomas Jefferson, and the Authority of Science" (May 6, 2008) www.tjscience.org/HemingsTJscience.htm.

Whether or not Hemings and Jefferson had children together, misreported DNA and misused statistics have skewed the paternity debate, discrediting science itself.

Perhaps the classic defense of Jefferson is a long essay by Douglass Adair, "The Jefferson Scandals," in *Fame and the Founding Fathers*, ed. Trevor Colbourn (New York: Norton, 1974).

Over the last thirty years most biographers have addressed James Callender's charges. Prior to the DNA experiments, most writers doubted the claims; biographies, for example, by Alf Mapp, Noble Cunningham, and Willard Sterne Randall; notable exceptions were Fawn Brodie and Annette Gordon-Reed. More recently shorter post-DNA biographies by Joyce Appleby, *Thomas Jefferson* (New York: Times Books, 2003), and Christopher Hitchens, *Thomas Jefferson* (New York: HarperCollins, 2005), have decided in favor of Sally. Supporting Jefferson's side are Rebecca and James McMurry, *Anatomy of a Scandal* (Shippensburg, PA: White Mane Books, 2002).

The so-called "Family Denial" consists of: 1) a letter from the historian Henry Randall to the biographer James Parton, and 2) a letter from Ellen Randolph Coolidge to her husband in 1858.

A particularly well-informed and scholarly series of essays is "Forum: Thomas Jefferson and Sally Hemings Redux," in the *William and Mary Quarterly*, January 2000; the essayists include Jan Lewis, Joseph Ellis, Lucia Cinder Stanton, Peter Onuf, Annette Gordon-Reed, Andrew Burstein, and Fraser Neiman.

Dr. Eugene Foster's findings of his DNA experiment were published in *Nature*, a British magazine in November 1998. The results were evaluated by a special Research Committee appointed by the Thomas Jefferson Memorial Society and published in April 2000, and available on the Internet. A conflicting report was published as the Scholars Commission sponsored by The Thomas Jefferson Heritage Society, which also published *The Jefferson-Hemings Myth*. *Myth* includes an essay on DNA by an early participant in arranging the DNA investigation, Herbert Barger, "The Jefferson-Hemings DNA Story." The DNA background is examined in "A Primer on Jefferson's DNA," www.pbs.org.frontline; this site also includes an interview with Dr. Foster. Also available on the Internet is an article that includes the diagram of the specific DNA markers: www.people.virginia.edu|jefthemm.html. "Defining the Possible Link: Between Thomas Jefferson and Sally Hemings: Lineages and DNA Markers."

SELECTED SECONDARY SOURCES

I have attempted to make a full accounting of all the material consulted and or referenced. I have examined Jefferson's correspondence in his hand, generally on microfilm in libraries, or by virtual research on the Internet. I gratefully acknowledge my frequent use of the online catalogues of the Library of Virginia, the University of Virginia Library, the Virginia Historical Society, Yale University, and the Library of Congress.

COLLECTIONS

Abigail Adams Papers, American Antiquarian Society.

Abigail Adams Papers, Carl Roach Library, Cornell University Abigail Adams Papers, Massachusetts Historical Society.

John Adams Papers, Massachusetts Historical Society.

John Quincy Adams Papers, Massachusetts Historical Society.

Ellen Randolph Coolidge Papers, University of Virginia, Alderman Library, Special Collections.

Carr and Cary Papers, 1785–39. Special Collections Department, University of Virginia Library.

Catalogue of the Library of Thomas Jefferson. Compiled by E. Millicent Sowerby. 5 vols. (Washington, DC, 1952–59).

Thomas Jefferson Randolph. Memoirs, 1974. Typescript in James A. Bear, Jr., Papers, ace. no. 5454-C, Special Collections Department, University of Virginia Library. (Letter from Thomas Jefferson Randolph, Thomas Jefferson's grandson, to the editor of the *Pike County* (Ohio) *Republican* (1874) (on file at University of Virginia Library, special collections), available at www.pbs.org/wgbh/pages/frontline/shows/jefferson/cron/1873randolph.html.

TJP-LC Thomas Jefferson Papers, Library of Congress.

TJP-WM Thomas Jefferson Papers, Tucker-Coleman Collection, College of William & Mary.

TJP-ViU Thomas Jefferson Papers, University of Virginia.

American Memory (Library of Congress) George Washington Papers, Thomas Jefferson Papers.

Family Letters Project (Papers of Thomas Jefferson: Retirement Series, Monticello).

John D. Rockefeller Jr. Library (Colonial Williamsburg Foundation) Virginia Gazette and index for 1736–80.

Thomas Jefferson Digital Archive (University of Virginia Library Electronic Text Center).

BOOKS

Adair, Douglass. "The Jefferson Scandals," in Trevor Colbourn, ed., *Fame and the Founding Fathers: Essays by Douglass Adair* (New York: Norton, 1974).

Adams, Charles Francis, ed. *Familiar Letters of John Adams and His Wife Abigail Adams During the Revolution* (New York: Hurd & Houghton, 1876).

———. *Letters of Mrs. Adams.* Vols. I–II (Boston: Little, Brown, 1840).

———. *The Works of John Adams.* Vols. I–X (Boston: Little, Brown, 1856).

Adams, Dickinson W., ed. *Jefferson's Extracts from the Gospels* (Princeton, NJ: Princeton University Press, 1983).

Adams, Henry. *History of the United States of America During the Administration of Thomas Jefferson* (original Scribner, 1889–91; reprint, New York: Library of America, 1986).

Adams, James Truslow. *The Adams Family* (Boston: Little, Brown, 1930).

———. *The Living Jefferson* (New York: Charles Scribner's Sons, 1936).

———. *New England in the Republic, 1776–1850* (Boston: Little, Brown, 1926).

———. *Revolutionary New England, 1691–1776* (Boston: Atlantic Monthly Press, 1923).

Adams, John. *Correspondence of the Late President Adams* (Boston: Everett & Munroe, 1809). Originally published in the *Boston Patriot* in a series of letters.

Adams, William Howard, ed. *The Eye of Thomas Jefferson* (Washington, DC: National Gallery of Art, 1976).

———. *Jefferson and the Arts: An Extended View* (Washington, DC: National Gallery of Art, 1976).

———. *Jefferson's Monticello* (New York: Abbeville Press, 1983).

———. *The Paris Years of Thomas Jefferson* (New Haven, CT: Yale University Press, 1997).

Appleby, Joyce. *Thomas Jefferson* (New York: Times Books, 2003).

Banning, Lance. *Jefferson and Madison: Three Conversations from the Founding* (Madison, WI: Madison House Publishers, 1995).

Bear, James A., Jr., and Lucia C. Stanton, eds. *Jefferson's Memorandum Books: Accounts, with Legal Records and Miscellany, 1767–1826. The Papers of Thomas Jefferson.* 2nd Series (Princeton, NJ: Princeton University Press, 1997).

Bear, James A., Jr., ed. *Jefferson at Monticello* (Charlottesville: University of Virginia Press, 1967). Includes "Memoirs of a Monticello Slave," as dictated to Charles Campbell by Isaac Jefferson, and "Jefferson at Monticello: The Private Life of Thomas Jefferson," by Reverend Hamilton W. Pierson. Introduction by James A. Bear, Jr.

————. *The Family Letters of Thomas Jefferson* (Columbia: University of Missouri Press, 1966).

Bedini, Silvio A. *Thomas Jefferson and His Copying Machines* (New York: Scribner, 1972).

Beran, M. K. *Jefferson's Demons* (New York: Free Press, 2003).

Betts, Edwin M., ed. *Thomas Jefferson's Farm Book* (Princeton, NJ: American Philosophical Society/Princeton University Press, 1953).

————. *Thomas Jefferson's Garden Book, 1766–1824* (Philadelphia, PA: American Philosophical Society, 1944).

Betts, Edwin M., and James Adam Bear, Jr., eds. *The Family Letters of Thomas Jefferson* (Charlottesville: University Press of Virginia, 1986).

Boyd, Julian, ed. *The Papers of Thomas Jefferson*. Vols. I–XX (Princeton, NJ: Princeton University Press, 1950).

————. *The Papers of Thomas Jefferson*. 26 vols. to date (Princeton, NJ: Princeton University Press, 1950–).

Brodie, Fawn M. *Thomas Jefferson: An Intimate History* (New York: Norton, 1974).

Burstein, Andrew. *The Inner Jefferson: Portrait of a Grieving Optimist* (Charlottesville: University Press of Virginia, 1995).

————. *Jefferson's Secrets: Death and Desire at Monticello* (New York: Basic Books, 2005).

Burton, Cynthia. *Jefferson Vindicated: Fallacies, Omissions, and Contradictions in the Hemings Genealogical Search* (Keswick, VA: self published, 2005).

Cappon, Lester J., ed. *The Adams-Jefferson Letters: The Complete Correspondence Between Thomas Jefferson and Abigail and John Adams*. 2 vols. (Chapel Hill: University of North Carolina Press, 1959).

Coates, Eyler Robert, Sr., ed. *The Jefferson-Hemings Myth: An American Travesty* (Charlottesville: Thomas Jefferson Heritage Society, 2001). Essays by John H. Works, Jr.; Rebecca L. McMurry and James F. McMurry, Jr., M.D.; Herbert Barger; David Murray, Ph.D.; White McKenzie Wallenborn, M.D.; C. Michael Moffitt, Ph.D.; Eyler Robert Coates, Sr.; Richard E. Dixon; and Bahman Batmanghelidj.

Comstock, George. *Television in America* (New York: Sage, 1980).

Corner, George W., ed. *The Autobiography of Benjamin Rush* (Westport, CT: Greenwood Press, 1948).

Crawford, Alan Pell. *Twilight at Monticello* (New York: Random House, 2008).

Cullen, Charles, ed. *The Papers of John Marshall* (Chapel Hill: University of North Carolina Press, 1984).

———. *The Papers of Thomas Jefferson.* Vols. XXI–XXIII (Princeton, NJ: Princeton University Press, 1983).

Cunningham, Noble E., Jr. *The Image of Thomas Jefferson in the Public Eye: Portraits for the People, 1800–1809* (Charlottesville: University of Virginia Press, 1981).

———. *In Pursuit of Reason: The Life of Thomas Jefferson* (Baton Rouge: Louisiana State University Press, 1987).

———. *The Jeffersonian Republicans in Power: Party Operations, 1801–1809* (Chapel Hill: University of North Carolina Press, 1963).

Dabney, Virginius. *Across the Years: Memories of a Virginian* (New York: Doubleday, 1978).

———. *The Jefferson Scandals: A Rebuttal* (New York: Dodd, Mead, 1981).

———. *Mr. Jefferson's University: A History* (Charlottesville: University Press of Virginia, 1983).

Daniels, Jonathan. *The Randolphs of Virginia* (Garden City, NY: Doubleday, 1972).

Dewey, Frank. *Thomas Jefferson, Lawyer* (Charlottesville: University Press of Virginia, 1986).

Dixon, Richard E. "The Case Against Thomas Jefferson: A Trial Analysis of the Evidence on Paternity," in Eyler Robert Coates, Sr., ed., *The Jefferson-Hemings Myth: An American Travesty* (Charlottesville: Thomas Jefferson Heritage Society, 2001).

Dorsey, John M., M.D., ed. *The Jefferson-Dunglison Letters* (Charlottesville, University Press of Virginia, 1960).

Dos Passos, John. *The Head and Heart of Thomas Jefferson* (Garden City, NY: Doubleday, 1954).

Du Bellet, Louise Pecquet. *Some Prominent Virginia Families.* 4 vols. (Baltimore, MD: The Apple Manor Press, 1976).

Durey, Michael. *With the Hammer of Truth: The Autobiography of James Callender* (Charlottesville: University Press of Virginia, 1990).

Ellis, Joseph J. *After the Revolution* (New York: Norton, 1979).

———. *American Sphinx: The Character of Thomas Jefferson* (New York: Knopf, 1997).

———. *Founding Brothers: The Revolutionary Generation* (New York: Knopf, 2001).

Fleming, Thomas. *The Man from Monticello: An Intimate Life of Thomas Jefferson* (New York: Morrow, 1969).

Flower, Milton E. *James Parton: The Father of Modern Biography* (Durham, NC: Duke University Press, 1951).

Ford, Paul, ed. *The Works of Thomas Jefferson* (New York, 1905; reprint, Irvine, CA: Reprint Services Corp., 2007).

———. *The Writings of Thomas Jefferson*. 10 vols. (New York: Putnam, 1892–1899).

Ford, Worthington Chauncey. *Thomas Jefferson and James Thomson Callender, 1798–1802* (Brooklyn, NY: History Print Club, 1897).

———. *Thomas Jefferson Correspondence* (Boston: from the collections of William K. Bixby, 1916).

French, Scot A., and Edward L. Ayers. "The Strange Career of Thomas Jefferson: Race and Slavery in American Memory, 1943–1993," in Peter S. Onuf ed., *Jeffersonian Legacies* (Charlottesville: University Press of Virginia, 1993).

Gaines, William H. *Thomas Mann Randolph, Jefferson's Son-in-Law* (Baton Rouge: Louisiana State University Press, 1966).

Gordon-Reed, Annette. *The Hemingses of Monticello* (New York: Norton, 2008).

———. *Thomas Jefferson and Sally Hemings: An American Controversy* (Charlottesville: University Press of Virginia, 1997).

Halliday, E. M. *Understanding Thomas Jefferson* (New York: HarperCollins, 2001).

Hitchens, Christopher. *Thomas Jefferson: Author of America* (New York: HarperCollins, 2005).

Hutchinson, William T., and William M. E. Rachal, eds. *The Papers of James Madison: Secretary of State Series, 1800–1801*. Vol. 1 (Chicago: University of Chicago Press, 1962).

Jackson, Donald. *A Year at Monticello: 1795* (Golden, CO: Fulcrum, 1989).

Jefferson, Isaac. "Memoirs of a Monticello Slave," in James A. Bear, Jr., ed., *Jefferson at Monticello* (Charlottesville: University Press of Virginia, 1967).

Johnson, Allen, ed. *Dictionary of American Biography* (New York: Scribner, 1958).

Jordan, Daniel P. *Political Leadership in Jefferson's Virginia* (Charlottesville: University Press of Virginia, 1983).

Jordan, Winthrop. *White Over Black: American Attitudes Toward the Negro, 1550–1812* (Chapel Hill: University of North Carolina Press, 1968).

Justus, Judith. *Down from the Mountain* (Perrysburg, OH: Jeskurtara, 1990).

Kennedy, Roger. *Burr, Hamilton, and Jefferson* (New York: Oxford University Press, 2000).

Kimball, Marie. *Jefferson: The Road to Glory, 1743–1776* (New York: Coward-McCann, 1943).

———. *Jefferson: The Scene of Europe, 1784–1789* (New York: Coward-McCann, 1950).

———. *Jefferson: War and Peace, 1776–1784* (New York: Coward-McCann, 1947).

Kissinger, Henry. *Diplomacy* (New York: Simon & Schuster, 1994).

Klingberg, Frank J., et al. eds. *The Correspondence between Henry Stephens Randall and Hugh Blair Grigsby, 1851–61* (Berkeley: University of California Press, 1952).

Koch, Adrienne, and William Peden, eds. *The Life and Selected Writings of Thomas Jefferson* (New York: Modern Library, 1944).

Kukla, Jon. *Mr. Jefferson's Women* (New York: Knopf, 2007).

Lamb, Martha J., ed. *Magazine of American History* (New York: A. S. Barnes & Company, 1887).

Langhorne, Elizabeth. *Monticello: A Family Story* (Chapel Hill, NC: Algonquin Books, 1989).

Lanier, Shannon, and Jane Feldman. *Jefferson's Children* (New York: Random House Books for Younger Readers, 2002).

Levy, Leonard W. *Freedom of Speech and Press in Early American History: Legacy of Suppression* (New York: Harper Torchbooks, 1963).

———. *Jefferson and Civil Liberties: The Darker Side* (Chicago: Elephant Paperbacks, 1989).

Lewis, Jan Ellen, and Peter S. Onuf, eds. *Sally Hemings and Thomas Jefferson: History, Memory, and Civic Culture* (Charlottesville: University Press of Virginia, 1999).

Lewis, Thomas. *The Fairfax Line: Thomas Lewis's Journal of 1746* (New Market, VA: J. W. Wayland, 1925).

Lichter, S. Robert, Linda S. Lichter, and Stanley Rothman. *Prime Time: How TV Portrays American Culture* (New York: Regenery Publishing, Inc., 1994).

Lipscomb, Andrew A., and Albert E. Bergh eds. *The Writings of Thomas Jefferson* (Washington, DC: Jefferson Memorial Association, 1903).

Lloyd, Stephen. *Richard and Maria Cosway: Regency Artists of Taste and Fashion* (Edinburgh: Scottish National Portrait Galleries, 1995).

Malone, Dumas. *Jefferson and His Time. Vol. One, Jefferson the Virginian* (Boston: Little Brown, 1948).

———. *Jefferson and His Time. Vol. Two, Jefferson and the Rights of Man* (Boston: Little Brown, 1951).

———. *Jefferson and His Time. Vol. Three, Jefferson and the Ordeal of Liberty* (Boston: Little Brown, 1962).

———. *Jefferson and His Time. Vol. Four, Jefferson the President, First Term, 1801–1805* (Boston: Little Brown, 1970).

———. *Jefferson and His Time. Vol. Five, Jefferson the President, Second Term, 1805–1809* (Boston: Little Brown, 1974).

———. *Jefferson and His Time. Vol. Six, The Sage of Monticello* (Boston: Little Brown, 1977).

Mapp, Alf, Jr. *Thomas Jefferson: A Strange Case of Mistaken Identity* (Lanham, MD: Madison Books, 1987).

———. *Thomas Jefferson: Passionate Pilgrim: The Presidency, the Founding of the University, and the Private Battle* (Lanham, MD: Madison Books, 1991).

Mayo, Bernard, and James A. Bear, Jr., eds. *Thomas Jefferson and His Unknown Brother* (Charlottesville: University Press of Virginia, 1981).

McCullough, David. *John Adams* (New York: Simon & Schuster, 2001).

McDonald, Forrest. *The Presidency of Thomas Jefferson* (Lawrence: University Press of Kansas, 1975).

McEwan, Barbara. *Thomas Jefferson: Farmer* (Jefferson, NC: McFarland & Co., 1991).

McLaughlin, Jack. *Jefferson and Monticello: Biography of a Builder* (New York: Owl Books, 1988).

McMurry, Rebecca L., and James F. McMurry, Jr. *Anatomy of a Scandal: Thomas Jefferson and the Sally Story* (Shippensburg, PA: White Mane Books, 2002).

———. *Jefferson, Callender and the Sally Story* (TomsBrook, VA: Old Virginia Books, 2000).

———. "The Origins of the 'Sally' Story" in Eyler Robert Coates, Sr., ed., *The Jefferson-Hemings Myth: An American Travesty* (Charlottesville: Thomas Jefferson Heritage Society, 2001).

McNeill, William H. *Plagues and Peoples* (New York: Anchor Books/Doubleday, 1976).

Miller, John C. *The Wolf by the Ears: Thomas Jefferson and Slavery* (Charlottesville: University Press of Virginia, 1991).

Montross, Lynn. *The Reluctant Rebels: The Story of the Continental Congress, 1774–1789* (New York: Barnes & Noble, 1950).

Morgan, Edmund S. *The Birth of the Republic* (Chicago: University of Chicago Press, 1992).

———. *The Meaning of Independence* (New York: Norton, 1976).

———. *The Puritan Family* (New York: Harper Torchbooks, 1966).

Morse, John T. *Thomas Jefferson* (Nashville, TN: Cumberland House, 2004).

Nock, Albert J. *Jefferson* (New York: Hill and Wong, 1926).

Oberg, Barbara B., ed. *The Papers of Thomas Jefferson, 1800–1801*. Vol. 31 (Princeton, NJ: Princeton University Press, 1951).

Onuf, Peter S., ed. *Jeffersonian Legacies* (Charlottesville: University Press of Virginia, 1993).

Padover, Saul K. *A Jefferson Profile* (New York: John Day, 1956).

———. *Thomas Jefferson and the National Capital* (Washington, DC: Government Printing Office, 1946).

Parton, James. *The Life of Thomas Jefferson* (Boston, 1874; reprint, New York: Da Capo Press, 1971).

Peden, William, ed. *Thomas Jefferson: Notes on the State of Virginia* (New York: Norton, 1982).

Peterson, Merrill D. *Adams and Jefferson: A Revolutionary Dialogue* (New York: Oxford University Press, 1976).

———. *The Jefferson Image in the American Mind* (New York: Oxford University Press, 1960).

———. *Jefferson's Writings* (Washington, DC: Library of America, 1984).

———. *Thomas Jefferson and the New Nation* (New York: Oxford University Press, 1970).

———, ed. *The Political Writings of Thomas Jefferson* (Woodlawn, MD: Wolk Press, 1993).

———, ed. *The Portable Thomas Jefferson* (New York: Penguin, 1983).

———, ed. *Thomas Jefferson: A Reference Biography* (New York: Scribner, 1986).

———, ed. *Visitors to Monticello* (Charlottesville: University Press of Virginia, 1989).

Pierson, Hamilton. *Jefferson at Monticello: The Private Life of Thomas Jefferson* (1862; reprint, Freeport, NY: Scribner, 1971).

Randall, Henry S. *The Life of Thomas Jefferson*. 3 vols. (1858; reprint, New York: Da Capo Press, 1972).

Randall, Willard Sterne. *Thomas Jefferson: A Life* (New York: Holt, 1993).

Randolph, Sarah N. *The Domestic Life of Thomas Jefferson* (Charlottesville: University Press of Virginia, 1978). Reprint of 1871 edition published by Harper, New York.

Rice, Howard C., Jr., ed. *Marquis de, Chastellux: Travels in North America in the Years 1780, 1781.* Vol I and II (Chapel Hill: University of North Carolina Press, 1963).

Rush, Benjamin. *Letters of Benjamin Rush.* 2 vols. (Princeton, NJ: American Philosophical Society, 1951).

Schachner, Nathan. *Thomas Jefferson: A Biography.* 2 vols. (New York: Thomas Voseloff, 1957).

Shuffelton, Frank. *Thomas Jefferson: A Comprehensive, Annotated Bibliography of Writings About Him (1826–1980)* (New York: Garland Publishing Co., 1983).

Stanton, Lucia Cinder. *Free Some Day: The African-American Families of Monticello* (Charlottesville: University Press of Virginia, 2000).

Vidal, Gore. *Inventing a Nation* (New Haven, CT: Yale University Press, 2003).

Wallenborn, White McKenzie, M.D. "A Committee Insider's Viewpoint," in Eyler Robert Coates, Sr., ed., *The Jefferson-Heming Myth: An American Travesty* (Charlottesville: Thomas Jefferson Heritage Society, 2001).

Wills, Garry. *Inventing America: Jefferson's Declaration of Independence* (Garden City, NY: Doubleday, 1978).

Wilson, Douglas, ed. *The Papers of Thomas Jefferson: Jefferson's Literary Commonplace Book* (Princeton, NJ: Princeton University Press, 1989).

Woodson, Byron W. *A President in the Family* (Westport, CT: Praeger, 2001).

Woodson, Minnie Shumate. *The Sable Curtain* (Washington, DC: Stafford Lowery Press, 1987).

ARTICLES

Banner, Lois W. Review of *Thomas Jefferson: An Intimate History*, by Fawn M. Brodie, in *American Historical Review*, 80 (1975), p. 1390.

Battle J. D. "The 'periodical head-achs' of Thomas Jefferson." *Cleveland Clinic Quarterly*, 51 (1983), pp. 531–39.

Bear, James A., Jr. "The Hemings Family at Monticello," *Virginia Cavalcade*, 29 (Autumn 1979), pp. 78–87.

Bowling, Kenneth R. "Dinner at Jefferson's: A Note on Jacob Cooke's 'The Compromise of 1790,'" *William and Mary Quarterly*, XXVIII, 3rd series, no. 4 (October 1971), pp. 629–48.

Britt, Donna. "A Slaveholder's Hypocrisy Was Inevitable," *Washington Post* (November 6, 1998), B1.

Brodie, Fawn M. "The Great American Taboo," *American Heritage*, vol. XXIII, no. 4 (June 1972), pp. 4–57.

———. "Jefferson's Biographers and the Psychology of Canonization," *Journal of Interdisciplinary History*, vol. II (Summer 1971), pp. 155–71.

———. "The Political Hero in America," *Virginia Quarterly Review*, vol. XL, no. I (Winter 1970), pp. 46–60.

———. "Thomas Jefferson's Unknown Grandchildren: A Study in Historical Silences," *American Heritage*, vol. XXVII, no. 6 (October 1976), pp. 2–33, 94–99.

Cauchon, Dennis. "Jefferson Affair No Longer Rumor," *USA Today* (November 2, 1998), 3A.

Cohen, Gary L., M.D., and Loren A. Rolak, M.D. "Thomas Jefferson's Headaches: Were They Migraines?" *Headache: The Journal of Head and Face Pain*, vol. 46, issue 3 (March 2006), pp. 492–97.

Corneliussen, Steven T. "Sally Hemings, Thomas Jefferson, and the Authority of Science" (May 6, 2008) www.tjscience.org/HemingsTJscience.htm.

Dabney, Virginius, and Jon Kukla. "The Monticello Scandals: History and Fiction," *Virginia Cavalcade*, vol. XXIX, no. 2 (Autumn 1979), pp. 52–61.

Foster Eugene A. "In Jefferson-Hemings Tie, a Family's Pride; Tenable Conclusions," *New York Times* (November 9, 1998), A24.

———., et al. "Jefferson Fathered Slave's Last Child," *Nature* (November 5, 1998), pp. 27–28.

———. "The Thomas Jefferson paternity case," *Nature* (January 7, 1999), p. 32.

Graham, Pearl N. "Thomas Jefferson and Sally Hemings," *Journal of Negro History*, 44 (1961), pp. 89–103.

Hamilton, Halmon. "Review of *Thomas Jefferson: An Intimate History*, by Fawn Brodie," *Journal of Southern History*, 41 (1975), pp. 107–9.

Hogan, Clifford. "How Not to Write a Biography: A Critical Look at Fawn Brodie's Thomas Jefferson," *Social Science Journal*, 14:2 (1977), pp. 132–33.

Hornblower, Margot. "Mr. Jefferson, With Passion: A Founding Father Revisited," *Washington Post* (August 28, 1975), B1.

Hyland, William G. "Creative Malpractice: The Cinematic Lawyer," *Texas Review of Entertainment and Sports Law*, vol. 9, no. 2, (Spring 2008), pp. 272–73.

Hyland, William G., Jr., and Hyland, William G. "A Civil Action: Hemings v. Jefferson," *American Journal of Trial Advocacy*, vol. 31 (Summer 2007), pp. 1–68.

Jefferson-Hemings Scholars Commission. Final Report of the Jefferson-Hemings Scholars Commission (April 12, 2001), available at www.tjheritage.org/SCreportl.html.

Jellison, Charles A. "James Thomson Callender: Human Nature in a Hideous Form," *Virginia Cavalcade*, 29 (Autumn 1978), pp. 62–69.

———. "That Scoundrel Callender," *Virginia Magazine of History and Biography*, 67 (1959), pp. 295–306.

Jordan, Winthrop. Review of *Thomas Jefferson: An Intimate History*, by Fawn Brodie, in *William and Mary Quarterly*, 3rd series, 32 (1975), p. 510.

Lander, Eric S., and Joseph J. Ellis. "Founding Father," *Nature* (November 5, 1998), pp. 13–14.

Leary, Helen F. M. "Sally Hemings's Children: A Genealogical Analysis of the Evidence," *Jefferson-Hemings, A Special Issue of the National Genealogical Society Quarterly* (NGSQ), vol. 89, no. 3 (September 2001), pp. 165–207.

Logan, Rayford W. "Memoirs of a Monticello Slave: As Dictated to Charles Campbell in the 1840's by Isaac One of Thomas Jefferson's Slaves," *The American Historical Review* (October 1952), pp. 131–33.

Malone, Dumas. "Mr. Jefferson's Private Life," Proceedings of the American Antiquarian Society at http://www.americanantiquarian.org/proceedings.htm.

Malone, Dumas, and Stephen H. Hochman. "A Note on Evidence: The Personal History of Madison Hemings," *Journal of Southern History*, 41 (1975), pp. 523–28.

Mayer, David N. "The Thomas Jefferson–Sally Hemings Myth and the Politicization of American History, Individual Views of David N. Mayer, Concurring with the Majority Report of the Scholars Commission on the Jefferson-Hemings Matter" (April 9, 2001) at www.ashbrook.org/articles/mayer-hemings.html.

Murray, Barbra, and Brian Duffy. "Jefferson's Secret Life," *U.S. News & World Report* (November 9, 1998), p. 58.

Neiman, Fraser D. "Coincidence or Causal Connection? The Relationship Between Thomas Jefferson's Visits to Monticello and Sally Hemings's Conceptions," *William and Mary Quarterly*, 57 (2000), pp. 198–211.

Onuf, Peter S. "The Scholars' Jefferson," *William and Mary Quarterly*, 3rd series, 50 (1993), p. 671.

Page, Clarence. "DNA Testing Puts Jefferson in a New Light," *The Times Union* (November 6, 1998), A21.

Pearce, J. M.S. "The Headaches of Thomas Jefferson," *Cephalalgia*, 23 (2003), pp. 472–73.

Smith, Dinitia, and Nicholas Wade. "DNA Tests Offer Evidence that Jefferson Fathered a Child with His Slave," *New York Times* on the Web (November 1, 1998), p. 24.

Swann-Wright, Dianne. "Report on Thomas Jefferson and Sally Hemings," Thomas Jefferson Memorial Foundation, January 2000.

Truscott IV, Lucian K. "Time for Monticello to Open the Gate and Stop Making Excuses," *New York Times* (November 5, 1998), F10.

Turner, Robert F., ed. "The Jefferson-Hemings Controversy: Report of the Scholars Commission," unpublished draft dated July 31, 2002. Published version forthcoming by Carolina Academic Press. Originally released as "Report on the Jefferson-Hemings Matter" (April 12, 2001) at www.tjheritage.org.

Veith, Gene Edward. "Founder's DNA revisited," *World* (February 20, 1999) at http://www.worldmag.com/articles/2654.

Wills, Garry. "The Aesthete." Review of *The Worlds of Thomas Jefferson*, by Susan R. Stein, in *New York Review of Books*, 40 (August 12, 1993), pp. 6–10.

———. "Uncle Thomas's Cabin." Review of *Thomas Jefferson: An Intimate History*, by Fawn M. Brodie in *New York Review of Books* (April 18, 1974).

Wilson, Douglas L. "Thomas Jefferson and the Character Issue," *Atlantic Monthly*, 27, no. 5 (November 1992), pp. 57–74.

———. "Thomas Jefferson's Early Notebooks," *William and Mary Quarterly*, XLII, 3rd series, no. 4 (October 1985), pp. 433–52.

Partial Excerpt from Appendix E of the
Thomas Jefferson Memorial Foundation Report

Table of Contents of Relevant Primary Documents, includes: "Except the typescript of relevant extracts from several James Callender articles (see following pages), these documents are not available as part of the .pdf version of this report. They are available in the publications and from the organizations cited below."

1802 James Thomson Callender, extracts of articles in Richmond *Recorder*, September through December Original, September 1, 1802 article Page 1 Typescript of extracts from several articles 3–5.

1805 Jefferson cover letter to Secretary of the Navy Robert Smith, July 1, 1805 Original, Missouri Historical Society 6 Printed version from *Thomas Jefferson Correspondence*, ed. Worthington C. Ford (Boston, 1916), pages 114–15, 7–8.

1850s Journal of John Hartwell Cocke, January 26, 1853, and April 23, 1859, extracts Originals, University of Virginia Library 9–12, Typescript of extracts 13–14.

1858 Letter of Jefferson's granddaughter Ellen Coolidge to her husband, Joseph Coolidge, October 24, 1858, Original, Ellen Coolidge Letterbook, pages 98–102, University of Virginia Library 15–19 Printed version from Annette Gordon-Reed, *Thomas Jefferson and Sally Hemings: An American Controversy* (Charlottesville, 1997), pages 258–60, 20–21.

1862 Recollections of Edmund Bacon, former Monticello overseer (original unlocated) Printed version from James A. Bear, Jr., ed., *Jefferson at Monticello* (Charlottesville, 1967), pages 28–117 (relevant page is 102) 22–23.

1868 Letter of Jefferson biographer Henry S. Randall to James Parton, June 1, 1868 (original in Harvard University Library); Printed version from Milton E. Flower, *James Parton: The Father of Modern Biography* (Durham, 1951), pages 236–39, 24–26.

1873 Recollections of Madison Hemings, *Pike County* (Ohio) *Republican*, March 13, 1873 Original, Ohio Historical Society 27–28; Printed version from Gordon-Reed, pages 245–48, 29–31.

1873 Recollections of Israel Gillette Jefferson, *Pike County Republican*, December 25, 1873 (original in Ohio Historical Society) Printed version from Gordon-Reed, pages 249–53, 32–34.

1874 Letter of Jefferson's grandson Thomas Jefferson Randolph to editor of *Pike County Republican*, undated Original, University of Virginia Library, Accession Number 8937 35–40, Typescript version 41.

Additional Sources Cited in
2000 OFFICIAL MONTICELLO REPORT

Farm Book Facsimile pages of Edwin M. Betts, ed., *Thomas Jefferson's Farm Book* (Princeton, 1953).

Getting Word project files Public records, newspaper accounts, interview transcripts, and other primary and secondary material relating to Monticello's African-American families and their descendants. Collected as part of Getting Word, Monticello's African-American Oral History Project, 1993 to the present.

1811 Elijah Fletcher to Jesse Fletcher, 24 May 1811, in Martha von Briesen, ed., *The Letters of Elijah Fletcher* (Charlottesville, 1965).

1826 Thomas Jefferson will and codicil, 16-17 Mch. 1826, in James A. Bear, Jr., *Jefferson at Monticello* (Charlottesville, 1967), pp. 118–22.

1858 Ellen Randolph Coolidge to Joseph Coolidge, 24 Oct. 1858, in Annette Gordon-Reed, *Thomas Jefferson and Sally Hemings: An American Controversy* (Charlottesville, 1997), pp. 258–60.

1862 Edmund Bacon recollections, in Bear, *Jefferson at Monticello*, pp. 27–117.

1868 Henry S. Randall letter to James Parton, 1 June 1868, in Gordon-Reed, *Thomas Jefferson and Sally Hemings*, pp. 254–57.

1873 Madison Hemings recollections, *Pike County* (Ohio) *Republican*, 13 Mch. 1873, in Gordon-Reed, *Thomas Jefferson and Sally Hemings*, pp. 245–48.

1873 Israel Jefferson recollections, *Pike County Republican*, 25 Dec. 1873, in Gordon-Reed, *Thomas Jefferson and Sally Hemings*, pp. 249–53

1874 Thomas J. Randolph letter to editor of *Pike County Republican*, post-25 Dec. 1873, University of Virginia Library.

1902 *Daily Scioto Gazette* [Chillicothe, Ohio], 1 Aug. 1902.

Lucia C. Stanton, Shannon Senior Research Historian, Monticello December 1998.

Boatner, Mark Mayo, Ill. Encyclopedia of the American Revolution. New York: David McKay, 1966.

Branyon, Richard A. *Latin Phrases and Quotations* (New York: Hippocrene Books, 1994).

Byrd, Robert C. The Senate, 1789–1989: Historical Statistics, 1789–1992. Vol. 4. Washington, D.C.: Government Printing Office, 1993.

Commager, Henry Steele. Documents of American History. 5th ed. New York: Appleton-Century-Crofts, 1949.

Dictionary of American Biography (New York: Scribner, 1932).

France: Eyewitness TravelGuides (London: Dorling Kindersley, 1994).

Harley, Sharon. *Timetables of African-American History* (New York: Touchstone, 1995).

Kennedy, Lawrence F. Biographical Directory of the American Congress 1774–1791. (Washington, D.C.: Government Printing Office, 1971).

London Michelin Guide. 1st ed. London, 1977.

Morison, Samuel Eliot; Henry Steele Commagerj and William Leuchtenburg, eds. *A Concise History of the American Republic* (New York: Oxford University Press, 1977–).

The Negro Almanac: A Reference Work on the African American. 5th ed. Ed. Harry A. Ploski and James Williams (New York: Gale Research, 1989).

Olmert, Michael. *Official Guide to Colonial Williamsburg* (Williamsburg, Va.: Colonial Williamsburg Foundation, 1985).

Purvis, Thomas L. *Almanacs of American Life: Revolutionary America, 1763–1800* (New York: Facts on File, 1995).

Wren, R. C. *Potter's New Cyclopedia of Botanical Drugs and Preparations* (Holsworrthy, England: Health Science Press, 1975).

INDEX